CW01064150

EVE BALFOUR

# EVE BALFOUR

*Founder of the Soil Association*
*&*
*The Voice of the Organic Movement*

A BIOGRAPHY BY

## Michael Brander

The Gleneil Press

First published in Great Britain in 2003 by
The Gleneil Press
Haddington, East Lothian, EH41 4QA

British Library Cataloguing in Publication Data
A catalogue record is available for the book
from the British Library

ISBN 0 9525330 5 7

Typeset by Hewer Text Limited, Edinburgh
Printed and bound in Great Britain by
Antony Rowe Ltd., Chippenham, Wiltshire

To my wife

*Evelyn*

Eve's niece and namesake
Without whose support this
(and over fifty other books)
would not have been written

# Contents

# Illustrations

# *Acknowledgements*

As author I must first acknowledge with gratitude a generous research grant from the Helene Horoys Literary Foundation, which materially assisted with the very considerable research necessary. My thanks are also due to many people, particularly to close members of the Balfour family, to the subject of this biography herself, who set me going initially just before her death giving me free access to all her papers and records, and also to her nephew, my brother-in-law, Gerald, 4th Earl of Balfour and Viscount Traprain, for giving me free access to the Balfour Mss in the Scottish Records Office, to Adam Fergusson for the photo-copy of his mother Lady Frances Fergusson's edition of the 'Balfour Book of Bosh,' to Peter and Diana Balfour, to Arthur and Tobina Cole and to many other members of the family for papers, letters and reminiscences. My thanks must also go to the very helpful Deputy-Keeper of the Records, Mr A.M.Broom, and to Dr. Frances Shaw and many other very helpful staff at the Scottish Records Office and once again to the Lbrarian and staff at the Scottish National Library; and to Mrs A.V.Morey, Student Records Officer, at the Registrar's Office of Reading University. I must also thank Patrick Holden, the director, and the staff of the Soil Association, particularly Sue Stolton, also Lawrence Woodward OBE, director of the Elm Farm Research Centre as well as the staff of the Henry Doubleday Research Association and many other individuals and firms; including the Librarian and Staff of the R.A.F Museum Library and the Librarian and Staff at Rothamsted Experimental Station; and the Librarian at the Centre for Human Ecology, at Edinburgh University: also Mr. Philip Attenborough, of Messrs. Hodder & Stoughton and my old friend Mark Hamilton of A.M.Heath, author's agents, who acted for Lady Eve in the 1930s; in addition Mr Matthew Evans and the archivist of Messrs Faber & Faber for digging up the old files on

The Living Soil. In conclusion I am particularly grateful to the late Mrs Elizabeth Murray, one of the founder members of the Soil Association, and her daughter, Mrs Helen Zipperlen, one of Eve's earliest pupils, also to Mr. John Marland, J.P., another of her early pupils and his son Mr. Angus Marland, of the Centre for Human Ecology at the University of Edinburgh, for their helpful comments. For her recollections and helpful comments I must also thank Mrs Carol Twinch.

The bulk of the research for this book, however, has come from Mss, letters and documents collected from as early as the late 19th century by Eve's seemingly indefatigable mother, Lady Betty Balfour, who was known to have written (and recorded) sixty letters in a morning. It was owing to her example, no doubt, that Eve herself collected almost every paper connected with her actions throughout her life. Lady Betty's mantle also seems to have fallen on her daughter-in-law, Jean, 2nd Countess of Balfour, a woman of similar very strong mind and principles. The amount was somewhat overwhelming, but proved a wonderful record for anyone such as myself trying to portray the life of someone now belatedly recognised as a pioneer in a field of ever-growing importance to mankind. I am most grateful to them.

Finally I must thank several readers for their patience in reading through an unfinished Ts, in particular, Mrs. Helen Zipperlen, the late Mrs. Elizabeth Murray, Mr & Mrs John Marland, Mr. Angus Marland, Mr. John Clark and, as usual, my very long suffering wife, Evelyn, and my son Andrew Michael. I am extremely grateful for their helpful comments. In conclusion, however, I must emphasise that for any errors, omissions, or mistakes I am solely responsible.

# *Author's Foreword*

I must first declare an interest over and above that usual between a biographer and his or her subject. Before we were married my wife was namesake to her aunt Lady Eve Balfour, the subject of this biography. I am thus related by marriage. I knew Eve for over forty years from 1947 to her death in 1990. Indeed my wife and I lived for three months in the late forties in her moated Tudor manor house at New Bells, near Haughley, in Suffolk, where the Haughley Experiment was conceived in the late 1930s and where the Soil Association was based from 1946 until it moved to Bristol in the 1980s.

My wife and I have spent most of our married life since at Whittingehame in East Lothian where Eve's father Gerald, was born and which Eve regarded as her second home as a child and where she and her sister Mary made their childhood decision to become farmers. To us she was never a formidable figure of international renown, but a close relative and friend, a loving great-aunt to our children with a splendid sense of humour and fun. She was always a welcome guest to our house on her regular visits north to Scotland, generally in the late Spring or mid-Summer and at New Year.

To put my relationship with Eve in perspective, there was an occasion when she visited us shortly before her ninetieth birthday which perhaps sums it up well. She had come into our sitting room where I was quietly reading in a corner and she stood in front of the two shelves containing my published books. She looked at them for some time before turning round, shaking her head, and saying aloud:

'Who'd have thought it?'

That I understood the implied compliment and laughed with her at the backhanded nature of it and that, on discovering me sitting there, she then laughed with me at herself should explain a great deal to the percipient reader about our relationship. To say that I was very fond of her is entirely true. She was certainly in my view the pick of my wife's aunts on that side and there were five to choose from. Equally I trust this will not be seen as in any way a work of hagiography, which is the last thing she would have wished.

As a professional author and her nephew by marriage, as well as a friend, it was, however, really inexcusable on my part that the idea of writing this biography never arose until we had celebrated her ninetieth birthday in our house here at Whittingehame. It was in fact suggested to me by one of my publishers' editors, John Beaton and seemed at once so obviously suitable that I was astounded I had not thought of it previously. I am most grateful to him for the timely suggestion.

Sadly it was not long after this that Eve suffered the stroke, which within a couple of months ended her life. Fortunately I had already discussed the broad outlines with her. She had agreed at least that I should be her official biographer and that her life should be set against the background of the many interesting and varied decades through which she had lived. This as far as possible is how I have written it.

After her death, however, when I finally got down to digesting the amount of material available I began to wonder whether it was possible to make sense of it all. Mouse-eaten letters dating from the turn of the century, jumbled up with reports of visits to Kenya in the 1970s and reports of the Soil Association from the 1940s side-by-side with details of the sister's lives in the 1920's and '30's. There were hundred-weights of damp and mildewed letters, papers, reports and miscellania, along with old photograph albums, as well as the very considerable Balfour Mss in the Scottish Records Office. At least it was all on hand, if much was in total chaos. The difficulty was to put it together coherently and depict her life as far as possible in Eve's own words, or those of close observers. That occasionally trivia had to be included to set a scene or background will I trust be excused as part of the larger picture of Eve the person, her life and achievements. Trivia is after all an inescapable part of everyone's life.

Eve was born in Victoria's reign, with in many ways an idyllic Edwardian childhood, and lived through two world wars to 1990. She saw and accomplished much in that time. As we had agreed, it is against the changing background of the century that I have tried to show her life and achievements. After her Victorian and Edwardian upbringing, her decision, highly unusual in a girl of her class and background at the time, to study agriculture at Reading University during the First World War, was followed by her experience in post-war rural Suffolk, then still virtually unchanged from the Victorian farming economy based on the horse.

At that time agriculture was still booming from the war years, It was not long, however, before the government decided to allow the unrestricted import of American corn and overseas butter, beef and mutton. Similar government decisions had caused the farming slump at the end of the 19<sup>th</sup> century and were to cause many hard-working farmers to go under during the twenties and thirties. In order to survive Eve was forced to turn her hand to running a largely female dance band in Ipswich in the evenings and to writing thrillers in co-operation with her long-standing friend Beb Hearnden, both of which ventures proved successful.

It was in the 1930s that she found herself fighting a now largely forgotten war against the payment of tithes to the church. Arraigned in court for riotous assembly one day and discharged, then facing a Royal Commission and making her points successfully on another, were experiences which taught her how to champion unpopular causes. Her decision to embrace the natural ecological cycle rather than the seemingly wonderful new artificial fertilisers then being introduced after the second world war seemed to most people merely a retrograde attempt to block the advance of science. To her it seemed absolute sense to cling to the first principles of sound soil management and wholesome living thus completing the natural cycle of life. She still found time to learn to fly during the later 1930s and gained her pilot's licence.

She had barely conceived the idea of forming the Haughley Research Farms in 1938 when the Second World War broke out, but not even that could prevent her turning her vision into reality and founding the Haughley Experiment. Its object was to compare three different systems of farming, organic, mixed and stockless, on a farm scale under identical conditions. Although a simple enough basic experiment to find out the long term effects of the different systems on crops and animals, it remains the only one ever carried out on a farm scale over more than twenty years.

During the war itself she somehow found time to write her classic book The Living Soil, published by Faber & Faber extolling the virtues of humus and spelling out the message that if we poison our crops we poison ourselves. It proved to be an unexpected best seller resulting in numerous letters from enthusiastic readers around the world. Soon after the end of the war she then gathered together a like-minded group, drawn from very varied sections of society, and formed the Soil Association, one of its' aims being the continuation of the Haughley Experiment.

Then came the post-war period when she propagated her views against a hostile and powerful chemical lobby led by ICI and Fisons and a powerful agricultural pressure group with the ear of the government. It was to be a protracted and hard fought battle. The odds were always against her and she grew used to being regarded as a crank. During the flower-power period of the late fifties and sixties some of her supporters were indeed cranks as she knew well enough and she did not mind being termed a crank herself, for, as E.F.Schumacher put it, the crank is a small and useful inexpensive instrument which causes revolutions.

She may have been accused and perhaps occasionally with justice, of having blinkered vision, but the same may be said of her opponents advocating the chemical approach to farming and she can never be accused of benefitting financially from her stand. Nor have her opponents very often had the saving grace of a sense of humour and of the ridiculous. Single mindedness and a sense of purpose and certainty can also often be confused with blinkered vision. The dividing line may sometimes be very narrow, To hold to a belief and stand by it with constancy in the face of mockery from accepted experts in the field requires great strength of character and self-confidence. These were qualities along with honesty and firmness of mind Eve never lacked. In religious circles in the past these same attributes have produced both saints and martyrs. They do not always make for a comfortable life and even in her own family circle Eve may not always have been the easiest of companions.

Yet without her single-minded approach to life and living Eve could never have achieved what she did. To say that she was a voice in the wilderness is not only a well-worn cliché but an understatement throughout the 1950's and 1960's. That, however, never stopped her. She was well aware that advocating chemical free farming was unpopular and that she could expect little support from governments conditioned to providing cheap food. Nevertheless she continued to point out the crucial inter-relationship of the soil, crops, animals and mankind undaunted by the powerful opposition arraigned against her.

From the 1970s onwards although officially retired, she remained an active force in the background, often called on for help and a catalyst for those who believed that something was wrong with modern scientific farming, depending as it seemed to do on ever-increasing use of sprays and pesticides affecting the organic and biological cycle. While today such issues are very much in the public mind and organic food is viewed as worth paying extra for rather than a passing fad it is only because of her stand and of those who joined forces with her around the world wherever she spread her message that we now have public awareness on a global scale of what are popularly known as Green issues. She is indeed entitled to be saluted as a pioneer and a visionary, the far-seeing founder of the Soil Association, The Voice of the Organic Movement.

# Family Tree

James Balfour (Younger of Balbirnie)
= Lady Eleanor Maitland

James Maitland Balfour
= Lady Blanche Gascoine Cecil

Eleanor
=H Sedgwick

Evelyn
= Lord Rayleigh

Arthur James
(1st Earl)

Cecil

Francis

Gerald
(2nd Earl)
= Lady Betty Lytton

Alice

Eustace
=Lady Frances

Joan   Oswald   Alison

Ruth
=William Balfour
(of Balbirnie)

Eleanor = Galbraith Cole

David   Arthur

Norah   John   Peter   Ann

Mary

EVE

Robert Arthur
(3rd Earl)
=Jean Cooke-Yarborough

Gerald   Evelyn   Alison

Gerald
(4th Earl)

Kathleen
=Richard Oldfield

Frances   Margaret

# Introduction

## 1800–1900

*'All Balfours are very slow developing.'* [1]

Blanche Dugdale, niece and biographer of
A.J.Balfour, quoted in the Balfour Book of Bosh.

AS A KEEN STOCKBREEDER herself, Eve would be amongst the first to agree that breeding has a great deal to do with development. It is therefore worth looking initially at her breeding and background. The Balfour family tree is included for precisely this reason, to show the various influences in her upbringing. The Balfours of Balbirnie in Fife were a minor landed family of coal-owners, and James Balfour, the founder of the Whittingehame branch, was a younger son, born in the late 18th century. As was often the case in Scottish landed families of the period the younger son who did not inherit the estate used his family influence to obtain a post in India, then regarded, following the example set by Clive and others, as the ideal place for a young man with no money to try for fame and fortune.

James was obviously a man without much grace or good fellowship, but with a keen eye to the main chance. After initially blotting his copybook by accepting too obviously a gift from a minor Indian prince in the shape of a thoroughbred Arab, which left him open to a charge of corruption, it is apparent that James adapted quickly to the system set by the English in India. In the manner of the single-minded Scot intent on making his own way regardless, he ended by beating them at their own game.

In those days the contract for supplying the Navy with provisions was granted to civilians and when the Honourable Basil Cochrane retired James Balfour obtained this lucrative sinecure, turning it swiftly into a major source of income. Whereas it was said by one observer of the social scene that Cochrane 'kept open house', the only things 'open' he noted about his successor's house were 'the doors and windows.'

Be that as it may, within four years James had saved the then immense fortune of £300,000 and had appointed another Scot named McConnachie to continue as manager in his place at a salary of £6,000 a year. If only as a man with a keen eye for the opportunities available and a determination to succeed in his aims, James Balfour, whether a particularly pleasant character or not, was clearly single-minded. He returned home in 1812, earning the title of 'Nabob,' then bestowed on all those who had come back from India after making their fortunes, whether by fair means or foul. In his case one may assume a certain amount of each was involved. It was generally accepted throughout the Georgian period, however, that anyone in charge of provisioning the troops, from their commanding officers downwards, was entitled to take his percentage within reason. From the days of Pepys onwards this had been the practice, but some pursued it with greater avidity than others and it is clear James Balfour took it to the ultimate degree.

On his return to Britain, following the tried and tested routine for a successful Nabob, James Balfour bought a house in Grosvenor Square. He continued to follow the usual pattern by marrying well. In 1815 he selected as his wife Lady Eleanor Maitland, a daughter of the 3rd Earl of Lauderdale of Thirlestane Castle near Lauder, a well-known and well-connected family in the Scottish borders who were no doubt happy to accept a wealthy son-in-law for a younger daughter with no dowry. His next step was to buy his own estate and establish his family seat. Initially he bought the small estate of Balgonie in Fife, close to his old family home at Markinch. He then negotiated to buy Ancrum in the Scottish border country, but the deal fell through at the last moment.

In 1817 he finally bought the Whittingehame estate from Colonel William Hay of Duns Castle. The Hays of Drumelzier had acquired Whittingehame in 1695 through marriage to Lady Elizabeth Seton, heiress to the estate. It then consisted of ten thousand acres extending from the wild moorland of the Lammermuir hills down to the lush farmlands of East Lothian, popularly known as 'the garden of Scotland'. The old Border Pele tower dating from the 12th century, which with later additions formed the Mansion House at the time, was falling down with dry rot and James selected the well known architect Sir Robert Smirke, who a few years later built the British Museum, to build a new mansion house on the opposite side of the steep-sided glen at Whittingehame. His directions were succinct. It was to be larger and more impressive than his old family seat Balbirnie House in Fife and it was to be faced, regardless of expense, with similar stone from a quarry on that side of the Forth.

It seems there had been little love lost between James and his elder brother and this was compounded by Lady Eleanor's refusal to visit Balbirnie on the grounds that crossing the Firth of Forth in the ferry made her ill. From this it may be deduced that she did not get on with either her brother-in-law or more probably his wife and it may be equally deduced that the Balbirnie Balfours were envious of their younger brother's evident success. Anyway there was clearly at this time considerable friction based on jealousy between the two branches of the family, which was not easily forgotten by subsequent generations.

The new house was completed around 1819 and although in a very beautiful setting still retains a slightly institutional look about it as did many of Smirke's buildings. The couple appear to have moved in immediately and their eldest surviving son, James Maitland, was born there in 1820, the first of six children. James Balfour's final step to becoming a substantial county landed gentleman was to stand for Parliament and from 1831 to 1835 he was elected as Member for Haddington. By this time he was clearly established as a powerful moving force in the area. Entertainment at Whittingehame was on a grand scale with Lady Eleanor to be seen 'in full panoply of bare shoulders, diamonds, crinoline and lace flounces.' Never was this more so than at the engagement party of their eldest son in 1843.

At the age of twenty two in that year James Maitland Balfour became engaged to Lady Blanche Gascoigne Cecil, daughter of the 2nd Marquis of Salisbury and sister of Lord Robert Cecil, subsequently 3rd Marquis and Prime Minister. Lady Eleanor, with all the matchmaking abilities of a late Georgian mother, had guided her son's choice carefully and well. James Balfour was also no doubt well satisfied with the match, but he died before the birth of his first grandson in 1848. The boy was baptised Arthur after his illustrious godfather the Duke of Wellington and James after both his father and grandfather.

3

James Maitland and Lady Blanche were to have nine children in the first eleven years of their marriage, which lasted only thirteen years before James's premature death from what appears to have been tuberculosis, one of the commoner scourges of all classes of society in those days. Lady Blanche was left to rear her large family of eight surviving children by herself, but she proved herself more than adequately equipped for the task while retaining strong links with her Salisbury relations rather than with the Balfour side of the family. It was probably a legacy of her strong personality that the ensuing generation of Balfours became subject to a decidedly matriarchal rule. The only two sons who married, Gerald and Eustace, were both influenced throughout their married lives by the strong personalities of their wives, although in the case of Gerald it may not have been so immediately obvious.

The first child to be born to James Maitland and Lady Blanche in 1846 was a girl, Eleanor, to be followed in 1847 by another girl, Evelyn. Arthur James Balfour, the eldest son born in 1848 and the heir to the estate, was eventually to enter politics as member for Hertford, backed by the power and influence of the Salisbury faction. In almost regular sequence, another brother, Cecil, was born in 1849 and another sister Alice in 1850 with a further brother Francis in 1851, to be followed by Gerald in 1853 and Eustace in 1854. All the brothers grew up to be good-looking and tall, making an impressive family group in their early twenties. The two elder girls were regarded more as handsome and striking than beautiful, while the third, Alice, was at first sight small and unremarkable, but with an inner strength of character which was to emerge in later years.

In 1869 A.J.Balfour came of age and inherited both Strathconan, an estate in the Highlands, which had been acquired by his father in 1841, and Whittingehame in East Lothian. In 1871 his sister Evelyn married his great Cambridge friend John Strutt, later Lord Rayleigh, who was to become a distinguished scientist. In 1872 his mother Lady Blanche died, just as he was taking over 4 Carlton Gardens as a London home for her. This remained his London base for the rest of his life.

In 1874 he entered Parliament unopposed as member for Hertford. The year after his election the girl he would almost certainly otherwise have married, May Littleton, died of scarlet fever. It is interesting to note that she was just such a woman as his mother with a powerful personality which obviously held a strong fascination for him.

Although not a man who easily betrayed his inner feelings he was overcome with grief at her death, all the greater for having no apparent outward release. Nor did he share his brother Gerald's subsequent strong interest in psychical research and belief in contact with the spirit world.[2] Thereafter this gifted and brilliant young man, destined to become Prime Minister, remained a confirmed bachelor, although possibly on more than one occasion in after years discreetly consummating an affair, notably with Mary Wyndham, Lady Elcho, later Countess of Wemyss, and known to him affectionately as Melcho, whose marriage was unhappy and unsuccessful.

In 1876 his eldest sister Eleanor married his Cambridge friend and tutor, Henry Sidgwick, notable as one of the founders of Newnham College for women, and a respected Cambridge academic name. He was also first President of the Society for Psychical research and the Balfour family's deep involvement with the Society stemmed originally from him. Eleanor, herself a brilliant mathematician, took over as second principal of Newnham in 1892 until her husband's death in 1900. She then continued her husband's work as Secretary of the Psychical Research Society for many years.

For five years following the death of their mother she had been the manager of the Whittingehame household. As such she had proved to be another brilliant organiser. The task thenceforward passed to Alice, the youngest sister, who appears always to have had a totally unnecessary if understandable inferiority complex about her management compared with that of her obviously outstanding predecessors.

From the original Lady Eleanor onwards the female side at Whittingehame, although always outwardly arranging everything for the convenience and satisfaction of the male side of the family, appear to have been notable for their autocratic command of the household, but it was under Alice and A.J.Balfour that the matriarchal rule reached its greatest heights. She was her brother's hostess from 1876 to 1930, becoming increasingly autocratic as the years passed. During A.J.Balfour's period as Prime Minister, from 1900–1905, she had a dress allowance of £2,000 a year, a very considerable amount in those days, while acting as his hostess at his London house. In 1889 she made an extensive tour of the United States and kept a graphic diary of her visit which still makes good reading. In 1894 she toured what was to become Rhodesia and from her letters produced a book beautifully illustrated with her own accomplished water-colours, entitled '1200 Miles in a Covered Wagon.' She was not only a water-colourist of professional standards, but a lepidopterist consulted by leaders in the field. Yet so great became her dislike of her own somewhat moth-like appearance in later years that she did her best to remove any photograph taken of her from the family albums, even going to the extent of erasing her face from them wherever possible.

The first of A.J.Balfour's brothers to marry was his younger brother Eustace. In 1879 he married Lady Frances Campbell, daughter of the Duke of Argyll. No doubt in those days, when useful family connections still governed much of politics, this ducal relationship provided a further political stimulus to A.J.Balfour's life, even if the Campbells were on the other side of the fence.

In 1881 Cecil Balfour, his next eldest brother, died not long after arriving in Australia, as the result of a fall from a horse. It is perhaps noteworthy that it was weaknesses regarding money and women, rather than the bottle, which caused him to be regarded as the black sheep of the family. He had on that account become something of an embarrassment in the family circle so that his early death was not greatly mourned.

The following year in 1882, however, the next eldest brother, Francis Balfour, was killed in an unfortunate and unexplained climbing accident in the Alps, where he had gone to recuperate after an attack of typhoid fever, prior to returning to Cambridge for the new term. Although only 31, his was a life of considerable promise, for he was already recognised as a biologist of the first rank in Cambridge academic circles. Professor of Animal Morphology, a chair which had been specially created for him the previous year, and F.R.I.C., he was the author of a number of highly acclaimed monographs. His death was a loss not only to the family but to the nation for in his field. he could well have eclipsed the subsequent fame of his elder brother.

Gerald, A.J.Balfour's eldest surviving brother, took a first in Classics at Trinity College, Cambridge and became a fellow and lecturer at the College. He and his brother Francis, fellow Cambridge academics although in different spheres, naturally gravitated towards each other and were great friends. Three years after Francis' death, in 1885, Gerald followed his elder brother into politics as member for Leeds. In 1887 he married Lady Betty Lytton[3], daughter of the 1st Earl of Lytton and Viceroy of India. As Chief Secretary for Ireland Gerald served in Salisbury's famous family cabinet, which contained eleven members all closely related to him, and later served under his brother when he became Prime Minister. After the defeat of the government in

1906, however, his interest in politics waned and he never stood for Parliament again. He became a Privy Counsellor, but his interests thereafter inclined particularly towards the Society for Psychical Research in which he played a considerable part.

The two families of A.J.Balfour's surviving brothers, Gerald and Eustace, were accustomed to visiting Whittingehame for a period of around seven months each year and naturally regarded it as their second home. The wives, whatever their feelings in the matter, put up with it and with the domestic arrangements organised by their sister-in-law Alice. To the children, regardless of any undercurrents amongst the adults, this must have been a heavenly place to visit each year. As the centre of their universe their beloved 'Nunkie' A.J.Balfour was naturally their favourite person.

It was however a classic feature of the Balfour household that every statement should be discussed, analysed and argued over before being either accepted or discarded. This was combined with a high degree of objectivity in both discussion and thought which could seem unfeeling to an outsider. This was noted by many observers, as for instance when one of the brothers' canoes was found abandoned by the river's edge with no sign of him. Rather than send out a search party a discussion immediately ensued at the end of which it was decided on the whole that he was unlikely to have drowned. The debate was only finally concluded by the appearance of the object of the discussion enquiring what the argument was all about.

It is more than probable that he was then informed that they had been arguing about whether he was dead or not. A high degree of insensitivity to the feelings of others was also a marked family trait. Tact was not a feature of the family and this could lead to quite unintentional rudeness, although Eleanor (Aunt Nora) and A.J.Balfour (Nunkie) were notable exceptions in this respect. Outstanding examples were chronicled in the family book of anecdotes, aptly entitled 'The Balfour Book of Bosh.' Two typical examples suffice:

1. 'Sir Ian Malcolm (Secretary to the Cabinet) at Whittingehame: 'I am afraid, Miss Balfour, I must leave tomorrow.

'Alice Balfour. That will suit me down to the ground.'

2. Gerald Balfour (to solitary lady guest) Do you play patience?

S.L.G. I am afraid I don't.

G.B. Oh I do. – and does.'

It must frequently have required a strong personality and an equally strong voice to hold one's own in the often animated family discussions when A.J.Balfour himself was not present. Nor were such discussions restricted to the male side of the family only. Indeed in this largely feminine household strong and animated discussion of this nature was latterly almost a female preserve.

The size of the household at Whittingehame varied considerably over the years, but any house of this magnitude was a major administrative problem to organise. The sheer logistics of keeping it running smoothly posed a considerable problem, approximately equivalent to that of organising a regimental-sized military barracks. Alice Balfour, in overall charge, was condemned to run the household, when she would probably much rather have travelled the world in the manner of Lady Hester Stanhope or similar great Victorian eccentrics.

Her staff at Whittingehame, under the supervision of a steward, butler and housekeeper, consisted in descending order of importance of a varying number of lady's maids, depending largely on the number of ladies living in the house, usually three or more, a cook, three housemaids, three kitchen maids, two stillroom maids, three laundry maids, two nurses, two nursery and schoolroom maids, as well no doubt as sundry local daily women for the rougher work and as stand-ins for grand occasions. Among the male staff were a valet and three footmen. Outside was a coachman and three stablemen grooms, latterly also a driver-cum-mechanic to look after the cars, which were to become an obsession with A.J.Balfour, even if his sister would only allow them to be taken out once a day, treating them on the same principle as the horses and carriages.

Outside staff also included the headkeeper with three or more underkeepers, also the head gardener with six or more under-gardeners and boys, as well as a head forester and six under-foresters. All these latter were nominally under control of the Factor, or estate manager, but were at call if required for the management of the household as when a ball, or reception, was taking place. It can be readily seen therefore that the smooth management of a household of this size posed considerable problems, calling for all the ability and arbitrary control of a quarter-master sergeant major.

Lady Blanche Balfour, the Cecil mother of A.J.Balfour, had clearly combined all these qualities and more, ruling the household and rearing her large family with little difficulty after the death of her husband, although with the ready help and assistance of her Cecil relations when required. On her death Eleanor the eldest sister took over with little or no apparent strain or difficulty. Alice, who was in control thereafter from 1876 to 1930, was cast in a different mould. This in turn probably led to exaggerated attempts to prove herself equal to the task, which resulted in some bizarre side effects.

The matriarchal rule of Alice, or 'Auntie' as she was known to all, was certainly all-pervading and rigid. The minute directions laid down for the proceedings governing the annual school-treat, already well known to everyone concerned, are fascinating reading. They cast a very revealing light on the character of the writer, who believed that motor cars like horse-drawn carriages should never be overworked or overloaded, as well as an interesting sidelight on the entertainments of the period:

'Black Maria (the covered van) to meet Bunch with Cinematograph and pianoforte player, East Linton 10.12 a.m.

Mrs Anderson to be taken directly after, in motor to see the Taits at Ruchlaw new cottages.

A motor to go to Garvald with things for Kingside school. Miss Sharpin knows all about these, and will give directions when consulted.

A motor to take Mr Gerald to Nunraw in the morning and fetch him at 4 p.m. Part of the household will be at the first performance of the cinematograph at 2 o'clock and part will be at the second performance beginning at 5, but all the men at the stables will be at the second performance. Therefore no motors, or ponies, or carriages, or horses must be out after the hour which will enable them to have everything cleaned up and put away before they come in to see the cinematograph.

The cinematograph performance must be sent down to Linton in the motor to catch the last train from Linton to Edinburgh. If they cannot catch that train they must be sent to Dunbar. Look out the trains as they may be altered. The new Bradshaw & Murray (the train time-table) ought to arrive from Douglas & Foulis (a leading Edinburgh bookshop) on Tuesday. If they do not come find out on Tuesday morning when the motor is down in Linton about the hours of trains.

Meals will be in the music room on Tuesday and possibly Wednesday morning (Better have breakfast late on Wednesday if more convenient for the servants) After dinner on Tuesday. servants' dance will take place in the dining room. The piano will be taken from the book room. Horsburgh knows about this and where to put it.

See that there are two hooded candlesticks on the piano.

Horsburgh will superintend the benches and chairs. See that low chairs are put in front.

Separate paper shows arrangements for cinematograph.

See that there are two Ajax extincteurs and one hand pump with pails of water close to the cinematograph at both performances in case of fire. I have "not" told Horsburgh this but it is imperative.

"Wednesday" The pianoforte player will have to be sent to Linton in the morning with Mrs Dugdale.

You will have to do your best to fit people in going down to the concert in the three motors. Whatever happens I do not want any of the three motors to be overloaded. There ought not to be more than six people besides the driver in either . . . But Eve might be thrown in as an extra . . . They can go backwards and forwards to Linton as often as you like. Miss Sharpin would like to go to the concert and some of the servants and if you can manage to take them down it would be a good thing.'

NOTES ON INTRODUCTION

1. *slow developing*: some Balfours could also be extremely dogmatic at times. This was indeed a marked trait of Blanche's generation and of the Campbell branch particularly. Blanche, generally known as Baffy, was the eldest

2. *spirit world*: A.J.Balfour retained her auburn hair, which had been cut off during her last illness, in a silver casket which he kept for the rest of his life as a treasured possession. The so-called 'Casket Letters' were subsequently the subject of an article in the Society for Psychical Research Journal by his niece-in-law, Jean, 2nd Countess of Balfour. See: The Proceedings of The Society For Psychical Research. Vol. 52. Part 189. February 1960. The Palm Sunday Case. P.79.

3. *Lady Betty*: Lady Betty was clearly another remarkable woman in the Balfour family circle. She may often have found it difficult to force her way into the voluble and vehement arguments, which abounded at Whittingehame, but as a letter-writer she was outstanding. Her habit of copying letters and filing them for reference, as well as her wide and varied correspondence, were an asset to any biographer.

# CHAPTER ONE

# The Background and the Early Days

## 1898–1914

*'Eve is exactly like a puppy, with a puppy's charm, a puppy's high spirits and a puppy's aggravatingness.'*

Lady Betty Balfour.

E VELYN BARBARA BALFOUR was born in London on July 16th 1898 at the tail end of Victoria's reign when the Great Queen-Empress still ruled half the globe and no-one dreamed of the slaughter to come in the half-century which lay ahead. She was the fourth daughter of the Rt. Hon. Gerald Balfour, M.P., a nephew of the Prime Minister, the Marquis of Salisbury.[1] Her mother was Lady Betty[2], daughter of the 1st Earl of Lytton, late Viceroy of India and grand daughter of Bulwer Lytton. At that time her father was Secretary for Ireland, crossing to Ireland each year with his family, to the official residence in Dublin, where armed guards protected them from extremists, as always a common factor in Irish politics. They also had a London house at 31 Phillimore Gardens above Kensington High Street. In those days this was almost on the edge of open country and little more than one of the small villages surrounding London, although already being steadily developed. It was here that they stayed when the House was sitting and Gerald's political duties required his presence in London.

With the passing of the Great Queen Empress in 1901 the glorious days of the brief Edwardian period were about to dawn and all seemed right with the world, as long as you were British or at the very least English-speaking. From 1901–1905 Gerald's bachelor elder brother A.J.Balfour succeeded their uncle as Prime Minister. (Hence the popular Music-hall catch-phrase of the day: 'Bob's your Uncle.') Even to live in North Britain was 'a good thing' and to be niece of the Prime Minister of Great Britain when it was still in its heyday must have seemed 'a very good thing indeed.' To all outward appearances this must have seemed a golden start in life.

Evelyn Barbara had three elder sisters, Ruth, born in 1887, Eleanor, born in 1888, and Mary, four years her senior, born in 1894. Mary, however, was a small, frail and physically weak child. Born with a cleft palate she was constantly prey to ailments such as eczema and asthma, which may well have been phsychosomatic. The much more robust and extrovert Evelyn soon established a moral ascendancy over her elder but weaker sibling, which continued throughout their lives, although there was always also a close bond between them.

It had, over the years, become the custom for Gerald with his wife and children to spend some seven months of the year from around June to January at Whittingehame, the Balfour family home in East Lothian, which his elder brother had inherited. The remainder of the year they spent at their own home in the south, latterly at Fisher's Hill, near Woking in Surrey, a house designed for him in 1902 by Edwin Lutyens. Making up the regular houseful of guests at Whittingehame during the Summer and Autumn months was the family of A.J.Balfour's youngest brother. Eustace[3], who in 1879 had married Lady Frances[4], daughter of the Duke of Argyll.

Eustace and Frances' family consisted of five children. The eldest Blanche, known as Baffy, born in 1880, took after her mother as a bossy, rather wild and volatile child. The eldest son Frank, born in 1882, was followed by Joan the next eldest daughter and something of a beauty born in 1884. Another son Oswald, born in 1890 and ultimately another daughter Alison born in 1892 completed this branch of the Balfour family. All of them to some extent inherited the wayward and mercurial nature as well as the commanding and autocratic attitudes of their mother.

In 1901, after a further interval of three years, Lady Betty finally gave birth to a son Arthur Robert Lytton. As the son of the eldest brother, he automatically became heir to the estate of the unmarried A.J.Balfour. Some evidence of the powerful undercurrents of feeling which pervaded this large and varied household of strong personalities may be gauged from the fact that Lady Frances, having borne two sons and convinced the estate would go to her side of the family, then showed the depths of her Campbell feelings by spitting into the baby's cradle on first viewing him. It was indeed some years before she could even force herself to stay in the same room as the infant Ral, as he became known. When he toddled into a room she immediately rose and left, so deep were her feelings on the subject.

There was to be one further daughter, Kathleen, born to Lady Betty in 1908. The two families when combined together at Whittingehame thus eventually consisted of eight girls and three boys, all of varying and disparate ages, but naturally forming cliques amongst themselves much in the manner of their elders. The older boys, Eustace and Oswald, were somewhat distanced from the rest as a natural result of boarding at public school. The four older girls, Blanche, or Baffy, and Joan, daughters of Frances and Ruth and Eleanor, or Nellie, daughters of Betty, formed a particularly close clique terming themselves somewhat ungrammatically, 'Us Four.' All somewhat older than the rest, they felt themselves rather aloof from the younger ones born around and after the turn of the century.

In this mixed household the adults all had their favoured names, bestowed on them by their numerous nieces and nephews. Thus A.J.Balfour, the pivot round which the entire united households revolved was known as 'Nunkie' or 'Nunk' to all of them. His brother Gerald, husband of Lady Betty, was known as 'Nunkie G' to the family of Eustace and Frances. The extremely arbitrary and increasingly eccentric controller of the household, Miss Alice Balfour, was known universally as 'Auntie'. Eleanor Sidgwick, who returned frequently to Whittingehame on the death of her husband Henry in 1900, was known as 'Aunt Nora' and Evelyn, who married Lord Rayleigh, but was also a frequent visitor, was known as 'Aunt Evelyn'. In an unusually percipient moment one of the nieces commented with evident truth but characteristic Balfour tactlessness; 'Aunt Nora never speaks without thinking, Auntie never thinks without speaking. Aunt Evelyn always speaks without thinking.'

The result, especially as Alice grew increasingly deaf, was frequent quarrels between the various sisters and their sisters-in-law. The task of peacemaker was usually left to Lady Betty, Nora, or in extreme cases A.J.Balfour himself. With an extremely strong will beneath her somewhat moth-like exterior, swathed in shawls, Alice however exercised an extraordinary control over the household including latterly A.J.Balfour himself, who with the indolence characteristic of the Balfour males, always did his best to avoid any confrontation whenever possible.

Although it must have been a heavenly place for children there can be little doubt that at times it was something of a straitjacket and even a minor purgatory for the adults, with considerable strains, stresses and undercurrents of feeling bubbling beneath the surface. Lady Betty wrote revealingly years later:' . . . none of us have ever been allowed to have a friend here. This is not done at Whitt. I have 'never' asked a friend here in all my life. Father once . . . asked S.H.Butcher (Professor S.H. Butcher an Ulster Protestant M.P.) and such surprise was shown by Auntie that he never did it again. You know what a fuss there always was when Aunt Francis tried to wangle a friend being asked to lunch or tea . . . Whitt is Whitt to take or leave . . .'

Fisher's Hill, also had its idiosyncratic life. The dining room and the kitchen were separated by a long L-shaped brick lined corridor so that all meals were announced long before the dinner gong by the sound of trolley wheels rumbling over the bricks of the passageway. Outside a stream tumbled down the hill and small fish, newts and frogs, as at Whittingehame, provided an interest. Unlike Whittingehame there were no long vistas to be seen from the main rooms, for here the Lutyens design had provided windows on the Elizabethan style at head height, which looked symmetrical from the exterior and allowed light into the room but no view. With rambling passageways and designed on several levels, however, Fisher's Hill provided another fascinating home for the young. The heaths and sandy countryside of Surrey, then still totally unspoiled by the advent of the motor car or ribbon development, also provided a splendid background for riding and walking.

With nannies and nursery-maids the children in the nursery were effectively segregated in those Edwardian days from the adult world. As they graduated to nursery-governesses to be taught their primary education there was little real change. When they graduated to a governess at the age of six or seven they might be separated from the nursery to some extent, but they still had not graduated to the full adult world. From then to the age of twelve or thirteen the daughters of the Edwardian household were still generally educated privately. It was through a series of governesses, sometimes shared with their cousins, and by the efforts of their own parents and relations, that the young Balfour girls were educated at Whittingehame and at Fisher's Hill.

The late Victorian and Edwardian households in which Eve was brought up, at Woking in Surrey and Whittingehame in East Lothian, thus had their totally individual characteristics and were like two different worlds. In each world, however, the background of the nursery and the servants halls were areas to which the children alone had complete access. Only they could freely pass between the rigidly segregated regions of grown-ups and servants quarters.

The attitudes of their wild Campbell cousins, flying into tantrums and savagely disciplined or scathingly tongue-lashed by their mother, were very different from the more ordered regime of the Surrey Balfours. The Campbell discipline was harsh and autocratic, stemming from the Campbell world of Lady Frances. To the more easygoing Surrey Balfours there was a certain fascination in this, just as there was always a fascination in visiting Whittingehame.

The transition from Surrey to Whittingehame must have been vastly exciting to a child. The packing of trunks for weeks beforehand built up the anticipation. Then at last the house was closed and the luggage, family, governess and nurse, all packed into a couple of horse-drawn cabs to go to Woking station, where their carriage was already booked on the regular local steam train to Victoria. There followed the journey by cab through the gas-lit chaos of London traffic to Kings Cross, with the clatter of horses' hooves and iron-shod wheels all round. At the station they found their private carriage booked for the entire family and the children were put to bed in their fold-down bunks, lulled to sleep eventually by the rhythmic sound of the iron wheels and the huffing and puffing of the steam engine, only occasionally woken by the shrill whistle as they entered a tunnel. In the morning there was the excitement of crossing the border via the great arches of the massive Victorian bridge over the river Tweed at Berwick. Then came the long-awaited stop at East Linton station where they were met by the frock-coated station master in his top hat and the familiar Whittingehame coachman. There followed the familiar hilly journey through the East Lothian countryside, with its rich red soil and with sometimes a faint whiff of gas from the East Linton gasometer leaking from the pipe by the roadside. At long last they passed the lodge into the entrance drive to Whittingehame house itself with the certain knowledge of a fresh voyage of discovery to follow round old familiar places and friends.

From July to January Whittingehame was thus filled by three differing and often conflicting groups, A.J.Balfour, his sister and their guests, along with his two brothers and their families. From January to June it was empty while the household staff took over the cleaning and renovation of the house. The blinds were drawn, the rooms were all closed and the staff started the annual cleaning process. The families themselves withdrew to their own worlds in the south and A.J.Balfour returned to his other residence at Carlton Gardens in London.

The attitude in the household at Whittingehame to children was indicative of slightly unusual and for the time very advanced thinking. Children were listened to with interest as long as they had anything original to say, but anything stupidly childish was likely to receive a severe set-down. To hold their own in any argument they had early to learn to speak up for themselves and refuse to be snubbed or over-ridden. For lesser spirits this could be a crushing experience at times. Anyone without something to contribute vociferously to the discussion in progress was likely to be ignored, but nevertheless Blanche Balfour, eldest daughter of Eustace and Lady Frances, was able to write with sublime belief in the truth of her own words, but total disregard for the facts:

'The profound respect for the individual which is characteristic of both Cecils and their Balfour cousins began early and was the foundation of social intercourse.'

From other outside and less biased observations it is clear that those unable and unwilling to hold their own robustly were unlikely to get a word in edgeways. Guests were expected to be entertaining and even if they were distinguished visitors they were not immune from criticism from this very self-contained family. The visit of Lord Kitchener was a case in point when it was more or less unanimously decided that he was something of a bore, a conclusion which was probably not far off the mark,

From comments made by Lady Betty Balfour to her mother, however, the way in which everyone listened to the slightest remark by A.J.Balfour appeared to the unbiased observer little short of idolatry. In an unguarded moment when visiting the Strathmore family at Glamis she was struck by the contrast with the free and easy family atmosphere there compared with that of Whittingehame. She referred to the 'deadly solemnity' with which 'Nunkie' was treated at Whittingehame.

The two young families of Gerald and Eustace nevertheless obviously revelled in their life at Whittingehame, where tennis, croquet, clock golf, walking, bicycling or riding, fishing or canoeing in the burn, and occasional shooting parties, were just some of the diversions available. In hot summer weather there was sea bathing nearby, or alfresco picnics in the hills. In winter there was skating, or toboganning down the steep-sided glens. Shooting or riding apart, A.J.Balfour took his full share in such activities whenever possible.

It was in this unusual environment that Eve spent much of her childhood unconsciously absorbing valuable lessons during those formative years. She learned very early that if she could make people laugh this was likely to result in at least punishment deferred. She also quickly learned not to be snubbed and to hold her own in any argument or discussion. In this volatile household any discussion, especially amongst the female members, was likely to degenerate readily into argument and 'the aunts' Alice and Frances, as well as Evelyn, had been known to descend to throwing buns at each other during highly-charged arguments at the breakfast table. Their nieces and nephews clearly found them both irritating and at times hilarious.

It was at Whittingehame as a two-year-old in a family pageant staged in 1900 that Eve was ushered in representing the new century. Appropriately enough her great uncle the Marquis of Salisbury[5] was ushered out as representing the old century. This must have been an ideal place for children to live during those halcyon summers and winters when the old assured world was unknowingly on the brink of dissolution. It was well described by Baffy;

'The nursery wing at Whittingehame opened on two staircases, leading down to the two separate worlds which make up the life of a great country house. The children of the family are the only members of the community who really have the freedom of both . . . On the first morning at Whittingehame my first visit was always to the house-keeper's room. Down the stone stairs, along the stone-flagged passage, smelling of paraffin and boot polish, where whistling footmen in shirt-sleeves popped across. On through the swing-doors which shut off the still-room and the store-room, a region scented with oranges and oatcakes on the girdle . . .'

All the same there were divides, which even the children were not expected to cross. This does not appear to have affected Eve greatly and her mother wrote in 1903 that Eve, aged 5, had given her a Christmas present of an almanac. She added; 'She has been funny about her gifts. Finding that she had not money enough to provide for all to whom she wanted to give she asked various members of the household, Joan, Ruth, Nannie, to give her back the present she had given them months ago then she wrapped it up in beautiful paper and gave it afresh!'

She went on to describe the Christmas lunch when the two dining tables, one for the adults and one for the children, were pulled together and the adults sat with the children instead of at separate tables as was usual. She continued; 'Directly after lunch the children with our presents (Frances and mine) went to the servants. Eve here again distinguished herself by breaking all 'the rules of the house' and marching into the servant's hall, where a solemn Xmas dinner was going on, and singing them a song!'

Already, even at that age, Eve was clearly proving a handful to her mother, for she wrote:

'At 4.15 ten of us started for the Biel (a neighbouring estate) Xmas tree all in one big brake – Alice much concerned for the horses – We promising to walk up the hills and then not being given a chance by the coachman . . . I had to go – though it is a shy making process to see that Eve did not disgrace the family. She was very comic, but quite good. When she left the Tree room and said Goodbye she forgot to thank her hostess but she had a second opportunity when her host conducted her to the front door. Then she said 'Thank you for my present, thank you for having had me, thank you for my good tea.' Then rapidly turning to me 'There Mother! I've done it!'

It was significant, however, that when a Christmas play was organised amid much trouble for the adults, the only ones who were noted as showing real acting ability were Mary and Eve, 'Mary almost the best of all, but of course difficult to understand.' The cleft palate must have made matters difficult for her, but she seems despite this and her undoubted frailty to have held her own in many respects, for she had undoubtedly a steely will of her own, although already tending to give way to her younger and more assertive sister.

One of the family relaxations in the warmer months was a trip to the sea at Ravensheugh, then part of the neighbouring estate of Tyningehame, owned by the Earl of Haddington (now part of the East Lothian John Muir Country Park) In September 1904 Lady Betty wrote; 'We kept Oswald's birthday here yesterday and had a luncheon picnic by the sea, Frances & I & the seven children . . . I, Alison and Oswald bicycled. Joan, Nellie & Eve went in one pony carriage with lunch packed up in a back seat. Frances, Ruth & Mary on the shafts went in the other pony carriage with the beautiful white pony. We went to Ravensheugh the favourite walk on the Tyningehame sands. The tide far out and though the day was lovely there was wind on the sea and it looked terribly cold in the water but all the children insisted on bathing . . . Eve got so far as the edge and put her foot in the water and then gave it up. It was too cold. I was glad for it gave me time to dress her again before the others came out. I haven't let her bathe again this year. Mary loves it almost the most and is never cold after it, but I don't know if it is very good for her ear . . . Eve had her luncheon perched on a rock at some distance from our sandy table and at that distance her voice was not ear splitting to Aunt Frances. Frances tries to be very stern with Eve but Eve is not the least afraid of her and Frances can't help being amused by her. . . .'

Along with Mary, Eve, in the early days especially, was mainly excluded from the older childrens' gatherings although tolerated on the fringes of them to the exclusion of her less assertive and sickly elder sister. As she grew older and more extrovert than her sister, however, she naturally gravitated towards the older group and was to some extent tolerated as an amusing if at times annoying appendage. She thus had a precocious upbringing endeavouring to keep up with her older siblings and consequently developed faster than would have been the case had she simply been amongst her equals. Riding six or seven miles to the coast to bathe in the chilly and often quite dangerous waters of the North Sea, or roaming the Lammermuir Hills, the children must frequently have taken risks of which their parents were totally unaware. It was a testing and hardy upbringing and as the youngest she must always have had to try that much harder than the others.

At the age of eight in 1906 Eve bicycled down to East Linton the small village two-and-a-half miles from Whittingehame, by herself for the first time and managed somehow to get lost[6]. She telephoned up to say that there was no need to worry about her as 'she would sleep with the bootmaker.' Such stories of her doings combined to make her a continual source of amusement to the family.

She continued to be something of a trial to her mother who that same year made her listen to a lecture being rehearsed by her Aunt Frances, which she intended to deliver in Edinburgh and was first trying out on the captive audience of the assembled family. Lady Betty noted in a letter to Gerald that it was 'good' and that 'Eve rolled on the carpet but kept silent, only saying when it was over that she thought it "too long."'

Towards the end of 1906, however, after watching a shoot at Whittingehame, when pheasants were shot near the house Eve was horrified by what seemed to her the needless cruelty involved in the keepers wringing the necks of wounded birds. Unaware that most of the birds were in fact already dead and not suffering pain she was appalled to see them flapping their wings as their necks were drawn. She attacked her father for taking part in this cruel sport.

'If you feel like that about it, you should become a vegetarian,' he replied, somewhat unfeelingly.

'What is a vegetarian?' she rather naturally demanded.

'A vegetarian is someone who does not eat meat,' he replied. 'And if you feel like that about killing animals you should be a vegetarian.'

'Very well,' she replied, somewhat struck by the idea. 'That's what I'll be.'

It says much for Eve's determination at an early age and also reveals a considerable amount about the households in which she was brought up, that when she expressed her intention to become a vegetarian, no-one told her that children of eight had to eat what was put before them. Her intention was duly noted and henceforth she was not forced to eat meat. Despite the inconvenience this no doubt caused on occasions to the domestic staff her decision was treated as that of an adult and duly respected accordingly.

In many other ways Betty Balfour stands revealed as an extremely imaginative parent for the time. In the summer of 1907, for instance. she arranged a lengthy tour of the Border area on bicycles, from Carlisle through Melrose, Lauder and Selkirk with Mary and Eve, stopping at lodgings on the way overnight. She wrote to her mother at some length in 1907, much of the letter about Eve. She wrote;'

'You ask me to tell you my heart's truth about the tour . . . I wished to break the common routine of life and do something new and rather more adventurous than usual. This I have done and deeply enjoyed, but it has been more expensive than I had expected. I hoped to do it for £15 and it will cost fully £20 and £5 more if I include my purchases. Then, though I wanted the children to feel as free and independent as possible I could not rid myself of conventional views about cleanliness and the daily washings . . . if I had not helped Eve she would never have washed at all and always have left her luggage behind. Mary does do everything for herself most neatly and conscientiously, but is 'very slow'. They take a good hour to get up and to go to bed. Mary has enjoyed it all more deeply than Eve. She is not at all bookish, has no memory and is always very childish for her age, but also very responsive. Loves anything she is told – anything that is read to her – especially poetry and has a genuine love for nature. Eve is exactly like a puppy, with a puppy's charm a puppy's high spirits and a puppy's aggravatingness. Wherever she goes she makes friends with animals, children. men and women and she likes them in that order. When in a rollicking mood she can be a frightful tease and when in a petulant mood very cross and rude and absolutely uncontrolled. On the other hand I think she is passionately loving – her ceaseless talking and thinking of Nannie and Ral have touched me – and though she is at times brutally selfish to Mary she always wants to be with her. Her dirtiness is a real fatigue. If ever there is a puddle she walks in it – if there is a dirty bit of furniture she wipes it with her hand. If she has dirty boots she will put them on a white counterpane; it seems natural for her to be dirty and an intolerable bore to be clean and the constant effort to make her so is tiring to her and her mentor. Would it be better to let her be as dirty as she likes for a time – till she herself wants to be clean?

'Physically I don't think I have ever overtired her; she has eaten well – slept well – and her average pace has been 5 miles an hour. Also Mary has been quite wonderfully strong over it. The food has been a bit difficult. We have had to depend on fresh eggs, bread, toast and milk and potatoes at practically every meal, very rarely being able to get a well cooked rice pudding. When Eve broke down at Selkirk I wondered if it was from underfeeding and they both have little gumboils and now comes your letter speaking of Anthony having exactly the same attack from overfeeding – so that I don't know what to think – children are an intense joy – their company more and more an all satisfying delight to me – but I do think they are an anxiety and seem to want quite ceaseless care. Perhaps I think this too much . . .'

Although Eve appears to have learned very early that to make people smile was a sound method of turning away wrath, she also seems to have had in her early days at least a pessimistic streak. This revealed itself very clearly around the age of ten when her elder sister Eleanor was taken ill and had to be left behind in the south. It was feared that she might have scarlet fever with all the complications and danger to life this disease involved. On their arrival at Whittingehame news of the invalid was impatiently awaited. Finally a telegraph boy arrived from East Linton, the nearest post office. Eve, impetuous as ever, ran out and seized the telegram and tore it open. The family assembling round her watched her face change dramatically. The telegram itself ran 'Nellie better. No cause for anxiety.' That was not how Eve saw it. She was asked what it said and replied.

'Oh, it's terribly bad news.'

What does it say?' her father demanded impatiently.

'Nellie better? No! Cause for anxiety!' she read out in tones of horror.

In a letter from 'Us Four' addressed to 'Dear Nunkie' and dated 18th October 1908 it is clear that the older girls had begun to adopt the by-then ten-year-old Eve as an amusing, if occasionally irritating hanger-on. In part it read: 'Eve spent the whole morning shopping with Ruth and Joan. She made them late for lunch and at lunch complained so of the things that she had not been allowed to do that she had to be taken back to Linton where she spent the whole afternoon . . .'

Another interesting excerpt from the same letter noted there was: 'A tramp scare going about. Three people have been attacked. We have never seen so many tramps going about. Mary and Eve are not allowed to ride alone . . .' Whether such an order would have stopped Eve from doing so is another matter.

It was in this way and against these backgrounds that Eve Balfour spent her childhood, half the year in Whittingehame and half in Surrey, with occasional excursions to visit her Lytton cousins at Knebworth and her Salisbury cousins at Hatfield. In each of these country homes Eve naturally had a pony, for it must be remembered that the Edwardian era was still predominantly ruled by horsepower, although the new-fangled motor cars were gradually being introduced by wealthy enthusiasts. Such names as Benz, Daimler and de Dion were being bandied about by the knowledgeable and snorting monsters were occasionally to be seen on the roads smelling strongly of kerosene. A.J.Balfour was amongst these early enthusiasts at Whittingehame.

It is an interesting point that musical ability and appreciation was an inherited trait in the Balfour family. A.J.Balfour was a highly skilled performer on the concertina, a musical instrument notoriously difficult to play. Eve herself mastered the flute, or recorder, from an early age and grew to become a more than competent player. Her musical ability was always to prove a source of relaxation to her and at one point in her career she was, when even more hard pressed financially than usual, able to turn it to profitable use.

An energetic horsewoman Eve was fond of riding through the wild Lammermuir hills above Whittingehame, or through the lush farmland of East Lothian, with its red earth and rich crops, so different from the then undeveloped countryside around Woking. Her intimacy with her aunt Alice and the chief gardener at Whittingehame may all have helped to sharpen the young girl's interest in agriculture and the soil. The contrast between the sandy Surrey heathland and the deep red soil of East Lothian was striking and must also have impressed her at an early age.

In both Whittingehame and Woking there were streams with frogs and newts and fish life in which, like any enquiring country child, she was naturally interested. She clearly had an affinity with animals from an early age. Kittens and puppies, cats and dogs, ponies and horses, were all naturally part of her upbringing. Breeding and caring for them followed as a matter of course on owning them. Her marked affinity with animals on the one hand was also balanced to some extent by an equal interest in the growth of the plants at both Whittingehame and Fisher's Hill, each of which had large gardens superintended by a considerable staff of gardeners and supervised in each case by the chatelaines of the house.

Eve's mother was a keen gardener as was Aunt Alice. Something of this interest in the soil and the growth of plants was undoubtedly imparted to most of the young at Whittingehame and Fisher's Hill, but notably so in the case of Eve. It is perhaps understandable in these circumstances and with this background that as early as twelve years of age she had resolved to be a farmer. In those days this was a somewhat eccentric ambition for any young female, let alone one with such a family background, where in the normal course of events she would be expected to marry well and rear a family. It is clear, however, that Eve had to a marked degree the family habit of making firm decisions. She appears to have shared this ambition from an early age with her elder sister Mary and when other girls of their age might have been contemplating an exciting future of balls and beaux they were playing at being farmers[7] and visualising sharing a dream farm.

Once again it was an example of the advanced approach to parenthood of both her mother and her father that when she announced her wish to become a farmer at the tender age of twelve in 1910 she was promptly entered for the Agricultural Department of Reading University College. Her schooling thereafter, although still by private tutor, was aimed at entering the university with this in mind. Her aim was to make sure of attaining her place in the college in 1915.

Around 1912, when her mother was away elsewhere, she was

allowed to accompany her father to Switzerland for a fortnight's winter sports. On her return her mother questioned her about her behaviour, fearing the worst.

'Did father never reprove you, Eve?' she asked.

'Oh, yes,' replied Eve. 'Sometimes he said, 'Manners, Billy, manners.'' '

'And when was that, Eve?' her mother persevered.

'Oh,' replied Eve dismissively. 'Only when I scratched too much in the restaurant.'

She appears early on to have had the Balfour habit of making dogmatic assertions, often combined with an assertive manner and an assured and forceful delivery, which was possibly developed early as a means of forestalling argument. The effect in discussion or argument on less self-assured and self-confident companions could be devastating, but it could also occasionally backfire. Thus on a well-remembered occasion she was in a greengrocer's examining fruit. Pointing an accusing finger at a melon she remarked loudly;

'That's not ripe.'

Her finger, thrust forcefully forward to prove her point, unfortunately went through the skin of the melon in question and she was forced to buy it, to her companion's amusement.

Although she learned in later life to restrain herself and to listen to the arguments of others and accept them when they were proved sound, she had by then an intimidating appearance and manner to those who did not know her. Her strong voice and commanding air gave a quite unintentional forcefulness to even minor statements. She was, however, always prepared to accept gracefully when she was in the wrong. As 1914 dawned Eve was aged fifteen and just at the awkward stage of growth, leaving childhood behind, but not really approaching womanhood. Her aims in life were, however, already firmly established in her mind. The fact that a world war was about to break out which would bring England to its knees and that a U-boat blockade would mean that farming became an essential war-time occupation was far from her mind at this stage.

Nobody brought up in the security of the Edwardian age could have visualised the appalling slaughter to come, when their entire world would be turned upside down. The very magnitude of the international struggle which tore their assured world apart during the next four years was something not even the wisest world-leaders could have foreseen. Amongst these was A.J.Balfour, who from this time on was to play the role of senior statesman, flitting from one cabinet post to another quite regardless of party in a manner remarkable by any standards.

NOTES ON CHAPTER ONE

1. *The Rt. Hon. Gerald Balfour M.P.*

Her father was then Secretary of State for Ireland and a member of the Marquis of Salisbury's notorious 'family' cabinet, which contained eleven close relatives of the Salisburys. The first two years of her life were thus spent partly in a heavily-guarded official residence in Dublin.

Subsequently, from 1900 to 1905, her father served as President of the Board of Trade in his brother A.J.Balfour's cabinet, but after their landslide defeat and the loss of his seat his interest in politics waned. He never stood for Parliament again. He became a Privy Counsellor and accepted various directorships, but he shared to the full the male Balfours' tendency towards indolence. His interests thereafter inclined particularly towards the Society for Psychical Research, of which he became President in 1906. His subsequent interest may have been stimulated by his affair with a notable medium Margaret Tennant.

2. *Lady Betty Balfour*

An outstanding correspondent throughout her life, she wrote as many as forty letters a day, retaining copies of the more important ones sent and received. Her younger sister, Constance Lytton, born in 1969 was a close friend and supporter of Sylvia Pankhurst and a leading figure in the Suffragette movement. The strength of character which was a notable feature of the Lytton sisters, was something that appears to have been passed on to Evelyn Barbara in full measure.

3. *Eustace Balfour*

At 6 ft 4 inches the tallest of the Balfour brothers, Eustace was an architect and keen member of the London Scottish Volunteer Force, which he commanded for a number of years until his comparatively early death in 1911 of dropsy, the debilitating effects of which caused him to grow enormously stout and lethargic. An excessive consumption of alcohol may have been a contributory factor. (It was noted that on his death in 1911 Alice entered his name in the departure column of the visitors' book without further comment.)

4. *Lady Frances Balfour*

She was perhaps typical of the Campbells of this generation, impetuous, opinionated, short-tempered, autocratic, subject to wild swings of temperament and capable of considerable charm as well as holding a grudge once formed for any reason good or bad. She also suffered from a chronic hip complaint which may have exacerbated her temper even more and with a tongue like a whiplash dipped in acid she was almost always at the centre of any family acrimony, clashing frequently with her sister-in-law Alice, or her other sister-in-law Evelyn, (married to Lord Rayleigh: see p.7) if she was present.

5. Marquis of Salisbury, 3rd Marquis and brother of Lady Blanche Gascoigne Cecil, who married James Maitland Balfour in 1844. Uncle of A.J.Balfour and Gerald, both of whose political careers owed much to his encouragement. Prime Minister

from 1885–1902 and notorious for the 'Family Cabinet' of 1890s, which contained eleven members who were related to him.

6. East Linton, though small, was an agricultural village, hub of a rich farming area. Amongst other features around this time it boasted two general practicioners, an apothecary (chemist), a draper's shop, a grocers shop, an ironmonger and dry-salters, a flesher (butcher), a saddler and harness-maker, a wheelwright and coach-builder, two or more cobblers and bootmakers, a sanitary engineer, several smithies, several dairies, a sawmill and undertaker, a police station, a sheep and cattle-market, a railway station o the main Edinburgh-London line, two Churches and two chapels, and three inns, the Railway, the Bull and the Queen's Head, the last a Mecca for artists eager to paint the picturesque Linton Water-mill. Although, to the casual observer it has only one main street leading off the old A1 London to Edinburgh road it would have been easy enough for Eve as a child to wander down one of the side closes down by the riverside and lose her sense of direction, or more probably, having befriended a bootmaker and bewitched by his craftsmanship, simply decided to spend the night with her new friend.

7. Playing at being farmers. In after-years Eve was to recall the far-reaching effects of the view from the Whittingehame road on reaching the top of the hill over-looking East Linton. From here the ground below is spread out like a flat relief map with the North Berwick Law and the Bass Rock standing out starkly. Beyond them the blue waters of the Firth of Forth are clear to the Isle of May and the coast of Fife beyond. This is the start of the truly lush East Lothian coastal fringe, often termed 'The Garden of Scotland.'

The fields are all plainly laid out, each clearly visible. Today toy combines may be seen working on the harvest or in the appropriate season toy tractors ploughing the rich red soil and sowing seeds for the harvest to come or cutting the hay or silage. It is easy to visualise these scenes as they were in Eve's childhood days when she took this road on horseback or in an open trap to East Linton or heading further afield to the coast at Ravensheugh for an afternoon's picnic and swim Then the fields would be full of labourers in shirt sleeves stooking the sheaves to dry for the harvest with the women also doing their share in their old fashioned sun-bonnets, known as 'Uglies.' (Still worn into the fifties and sixties.) Teams of horses would be hauling wagon-loads of corn or hay or alternatively hauling the ploughs and turning the rich red soil. Each farm with its' square of neat buildings and their red pan-tiled roofs, at one corner its' distinctive tall brick donkey-engine chImmney smoking gently and the bustle of activity visible all around, all laid out in a toy landscape beneath them, would have been enough to grip the imagination of any child and give rise to the wish to be a part of such a scene. Understandably Eve and Mary played at 'Farms' rather than with dolls in the nursery.

2. Front of Whittingehame House 1898

3. Back of Whittingehame House 1898

4. Family Group in 1904 winter on steps of Whittinhgehame.
*Back row: L to R.* Eleanor, Joan, Ruth with Ral.
*Front:* Mary Eve aged 6 (centre) Alison.

5. Portrait by Neville Lytton of Eve aged 13 years.

6. Eve in side-saddle habit aged 17 in front of
Whittingehame training a pony on the lunge line.

# CHAPTER TWO

# The War Years

## 1914–1918

*'I am enjoying the work and life quite enormously, and feeling most remarkably well . . . Shows what an outdoor life and lots of exercise does.'*

Eve in a letter home from Reading.

THE BOER WAR had shaken the complacency of the British concerning the might of the British Empire, but unfortunately it had taught the ageing Generals in charge of their army little about tactics or strategy. They were all old men still largely products of a system of promotion which rewarded age and seniority rather than ability and for the most part incapable of adapting to modern warfare. Yet the patriotic fervour of the Empire was such that hundreds of thousands of gifted youths flocked to join the armed forces and died before reaching full manhood. As the war progressed boys and middle-aged men were pressed into service on both sides. Women too took their share of the war in ways which would have seemed inconceivable only a few years earlier. A different, more realistic, lifestyle was forged in the crucible of war.

It is hard today to conceive the anxiety and worries of those left at home in a Britain faced with ever-longer casualty lists as men died in hitherto unimaginable numbers, slaughtered in the fields of Belgium, France, the Dardanelles and even further afield, in places where the names meant less than nothing to the average man-in-the-street. Yet all the while the U-boat blockade intensified its grip on Britain and rationing was imposed to prevent the nation being starved into submission, a state of affairs which had never been conceived by a people who sang of 'ruling the waves.' Under such pressures the nation rose to face the challenge in a way that had never been seen before. Eventually conscription was introduced, women joining men, shoulder to shoulder, serving in the forces, driving ambulances, working in munitions, or on the factory floor, or serving in hospitals or on the land.

The patriotic fervour which swept the country at the start of the war and gathered many of Britain's youth into the armed forces had as strong an appeal to women. The first-aid nursing auxiliaries flooded the hospitals, the army took on its first women cooks as volunteers in khaki, appeals were made for women to help on the land and in making munitions and in other jobs previously regarded as male preserves. The spirit which had fired the early Suffragettes during the Edwardian period to demand the vote was now harnessed to the war effort. Anti-German feeling and spy mania was at its height in these early days.

Eve was being crammed for her entry examinations for University during 1914 and in an undated letter to her mother in this period gives an account of collecting moths with 'Aunty' in the car headlights. She wrote:

'Darling Mum,

. . . I have not sent Court Life to Miss Gardner because I thought I ought to wait till I had done the whole paper. But now I will send 'Court Life of George II and Conditions in France before the Revolution' together as soon as the latter is finished . . . It is so difficult you know, I do them as shortly as possible, but if she will give me such large subjects I can't skip over them. I don't mean that I don't like large subjects, I do and I love doing my papers. They are enormous fun and very interesting. But not having my full and uninterrupted lesson hours here I can not do them very fast. I only hope Miss G doesn't mind . . . I do feel that I have learned more since the summer than ever in the same time before. And that I think is the great thing . . .

Did I tell you about Mothing with Auntie? . . . We did it all up and down the road to Linton! At first we walked in front of the motor. (What people thought! Spies I'm sure ) and when a moth appeared Mills blew the horn. Or Aunty examined the hedge for females! After that we walked one on each side just behind the lamps. Its very difficult you know to keep a car exactly even at a snail's pace up and down hill. However if Mills got an inch behind Auntie she said 'Come on Mills a little faster' or if he got an inch in front 'You're going too fast now.' At intervals she called a halt (generally in the middle of a steep hill) and we stood like sentinels nets over shoulders one on each side for 10 minutes on end. Waiting for moths which never came. The only two which we saw were sucked into the engine! Once Auntie leant over Mills and said 'You know Mills the females of these moths we're trying to catch have no wings. Very curious isn't it' 'Yes Miss,' said Mills. I love Mothing with her it is always such an endless source of amusement . . . Tea time. Yours devotedly . . .'

Subsequently in 1914 Eve sat and successfully passed her Junior local Cambridge examination to qualify for University. It says much for her private education that she passed in History, Geography, French, German, English Literature and Scripture. With such an academic family background it was natural enough that she turned to higher education, but she was already determined to be a farmer. At the age of seventeen in 1915 she enrolled as a student at Reading University College for the Diploma of Agriculture, amongst the first women students to do so. Her beloved elder sister Mary had started work as a VAD, a nursing auxiliary, but the two sisters had already decided on an ambitious plan for the distant future 'after the war' to own and run their own farm. With this in mind Mary in 1918 gave up her VAD work and enrolled at Reading just before Eve had completed her course, taking a short ten-week course for a Certificate in milking husbandry rather than general farming as in Eve's case. In October 7th 1915 Eve was writing to A.J.Balfour from University College Reading with characteristically erratic spelling:

'Darling Nunkie

I was so miserable not to see you on Tuesday . . . It is no good telling you the latest news of Whitt and the journey as Joan and Nell are sure to do that . . . I have been here three days and am feeling quite at home. Today was my first day's work and I enjoyed it emensly . . . I do hope we can see you on the 17th, Your loving Eve.'

In the early stages of the war A.J.Balfour had been appointed First Lord of the Admiralty. When he visited Whittingehame the family there was accustomed to obtaining news of the war through highly secret despatches not normally seen by civilians. Soon after Eve went to Reading Nell wrote with a characteristic Balfour lack of under-standing of her sister's feelings at being stranded in a university where any news there was came at best through newspapers and rumour:

'Eve's letters from Reading continue to be priceless . . . she says what she misses most is being 'cut off from sources of information . . .'

One of the reasons for family mirth at her letters was Eve's always eccentric spelling.[1] On Saturday 23rd of December, 1915, she wrote again to A.J.Balfour from Whittingehame. To judge by the under-linings, however, her spelling was still a sore subject. Although the old Balbirnie and Whittingehame rivalry still seemed to exist amongst the older generation her elder sister Ruth, now qualified as a doctor, had gone a long way to resolving it by marrying her first cousin, the heir to Balbirnie, William Balfour, known as Bill. Eve wrote:

'Darling Nunkie

It is beastly not to have you for Christmas. We are a very reduced little party. Joan does not arrive until the 27th so that there are only Baffy and myself and the 3 babies, besides Auntie. On Thursday I went for one night to Balbirnie (for the first time in my life) to be with Bill and Ruth. Cousin Teddy whom I had never seen before more than came up to the numerous reports of him. Some of his remarks at dinner were:

1. Did you ever see such pheasants as these?

2. Aren't these magnificent potatos?

3. Have a marrow bone, Never eat anything in your life like these marrow bones.

4. Isn't this pudding dilicious? Never get a pudding like this.

5. The other day we had fifteen vegitables at one meal.

6. This last is to go into the Book of Bosh as Teddy's War Economy.

The next morning I was taken over the farms after having been given accounts of the last three years to inspect the evening before. I was really much impressed with the improvements in plant and labour saving appliances which Teddy has put in. Such things as new sheds and thrashing machine and chaff cutting and cake breaking machines. All run by electric power which he has tapped and which carry the various foods and drop them just wherever they are wanted. By this one man feeds nearly 80 head of fatting cattle in the covered yards. It also means most of his labour is skilled labour.

When Auntie heard I was going to Balbirnie the first thing she said was 'You'll – find it a very dull place compared with this.'

There have been many humours of course. It is impossible for 2 Bs (Balfours) to collect without their occuring . . . I hope to be able to lunch with you on my way south if you are free. Your loving Eve.'

The syllabus for the first-year course at Reading was a stiff one consisting of Farm Management, Agricultural Botany, Land Survey-ing, Book-Keeping, General Chemistry, General Botany, Zoology, Geology, Physics and Meteorology, along with Veterinary Hygiene.

The syllabus for the second year was even more demanding, consisting of Agriculture, sub-divided into Farm and Estate Management and Farm Economics, Live Stock, Dairy Farming, Land Drainage, Agricultural Law and Practical Farming. In addition there was Book-Keeping, Surveying, Agricultural Buildings and Machinery, Agricultural Chemistry and Botany and Veterinary Hygiene. Finally it included Agricultural Entomology and Practical Work.

During 1916 and 1917 Eve was closely in touch with her Lytton relations at Crabbet Park. Judith Wentworth, her cousin, was to become the noted Arab horse breeder. Eve, of course, was greatly interested in her work and enjoyed visiting her. She even contemplated leasing one of the Crabbet Park farms in Sussex and went as far as discussing the possibility with Judith. At this stage her inclinations were strongly towards eventually taking a farm in Sussex, but, of course this was looking far ahead. She still had her practical year on a farm to fill in.

This last, as today, was intended to provide practical farm experience and involved a year's practical training as a farm pupil after her diploma had been gained. In the course of this she had to learn practical milking, all done by hand in those days, and ploughing, all accomplished by horsepower at the time. Two-horse ploughing required considerable stamina and strength, but fortunately Eve was unusually strong for her sex. Indeed in 1916 her sister Eleanor, Nellie, felt constrained to write to her on this subject. She wrote:

'Jan 19 1916: Darling Eve,

I was rather horrified at your letter . . . I do honestly think you are too old now to act in 'modern' man's costume . . . I and Ruth did it when we were 14 & 15 but even then – tho' I was slighter than you, I vowed I would never do it again. You must remember that however much you wish you weren't, the fact remains that you are a woman . . . I understand that Neville said you were getting more and more like a man. I expect you took this as a compliment but I feel quite sure "he" did not mean it as such . . . A boyish girl is not without charm, but a masculine woman is . . .'

This 'tirade' as Nellie herself termed it went on for six pages and included some interesting sidelights on the attitudes of the age such as: 'You know I am no feminist . . . but . . . to have a woman apeing the ways of a man is . . . nearly as horrible as a man who is like a woman . . . with little girl's voice and mincing ways etc. You know what your feelings would be about such a creature . . .'

Their cousin Neville (Lytton) mentioned above was the artist who drew the notable likeness of Eve pictured at the age of fifteen in 1913. It is somewhat difficult looking at this very feminine picture to visualise her as being the object of this lecture from her elder sister only three years later. It is significant, however, that this letter should have been kept for nearly eighty years, amongst Eve's collection of family letters. In the Book of Bosh, Neville Lytton was also noted as saying before taking Eve to a play about this time 'that it was scarcely "jeaune fille" but then Eve was almost "jeunne homme".'

Neville Lytton's artistic eye undoubtedly depicted Eve accurately. His later comment was merely a somewhat feline play on words, but Eve was always sublimely unconcerned about outward appearances. In later life to the casual observer who did not know her well she must frequently have appeared to be the archetypal Lesbian with her Eton crop, loud voice, trousers and general carelessness about her appearance. The fact that she lived happily for many years with a female companion may have confirmed this impression for some superficial observers, but in any mixed gathering even in advancing years she was invariably the centre of considerable male attention sometimes to the obvious chagrin of other females present. The often forgotten explanation was that in her generation almost all the eligible young men had died between 1914 and 1918. That Lytton portrait was a good insight into her true sexual libido.

Quite aside from the portrait, some idea of Eve's very attractive appearance at this stage may be had from an interesting encounter her sister Ruth had in London. In April 1917 Ruth wrote to her at Reading describing a remarkable double co-incidence which had occurred as follows:

'Dearest Eve,

. . . Walking back from dining with Dr Jane a week ago about 10.30 I passed a woman who called out to me 'Hello Eve'. I turned round and she approaching me exclaimed' Oh, I'm so sorry I thought it was Eve Balfour.' 'I am her sister, 'I replied. 'Well that's most extraordinary.' she remarked. 'You must be very like her.' and after she had a good look at me. 'Yes, you are very like her. 'As she was now standing quite close to me I observed . . . a faint aroma of whisky hung around her though she was respectably dressed. Who is this strange acquaintance of Eve's I thought. 'Did you meet her at Reading?'I asked. 'No,' she said looking puzzled and after a pause. 'You do mean Eve Balfour the Cinema actress don't you?' She was amazed when I explained there was another Eve Balfour and repeated I was very like her. Should I feel flattered by this?! Uncle Neville has sent you her portrait before now hasn't he? . . . Even father was struck by this remarkable double co-incidence . . . loving Ruth.

After nearly two years' study Eve gained her Farming Diploma in 1917 and moved from St. Andrews Hall in the University into 'digs' in Reading at 102, Basingstoke Road. She now had to do her practical year's work on a farm and she wrote to her mother with her usual erratic spelling and incurable optimism:

Darling Mum, Saturday,

On reciept of your letter I have been and fixed up with my landlady, but you will be pleased to hear that in view of my being a vegitarian I have brought her down to 30/ – without any difficulty.

I am afraid if I payed everything it will be more than you say. You must have misread my letter. The Farmers charges are per week changing at the end of a month. The most therefore that I could cost is as follows;

| | |
|---|---|
| Lodgings 30/- per week 52 weeks | = £78 |
| Tuition 1 month @ £1 per week | = £4 |
| 1 month @ 17/6 per week | = £3 – 10s |
| 10 months @ 15/- per week | = £30 |
| | £115 10s |
| Dues, if as this year | £60 |
| Gross Total £175 10s | |

But I think I can safely reduce this to £150 – your estimate) because I dont think the farmer will charge me 15/- p.week for v. long if I work hard. A pupil he once had started by giving him £1 per week and in a short time the farmer was giving 'him' £1 per week. I dont hope for this, but I think by the end of the twelve months he may be charging me nothing perhaps. Also my dues will be less so that if you start me in October with £150 for everything I am sure I can manage with that till the following October and after that I shall be earning 'About Mar' (her sister Mary), there isn't another room available but I have chosen the large bedroom (really quite a nice room especially when I get my own things in it). This has another small bed in it which they are going to leave there. Mar won't mind sleeping with me. The room is really quite big. It will be cheaper so, too, and also when she is not there any of you could come down for a night if you felt inclined. The bedroom has a southern aspect a little to the east and the sitting room opposite i.e. North westerly. Furniture quite comfy (Piano in the sitting room)! . . .'

At this stage Mary was still working as a VAD, but she had been planning to join Eve at Reading for a short course in poultry keeping. She was, however, in the middle of a very intense, if largely spiritual, love affair with a bedridden poultry geneticist and felt unable to leave him. This does not appear to have affected Eve, for not long afterwards she was writing enthusiastically about her work on the farm as follows:

'102 Basingstoke Road, Reading: Oct 3 '17.

. . . I am enjoying the work and life quite enormously, and feeling most remarkably well . . . Shows what an outdoor life and lots of exercise does. . . My day is as follows: On the farm by 6 a.m. – plough till 8. Then home to breakfast. Back by 9. and then plough till 3 p.m. stopping for half an hour at 12.30 to eat lunch which I take with me. The men stop from 10 – 10.30, that is the only half hour I waste and I am quite glad of it at present. (I eat a biscuit) At 3.30 I go to the cattle-man and help him feed and water the stock etc till 4.30, when the men come back from their dinner, then I clean two of the horses we have been using, help to feed and after they are turned out sweep up the stable, so that I usually leave the farm at 5.25 about. The big meal of the day I have at 8 p m. which just leaves me time to get off my boots and tidy. Then at 9 p.m I have milk and biscuits – so I have a 'bear' two hours to do anything out-side actual farm work. I want to do my own things from 6.30 – 7.30 and then agricultural reading from 7.30 to 8.30 and then turn in. Of course if I go out in the evenings I have time for neither of these . . .'

A combination of the natural hunger of a growing teenager during the difficult period of rationing in wartime, especially one taking a great deal of outdoor exercise, combined with her landlady's distrust of her diet, finally overcame, at least partially, Eve's determination to remain vegetarian. Reluctantly she ate occasional fish and meat dishes when nothing else was available. In the circumstances this was scarcely surprising. Thereafter, although sticking to a mainly vegetarian diet, she would eat meat and fish dishes when nothing else was available.

It is apparent that A.J.Balfour, the revered 'Nunkie,' had raised somewhat the same questions as her sister Nellie as to the possible coarsening effect of this life on her for Eve wrote interestingly:

'102 Basingstoke Road: October 11th 17:

Darlingest Mother, I didn't really mean to write home today, but I must answer your letter . . . About Nunk. I was most touched. Darling you need have 'no' fears. The life I am now living only makes me care more about the other and be more interested in it. It quickens and makes more sensitive my perceptions thoughts and feelings rather than having the other effect. The life has three sides to it:

1st: that joyous feeling of acquiring knowledge which I felt so keenly on first going to college and I am learning things fast and applying the theory I have learned to the things I do. Combined with this is the delightful feeling of working for a fixed aim and learning so that I can one day say, these are 'my' horses, I have been ploughing 'my' wheat field, these are Mary's calves and its 'our' farm.

2nd There is the joy of perfect health and the invigorating feeling of air and exercise . . .

3rd There is the human aspect. You can't think how it thrills me to get into the working class mind – see how it moves and thinks and to hear questions concerning their class discussed from their point of view . . . the foreman and Farmer don't treat me as a labourer and the ploughmen don't treat me as any form of employer; so that I hear the foreman and Chettle (the farmer who had taken her on as student) discussed from the men's point of view and I hear the men discussed from Chettle's point of view . . . I am quite sure that when I come to be an employer of labour myself that the experience I am gaining here will be invaluable . . .

'Nunkie may be right about 9 farmers out of 10 never having touched a plough, but I am sure that those 9 are the unsuccessful ones and the 10th is the one who makes his farm pay; besides when we start . . . I shall have to plough and reap as well as my employees and I want to start so. Anyone can make a farm pay if they start with lots of capital . . .

'Then to refer to a quite minor detail; i.e care of my own person and things, you may remember nannie saying a little time ago that I had got so much tidier both in my room and my clothes. Well I 'am' better if not really tidy and I have begun to care about cleanliness and order etc., but the date of my first 'caring' dates from my first real practical work upon a farm. When one is out all day and gets covered in mud, its a genuine pleasure to get really clean and into decent clothes. Also one cares for the respect of the men working under or with one and that makes one work in tidy clothes as far as possible . . . Being away from my kind and my own folk only makes me care more about them, one has got to be away from all good things to appreciate them properly . . .

'You needn't worry. Good heavens! because I have chosen a life that "does" instead of merely "is" in order to feel justified in being in the world at all, and wish to train for that life "properly," so as to be some use, and if part of that training takes me away from the atmosphere I was brought up in do you think it means I am going to renounce that atmosphere altogether and let myself become unfit to associate with it! I shall think not indeed!

'It is simply darling of Nunkie to take an interest in the way he has. You may send him this letter if you think it would quiet his fears . . .'

In early January of 1918 she wrote home enthusiastically about a change of farm work:

'January 7th 1918:

Darling Mum,

I have got a new and most delightful job on the Farm. I am in sole charge of twenty six colts in three lots. Ten 2 – 3 year olds, six yearlings and ten foals. They are in meadows with sheds. The hay stacks are on the spot and I have to cut and carry the hay for them every morning. It takes me over two hours to feed the lot. While I am doing that I do not care how cold it is. Getting hay makes me sweat in three minutes in the coldest weather. But when I have to stand about as I did some of the coldest days in the cow sheds doing nothing but taking temperatures all day preparatory to the tubercolosis test I did get 'frozen.'

'I have got another cold but am feeling quite well in spite of it. One of the joys of my present job is that I don't have to be at the farm till 8 o'clock. This gives me an hour longer in the evenings. My diploma Certificate has arrived and makes me feel so important.

Devoted Eve.'

Although a vegetarian, in common with most hungry teenagers, she found the effects of rationing were something that occupied her thoughts a great deal. It was particularly intensified for her, of course, since she had come from homes in Surrey and in Scotland where the effects of rationing could be cushioned with the aid of fresh milk from the cows and of course vegetables and fruit grown in the gardens. In an industrial area, even working on the Reading University farm, the effects of rationing were felt much more intensely and as a vegetarian possibly they affected her even more deeply than most. She wrote to her mother in 1918;

'Darlingest Mum, Jan 26 1918

Many thanks for the 15/- most welcome . . . I have a host of questions to ask . . .

1. Will you send me the receipts of some of our nut dishes?

2. What are the terms of the Woman's Suffrage clause in the reform bill . . . This a question on behalf of Mrs Wheeler.(Her landlady)

3. Is the fat ration 1/4 lb 'total' for every kind of fat?

4 – there 'was' a fourth but I have forgotten it.

'Are you keeping your fat ration?' I find the only way to do it is on the days when there is any fat in the cooking, I must eat dry toast. If I have butter on these there must be no fat in the cooking. It is the hardest of all the rations. The milk I have not till now kept, but I am starting tomorrow. It means milk with grapenuts or porridge only. Everything else, coffee, milk pudding etc., has to be done with condensed milk. I am told Cow & Gate is the best. I shall be keeping all my rations then except eggs and I am going to let myself exceed in those because I eat no meat. This is legitimate isn't it?'

She reported back in letters home about the discontent with the unfairness of the rationing which was felt in the working class in Reading. She wrote:

'. . . it is distressing (tho' not unnatural) to see how the attitude about the war of some of my staunchest working class friends is changed by the present food crisis . . . Of course it is very natural they should feel worried when their wives go four days running and can get neither meat nor butter and 1lb of meat is not much to the man who can't get substitutes like we can . . .'

She described the state of affairs at one point in grim terms; 'Many shops have been raided in Reading and the biscuit factory and gas works either have or are coming out on strike. They are the mainstay of Reading. Their example whatever it is sure to be followed . . . However when they talk of a revolution one has only to remind them of the result of that course in Russia and they are silent. Others again are unaltered by the difficulties and if you speak of rumours of revolution exclaim. 'Oh we doesn't want none o' that here be God.' My work up till now has been finding colts . . . This week I am to desert the colts and do some 2 horse ploughing.'

She was at this time acting as one of the Manor Farm ploughmen and as such worked under Bill French the foreman. She was obviously on very good terms with him and clearly he was pleased to have such an unusual and keen pupil. She wrote of his wife, Mrs French:

'She feeds and houses 7 and clothes 5 on 33/- a week. 'That's quite usual,' you'll say. But listen to the extras she has to face. The boy in France continually writes home for things. She sends a parcel oftener than once a month. They usually cost, all told, 5/- to 7/-. She gets no money for that.'

She went on to detail other expenses that resulted from the actions of thoughtless employers, showing that even then she was interested in every detail of any subject she investigated. At the same time it is mildly interesting that although strongly interested and supportive of Mrs French the case was detailed quite clinically and even with detachment, showing that she was even then prone to dispassionate judgements.

It is an interesting sidelight on the 1914–18 War often forgotten today that before the days of the radio the only reliable news of events available was through the daily newspaper. This was seized on eagerly by the family each morning and practically snatched from those who had first obtained it. Rumours were also widespread, especially in country districts. Everyone knew someone who knew something about the way the war was being managed or mismanaged. Eve herself gave detailed accounts, which must have been typical of many others throughout the country, of government and bureaucratic mismanagement. Her landlady's brother-in-law was an agent for the Board of Agriculture buying horses throughout the country, a subject which interested her greatly; she noted with amazement:

'£80 is the sum he 'must' pay, not less, not more. He say's 'I'd like to give £70 here and £90 there. But it's not allowed. The consequence is I don't buy this horse because he's not worth £80 or that one because I can't get him for £80. He is given passes to go and buy at special places and costs the Board a lot of money travelling and motoring about to do this and yet again and again when he arrives he is told 'Oh but a Representative of the Board has just been here and bought them.'

In trying to be as economical as he can be he had lunch once in a simple way and sent up with his account Chauffeurs lunch 1/6. The immediate reply came 'We don't understand this item Chauffeur's lunch 1/6. The lunch allowed for the Chauffeur is 2/6 and he had to change that although he hadn't spent it . . .'

Not surprisingly her father, Gerald, said to her mother: 'Eve writes a most uncommonly good letter. You must keep these letters from Eve. They will be a very interesting record.'

This appears to have been unnecessary advice since in her customary fashion his wife Betty was busily copying these and other family letters and circulating them around the family circle. Thanks to this habit there is an unusually complete record of Eve's early life.

NOTE ON CHAPTER TWO

1. *Spelling*

    This was a family failing amongst the younger Balfours, possibly the result of an indifferent governess at an early age. Eve's elder sister Mary could seldom spell either, nor could her weakly younger brother, known as Ral. In his case it was possibly a form of dyslexia since at the age of 12 he was noted as spelling 'Useful' as 'Yousphel'. In 1916 having been sent to Eton he begged to be allowed to enter Osborne to join the Navy, but although he managed to pass the medical at the second attempt he failed the entrance exam by signing his name Arthur Robert Lytton as Arther Robart Lyton. Rather than interrupt the text by noting the frequent spelling errors these have been left as written.

# CHAPTER THREE

# The Farm at Newport

## 1918

*'Every day's farm work convinces me still further that I have chosen the profession which really suits me. I love it more and more.'*

Eve in a letter home from Monmouthshire.

IN MARCH 1918 MARY was still deeply involved in her unfortunate but very intense love affair with her poultry geneticist. He had the unlikely name of Oscar Smart and was many years older than she, eventually dying of consumption. During the four years it lasted, however, the affair had an intense spiritual effect on her. At this stage she had given up work as a VAD and started a short ten-week course in dairying at Reading University, joining Eve at 102 Basingstoke Road.

By the end of May Eve had graduated from college and almost finished her year's practical farming. She was determined to obtain a post in charge of one of the farms run by the government as part of the war effort. With this in mind she went up to Oxford to see a Dr. Allen who was part of the selection board for such posts. After taking her luggage to the lodgings provided, she gave a cri-de-coeur which many others, at a similar age, must have felt;

'Nice room of the usual lodging house type. My thoughts flew to Lauder, Winchester, Dorking. Sometimes I think innkeepers and landladies must be a special breed of mankind who manage to create rooms exactly similar in every detail to every other room of the kind.'

It may have been on this visit to Oxford that her interest in flying was first kindled. She met a young Scottish Naval Flyer, 'Dennis Murray, son of Gilbert Murray.' She noted: 'He is . . . back for a month's holiday from Internment in Holland. Don't you think that is an amazing thing? He has to go back in July. He had an accident in the North Sea quite early in the war and was picked up by a Dutch Ship . . . he tried to escape before an order came from England warning officers not to do so and that they would be sent back if they did . . . A millionaire he said could have done anything. For £50,000 you could have been conducted to the frontier in the Governor's car and sent over the channel with an escort. He said the Dutch were very nice to them now but were beastly at first. The feeling . . . is . . . pro-French rather than pro-English. He has been spending his time at home flying. He says the latest machines are 1,000 horse power and will go up to 180 miles an hour . . .' She added triumphantly; 'After dinner we went to the upper common room (strictly forbidden to females.)'

In June 1918 Eve applied for the post of supervisor at a small fifty acre farm in Monmouthshire, near Rogerstone above Newport, advertised in the 'Farmer & Stockbreeder'. The farm had been taken over by the Monmouthshire War Agricultural Executive Committee, when the original tenant had been turned out by the Board of Agriculture for bad and inefficient farming. They had handed over control to the Monmouthshire Women's War Agricultural Committee. Eve was duly interviewed by the Chairwoman of this Committee, a Lady Mather Jackson of Llantilio Court, Abergavenny and wrote:

'Queen's Hotel, Newport, July 17 1918

Darlingest Mum,

The momentous interview is over, but I do not yet know my fate. On arriving at Newport I went to the Labour Exchange and asked for Lady Jackson. Had some time to wait in an office like Miss A works in. Land posters on the walls and earnest females rushing in and out with official looking documents. Mrs Williams, Vice Chairman of the committee who is to take me over the farm this p.m. was the 1st to appear. Later Lady Jackson came and we three solemnly went off to a private room leaving the rest of her committee sitting without her. The interview was much less alarming than it might have been and neither of the inquisitors the least alarming. They were as much surprised as anyone at my age and Lady Jackson said 'I think we had better keep low about the age. I was asked 'Have you got parents?' to which I replied 'Yes' but kept quite dark as to who they were. The farm, even before I have seen it, will I can see take a lot of work, but I think it will be extremely interesting and stimulating work to do. I shall have to be housekeeper as well which will be extremely good for me. The five workers taking it in turn to do the housework. I am given their wages out of which I have to take 15/- a week to board them on. My salary is 30/- a week – 15/- for board which is good as a start. I shall have a bedroom and sitting room to myself.

Meanwhile I am waiting at this Hotel for Mrs Williams while she and the rest of the committee are discussing my case. I think I shall get it. If I do it will need doing, but I will put heart and soul into making a success of it. I'll tell you more later.'

This somewhat disjointed, but triumphant, letter then continued without stopping:

'In the train on the way home to Reading without a change 'Marvelous!

I lunched with a large party of the committee people. I like them. They were human had a sence of humour and were as free from Red tape as the restrictions of the board will let them be.

'So far as the Monmouthshire committee are concerned I have got the job. But of course it has to be submitted to the men's committee and also to the Board. When all this has been got through they'll let me know, in a few weeks I expect. If I go I have decided to go on Oct 12th. And as I shall try to get away from the Manor Farm in the middle of Sep: I shall get about 1 months holiday. One clear week of this I would like to spend at Whitt exclusive of travelling and the rest of the time with you and Father at home. It isn't long I know but then they urgently need someone and if I put it off any longer I might lose the job. And I can't leave Reading much sooner or I shan't have learnt the two things remaining for me to know, binding and thatching.'

Clearly her mother had discussed the prospective job with her at length and had tried to point out some of the obvious disadvantages to her ever optimistic daughter, for she continued:

'It will be as you said a year of real separation, for I don't see how I am to get away even for a night as I am in charge 'indoors' as well as out, but Mother, it's worth it. There is a 'mine' of experience to be got and if I can make a success of this place I shan't be afraid of anything.

'I shan't have whole responsibility for the entire management, which is rather a comfort seeing that the vice chairman is going to be a friend, otherwise it would be rather a bore.

'Feeding stuffs, manures etc., will be bought thro' the committee, who will also decide on the cropping etc. Mrs Williams and her bailiff come over once a week to see how things are going. I am pretty sure Mrs Williams is a friend and I think if I have any schemes and talk them over with her that I shall get them worked. I have allready interested her in my pet cash cropping system which is quite new to this part.'

She was glowing with enthusiasm and went on to extol the farm itself, but had the sense to minimise the fact that the conscript girls were mostly pretty tough semi-delinquents.

'The farm is in a 'lovely' bit of country. High up and higher hills all round. Dear friendly old red sandstone soil. 'Excelent' buildings and 'very' nice tho' small house. If any of you ever come to stay with me you'll have to bring a camp bed and put it up in my sitting room.

'I think the only thing I shall really miss is my long hot bath, but one can't always live in the lap of luxury and it will do me no harm. I am told the girls are a handfull to manage sometimes, but I am not afraid of that. I think whatever my faults I am fairly tactful and I usually get on with people.

'They are going to rear and breed calves to my great joy for I love this side of it. The farm has got in a bad state and will need pulling together but I think I can do it . . . I will tell you all more details when I come Friday night . . . If I get this job next year I shall be 'rich' if you give me 1/3 of my present allowance. And I could do on none at all. Just think what fun to be earning my own living. I shall have to get Mrs Wheeler to give me some lessons about catering . . . Devoted, Eve.'

With the prospect of taking this job it is clear that Eve had now determined to have her long hair cut off into a short and then fashionable Eton crop. On 28th July she wrote yet again to her mother indicating that matters had been moving behind the scenes with her employer at Reading taking a hand:

'. . . Many thanks for yours. 'Delighted' that you have got an appointment with the hairdresser for Wed . . . There have been considerable developements over the Newport job since I left. While still at Fishers hill I had a letter from Lady Jackson asking me for my views about the farm which I answered by return.

'On Friday Chettle (the farmer who employed her) showed me a letter he had received that a.m from her. Chettle had very kindly written to a country man of some influence asking him to support my application if he got the chance. This letter Lady Jackson had forwarded to her. She said that it confirmed the oppinion she had formed of me at the interview, that she had been much impressed with me, that I had a 'knowledge and bearing far beyond my years.' and that I had evidently benefitted to the utmost from my excellent experience and then asked T.C for a few more particulars. When I got home I found a letter from her to me too in which she agreed with all I had said about the farm and said she would now have to send my application to the Board of Agriculture and that Mrs Baynes who is chief inspector of the Woman's Branch of the Food Production dept (B o A) might demand an interview. Then as a P.S she said; 'I might say that as a committee we are all willing and anxious to appoint you.'

'Yesterday I had a letter from Mrs Baynes asking for an interview at the B o A offices on Tuesday. Its an awful bore but I fear I ought to go, At anyrate I hope she will be able to seal my fate. I shall go to Derry & Toms (a well known apartment store) about the hat and am trying to lunch with Nunkie. . . .'

The sequel was written 'in the train' after the Tuesday interview. 'Darling Mum . . . I saw Miss A for a second before my interview and then went up to Mrs Baynes room. She was very nice to me . . . As far as I can make out keeness in the object of the place and interest in the work was what she most cared about. She was just as surprised as everyone else about my age and said . . .'I don't mind your being young. But you must have an official age of 25 as well as a real one because the girls will be older than you.'

'We agreed about what needs doing on the farm and she wants me to go down to Newport once more before my holiday (when she will try to be there too) with a thought out plan of action, so that necessary things may be got before I come. This is a good plan and will give me a much fairer start . . . No time or ink for more Love Eve'

Her next letter was in the following Sunday from 102 Basingstoke Road.

'Darling Mum, Every morning and every evening I count the hours till the time when I shall no longer have long hair. Ever since the date has been fixed I cannot understand how I have stood the burden so long . . . I don't know how father can think they have little work at the Food Production dept. Women's branch. Does he realise that they have the organisation of the entire Land army all over the country, the members of which run now into millions I think, The recruits for the 1st week in July alone were 1,000. The chief business of the chief inspector (Mrs Baynes) as the title implies is to travel from centre to centre to see how things are going. Besides this the board owns four farms which are being run as an experiment with only women labour under women bailiffs and the Newport farm is one of these. Of course she has to inspect this . . . Best love Eve.

She was given the post as Bailiff with '2 paid Land Army Girls and 3 pupils (6 weeks training at a time).' Lady Mather Jackson also explained to her that the 'Monmouthshire War Agricultural Committee, Ladies' Committee' was 'responsible to the Men's War Agricultural Committee' and added emphatically 'we have to make the Farm pay.' This was only a foretaste of what was to come.

Soon after her arrival, having begun to see what she was in for, Eve wrote: '. . . now you see the kind of medley of committees that I, their unfortunate agent have to deal with. There is first the M.W.W.A Committee (Women) the M.A. Executive Committee (Men) (All finance matters have to go through them) Then the Small Holdings committee who deal with repairs. Then the Inspector of the Board of Agriculture and lastly Lord Trafalgar's agent. So I have a gay time of it.'

Commenting on the state of the farm itself she wrote; The place as you can imagine from its history is in the last stages of neglect. When I took possession . . . as Forewoman, there were four acres of cornland which had grown a decent crop but had been ruined in the harvesting. (This ground is very dirty) Two acres with a good crop of swedes (for the season) Two acres under potatoes. No start had been made at lifting these last. All the rest was grass, poor and starved and full of coarse bents and bracken. Worse than all there was no one fence in the place worthy of the name. The cattle could just walk through wherever they chose. The one redeeming feature was the beauty of the country . . . surrounded on three sides by the most lovely rolling hills more like the Lammermoors at home than anything I have yet met . . .'

She sent the Committee a detailed scheme 'which I had worked out for the future management of the farm in which I had urged the purchase of more stock . . . My scheme was more or less accepted and finally the purchase of two new cows and four heifers sanctioned . . .'

She admitted; 'I had a most unlucky three weeks start . . . I started potato picking in earnest. I had no lifter or potato plough so ploughed them out with an ordinary plough. I then discovered that my team, our splendid little Welsh cob, who really is a treasure, and the broken winded greasy legged cart horse had never worked together before . . . also Maisie the cob had never done any sort of ploughing before. However, I persevered and after a lot of swearing and much pulling about they really learnt quite quickly what was wanted . . .'

Two days later she went down with what she described as 'one of the heaviest colds I ever had . . . feeling as if a cheese grater were working up and down inside my chest.' Then the first girl went down with flu. The next day they were all sick with flu and she was working the farm single-handed as well as nursing the invalids. Then the bull got loose, and when it had been cornered all the other cattle broke out. As she noted 'the invalids got sadly neglected that day . . .'

Thereafter for a fortnight she was milking six cows night and morning with all the stock to 'chaff and pulp for' with a rick a quarter of a mile away. As she wrote graphically 'you can imagine the life, between watering the horses and cleaning out the pigsty, dashing indoors to take a temperature and administer a dose.' It must have been a hectic introduction to the real business of life on a farm after the ordered life at Reading.

Her day started at 5.30 milking the cows and ended again at 6.00 in the evening after another round of milking with feeding stock, mending fences, picking potatoes and nursing the invalids at intervals throughout the rest of the day. It was a full day by any standards but for a nineteen-year-old girl it was indeed a testing time.

On the 10th of November, on the day before the war ended, she wrote to her mother as follows: 'Grove Farm, Rogerstone, nr Newport, 10th November.

Darlingest Mum, I have left you till the last tonight (the 14t letter) so that I can enjoy writing without the knowledge of all the other letters to be written on my concience. I have been here just a month. I can hardly believe it. The time went fast enough at Reading but it is going twice as fast here. This has been my first Sunday off and I 'have' enjoyed it. Breakfast in bed in the good old style and time to get some letters off my chest. First to answer your's in order . . . the girls 'love' the flute and sing with it. I have taught them 'Drink to me only.' . . . I have not much farm news. All my hands are well again thank goodness. I have ploughed out all my potatoes at last and hope to get the wheat in by the end of this week. We had three fine days and I engaged 4 small boys off my own bat at 3d an hour to come and help pick up. I hope the committee will aprove, but I don't much care, its done now and made the whole difference to getting up the crop which after all is more important than any red tape nonsense.

'Isn't the war news wonderful. Perhaps by the time you get this the armistice will be signed. Monday night it ought to be in the papers, the answer of the delegates, but I shan't know till Tuesday . . . The committee registrar Miss Fox asked me the other day if I was the Balfour whose mother had been a Lytton because she knew the ones that used to be at Knebworth. Its a small world . . . Best love to all at home. Devoted Eve'

The landgirls had recovered by this time and some had been sent on sick leave. Further conscripted replacements were due to arrive on the following day, Monday 11th November, the very day the war ended. Scarcely surprisingly they did not arrive. Unconsciously revealing that streak of latent pessimism which afflicted her at times, though never for long, Eve wrote:

'It is an out of the way spot and I do not get my papers till the day after. I had assumed gloomily that I should not get the news of the famous event till the Tuesday. On Monday morning three of us were down in one of the lower fields mending a fence around the hayrick which the cattle had broken down. At 11 o'clock one of the factory hooters (we are within earshot of five) began to blow, we paid no attention, thinking it merely the eleven o'clock hooter, but when after 5 minutes it and the other four were still blowing we began to notice after another five minutes it and the other four were still blowing we began to think, then the church bells started too and we began to hope, and then all the detonators on the line started going off with their sharp pop! pop! Then we got excited. Even so I did not dare believe it as I thought the news could not reach this country till the evening, but after half an hour and the noise still going on it finally dawned that it could mean nothing else and we became delirious. Continued hooters is really a most moving sound, it affects one like a cheering crowd and on this occasion meaning all that it did mean it very nearly made me weep.'

She had her own local celebration and wrote:

'All the small children of Rogerstone are great friends of mine and have rides on the cart when I have not got too big a load on. On this occasion all the children had run out of school and all the men had come out of the factory so that the little one street town was one seething mass of joyful humanity waving flags (Goodness knows where they had all come from) cheering and yelling Rule Britannia at the top of their voices. My cart was quickly filled with all the children it could hold, over a dozen, all yelling and waving flags. Poor Maisie couldn't make it out at all and was prancing on her toes and pulling like the dickens. There is one of my small boy friends who usually says 'This cart used to be driven by a woman and a girl.' (I wonder what he thinks I am) On this occasion he exclaimed 'Isn't it good about the war bein' over – why don't you dress her up?' So we bought some flags and fastened them to Maisie's bridle and in the cart. My workers I need hardly say did not turn up and I drove my little crowd half the way home . . .'

'Next day the new hands had not arrived, so that once more I was short handed . . . Four days this continued . . . At last two turned up . . . having been caught on the streets . . . and carried off to the train and guarded there till it started. These girls having twice before torn up their warrants. All this they told us quite unabashed within 5 minutes of entering the house and they arrived with nothing save the clothing on their backs!

'Then arose a difficult situation. The night of the day they arrived there was to be a torchlight procession in Newport and it soon became quite evident that these two were quite determined to walk in it. It was equally evident that if I forbade it they would take French leave. On the other hand if I said yes the odds were 1000 to one they would never come back. There seemed nothing for it but that we should all drive in so that I could keep an eye on the truants and with a little luck bring them back again. I did not at all relish the idea. I was extremely tired that night for one thing and for another I hate crowds. I had gone into Newport on Armistice night because the girls wanted to and that was quite enough to last for months. Besides there was a certain excitement then to keep me going. None now . . . that other time there was something rather wonderful about it . . . Groups of people dancing held up the traffic and . . . one knew in that vast crowd what ever single member of it was thinking about. But this second outing was pure nightmare from start to finish . . . we all got home somewhere round midnight . . ."

Although Eve was not given to complaining unduly it seemed the members of the committees were inclined to be obstructive and interfering. As anyone who has ever worked for or with a committee will know it is seldom possible to get all the members to agree. No doubt this was good training for later life, but there were other features which combined to make life difficult, Most of the horses she was supplied with were worn out and useless. The two new girls were lazy and most people would, one feels, have given up. However she persevered and wrote later with her usual optimism.

'. . . now I have really got a very good little horse and with him have finished the first ploughing for my potatoes, but it was a tough job as it is a steep hill and full of bracken and gorse. I wore out two shares in two acres!

'The last excitement has been building my new intensive poultry house and the arrival of my new stock. I have sold all the old mixed lot of fowls that was here when I came and started a pure breed and good strain.

'I hope to get the place straight in time. but it is rather a grind sometimes. I don't get depressed except when the committee thwart one and then I do sometimes want to give it all up. The latest is that when I sent in a list of manures that I need for my spring crops they say that they think we'd better go in for basic slag instead of sulphate of ammonia because it is cheaper! Aren't they simply wonderful?'

Eve's upbringing had already moulded her character. Although barely out of her teens she was prepared as a matter of course to stand up for herself and justify her opinions in any company. She would not be browbeaten and she could get along well with people of all classes. Her training at Reading had grounded her in the theory of farming. She had already gained her first experience of the pitfalls of the real thing. She was learning to deal with people, especially with the intricacies of committees, and at other people's expense she was also gaining valuable experience in the basics of practical farming. It was all good training for her later life and already it is plain that in the main she was winning her battles. In December she suffered an acute, if delayed, attack of homesickness, She wrote;

'Dec 1st. Darlingest Mum,

No letter from you to answer this week. My Sunday off again. I 'do' enjoy them. I am going for a ride this p.m. on our Cob as she hasn't had much work this week. Being in my habit feels like good old holiday times again . . . I had an awful fit of depression this morning (it has passed now) The first since I have been here. I am 'longing' to see one of the family and have a good talk . . . If you can spare Mary 'let' her come to me the week before Xmas. 3 weeks on Wed. Xmas day, can you believe it. The 1st of peace and the 1st of all my 20 years spent without the family . . .

Typically she pulled herself together at once and continued: 'Every days farm work convinces me still further that I have chosen the profession which really suits me. I love it more and more. I even dont mind turning out at 5.30 a.m. in the dark winter mornings now. If I am so perfectly happy here, just 'think' of the happiness of our own farm when I am no longer away from the family . . . always devoted, Eve.'

She was, however, still very young and in some ways quite naive, especially commercially and in the ways of the world. Her sister Mary, although older, had always tended to play the secondary role and was very much the younger mentally. At no time in her life could Mary have been termed worldly, although never without a surprising ability to turn her hand to the most unlikely tasks for one so apparently frail. Between them the sisters had learned a lot which would never normally have come their way, but they still had a great deal to learn.

The end of the war also eventually brought about the end of Eve's job. Although she continued to run the farm until October 1919 to complete her contract, the end was inevitable. Gradually the Woman's Land Army was wound up and her 'girls' all departed, some no doubt thankfully and others with regret, back to their civilian occupations.

Before the winding-up process had really begun, however, in May 1919, Lady Betty visited Grove Farm to see for herself how her daughter was getting on. Unfortunately she did not leave a record of her impressions, but it is clear she was appalled by the primitive domestic arrangements for it is significant that Eve wrote;

' I will try to answer your questions. Yes the mangels are in. Also the clover seed and my wheat. Potatos will be this week and then I shall really have caught up. Polly died alas. I am expecting Peggy to calve any moment.

After, typically, placing first things first as she saw it, she continued with more mundane matters, which were no doubt of greater interest to her mother:

'We have stained all the floors and with your money have so far bought – O-Cedar mop. Stuff for chairs. Chamber for my room. Bucket for ashes. Pot cleaning things and swabs. . . .'

With the end of the war a certain amount of time for relaxation seems to have been acceptable. Soon after her mother's visit Eve organised a fancy-dress party for her farm staff and a number of local people including some wounded soldiers from the local hospital. It was an ambitious affair considering the size of the farm, with nearly fifty present. The food 'looked very appetising all spread out on the ground, large bowls of fruit salad and jelly and plates of sandwiches and cake . . . lasted out very well, much better than I thought it would . . .'

She noted; 'There wasn't much variety in fancy dress. Three male pierrots, 2 cow boys, two sort of hungarian gypsy dresses . . . everyone else was either in khaki or blue . . . All 'our' dresses were a tremendous success . . .'

She must have put a great deal of effort into this party for she also noted: 'I was making up from 2–30 till 5–30. After which I dressed and made myself up with lightning speed in about 1/4 of an hour. They played the gramaphone . . . and stood about in groups until I came down when I made them all dance Sir Roger playing the flute. After that we had the meal.' She added, with amusement:' . . . Someone asked if I was the father of the two children!' With her Eton crop, her impressively resonant voice and fancy dress, this was not surprising. At around five foot eight she was quite tall and clearly even then had considerable self assurance. It was not the last time people were to make a similar mistake.

With the end of the war the urgency which had inspired everyone to extra effort suddenly eased. Very soon the supply of new recruits for the Women's Land Army ceased. The various War Agricultural Committees also began to wind down their activities. In order to get in her harvest in 1919 Eve was forced to employ returned ex-servicemen eager for any job. One of these, George Pitt, who had a wife and two children, proved a good worker and Eve went so far as to promise that if and when she had a farm of her own she would do her best for him.

As her year's contract ended in October Eve was left to wind up the farm and sell off all the live and dead stock as well as the farm itself. It was at this stage that she was joined by her sister Mary, who after completing her course at Reading had attended the final demise of her Oscar. The sisters immediately started looking for the farm which they had dreamed of setting up together for years and once again Eve's first choice was for Sussex.

Mary described the occasion later. They were ensconced in Eve's small room where she had lived as bailiff for a year. Mary, typically, was darning Eve's stockings. Eve entered with a sheaf of estate agents' particulars of farms and announced that they were quite useless. She had asked for particulars of farms to let in Sussex, with a view to being near their Lytton cousins at Crabbett Park, the notable Arabian Stud. The estate agents had sent them particulars of farms for sale in Dorset and Suffolk.

The two sisters, with little left to do before the sale of the farm, read through the leaflets and found one particular farm at Haughley in Suffolk, which particularly attracted them both. It was 157 acres, just the size they required, with a moat and a Fifteenth-century timber and plaster house.

Mary wrote later:

'You know,' Eve remarked. 'We think nothing would induce us to live in Suffolk, but we've never been there. It may be dead flat, but I've had enough of these Welsh hills and ploughing would be a mug's game there.'

At this stage Mary told Eve for the first time that their father had said that if they found the ideal farm but it was only for sale they need not necessarily turn it down just on those grounds. The two sisters decided then and there to go to Haughley at once, but there were two inhibiting factors. Firstly the sale of the Monmouthshire farm had to be completed and Eve had to stay for a further thirty-six hours to finish her contract. Secondly there was a nation-wide rail strike and few if any trains were moving.

They decided to bid for the Welsh cob, Maisie, which Eve had used on the Monmouthshire farm at the sale the next day. They also bought a very second-hand dog cart for £5 which they discovered lying in the yard of a local blacksmith. At the sale they bought the cob and after a night sleeping in the hayloft they left the Monmouthshire farm in the early hours of the morning 'rattling along the road to Gloucester.'

Mary wrote: 'The first night we stopped at Lydney.' They had thus covered the best part of twenty-five miles being passed by numerous motor vehicles and faster conveyances. There was a local celebration taking place at the town and all the inns and lodging houses were full. Furthermore no-one had stabling available for a horse. Mary noted;

'At last we found a disused stables with some musty hay. For Maisie we bought two packets of Quaker oats. For ourselves cheese and chocolate.

'As we scrambled through the hole above Maisie's head to seek a bed in the loft an angry voice brought me slithering back into the manger.'

It was the owner of the stables demanding an explanation of their presence. On discovering that the trespassers were two girls alone and unable to find lodgings he good-naturedly assured them he would find them somewhere for the night only to discover as they had that everywhere was full. In the end he loaned them an old fur rug to sleep under and Mary maintained that they slept well 'to the accompaniment of Maisie's whinnies and the smell of musty hay and camphor.'

The next night they spent with friends near Gloucester, with only two days left to reach Haughley before the sale was to be completed.

The friends attempted to point out that no-one ever bought the first farm they looked at and that it would not be the end of the world if they failed to get there, pressing them to stay longer. Both sisters were, however, determined to follow up the advertisment.

Leaving Maisie behind they managed to find a train which took them into London after dark. There they spent the night with Beryl Hearnden, a doctor's daughter and an old friend of Mary's from her days as a VAD, who proved a sympathetic and receptive audience to their plans. She even suggested the possibility of joining them as a partner in the venture and they went to bed very late after building castles in the air.

The following morning hanging around the gloom of Liverpool Street Station waiting for a train to Ipswich their spirits sank somewhat. On their eventual arrival at Ipswich, however, they were picked up at once by the owner of the farm, a young man, who seems to have had all the natural abilities of a second-hand car salesman and who was as anxious to sell as they were to buy. Although he claimed to have another purchaser on hand the likelihood is that the young sisters were the only really serious buyers he had encountered. Certainly the market for run-down small farms in Suffolk at this time was not booming, to say the least. Anyway it is clear that sensing that he had a pair of keen prospective purchasers in hand he spent considerable time showing them round the semi-derelict property. He assured them he was only interested in selling not letting, but their interest in buying must have been obvious to him for he eventually agreed to allow them until ten the following morning to give a firm answer.

They spent the night in lodgings in Stowmarket. The following morning they rang their mother at Fisher's Hill from the local post-office and Eve explained the situation. Mary described the conversation thus:

'That you mother? It's Eve . . . No I've left Monmouthshire. I'm speaking from Suffolk . . . yes Suffolk! We're both here and, listen, we've found the farm we want . . . no I'm not joking . . . only Mother, it's for sale . . . No, he won't let. Wait and I'll tell you the details . . .' Here she burst into technicalities . . . broken off suddenly to tell me Mother had gone to speak to Father. Five interminable minutes then Eve swung round to the mouthpiece and I, watching, knew that miracles were happening. At last she rang off and turned to me. 'When mother told him father was shaving. She said he considered for a moment then said "Tell the children to pay the deposit, then come home and we'll see how it's to be done." '

We stared at each other.

'I suppose,' Eve added thoughtfully.'It's the greatest compliment we've ever been paid.'

The cost of the farm was to be £25 an acre, a stiff price, and the £4,000 was to be deducted from the legacies they could have expected. In the manner of the Victorians, their father, Gerald, set up a Trust for overall control of the farm, the Trustees consisting of himself and Eleanor Sidgwick. Thus it was that Eve and Mary eventually moved to Suffolk and took over the farm of New Bells where subsequently the Haughley Experiment was to be set up and the Soil Association founded.

7. Fisher's hill the family home in Surrey 1920.

8. Eve with 2 horse plough c. 1920.

9. Bullett the foundation stock bull of the milking herd in front of the moat at New Bells. c. 1922.

10. The Pickwick Dance Band in action 1923.
*L-R* Bunny (piano) Mary, Beb, Eve on saxophone, Derry on drums.

# CHAPTER FOUR

# The Early Days at New Bells

## 1919–1923

*'It was a singularly easy and happy intimacy without sex complications or a tinge of jealousy.'*

Eve, recalling these days.

ALL THE ARRANGEMENTS for the Trust and completion of the purchase meant spending some time at Fisher's Hill, but it is understandable that the sisters returned to Haughley to take possession of their new acquisition as soon as possible. Mary described how, on their arrival at Haughley they were the only people to get off on the wet station platform. They dashed to the rear of the train to ensure the removal of their considerable baggage from the Guard's van. Then to their surprise they were greeted by name by the courtly station-master who took their tickets, superintended the stacking of their bags to await their collection later and expressed the warm hope that they had come to stay. They were still unaware at this stage of the speed with which news travels in remote country districts.

Of course in those days even a small farm required quite a large staff to run it and with their purchase they had also acquired a number of employees living in tied cottages, who were anxiously awaiting to know whether their employment would be continued or not. The most important member of their staff at this stage consisted of the foreman, Bob Aldiss, who had worked for the previous owner, but who proved himself to be a very able and very loyal friend for many years. Mary, already afflicted by the deafness which was to grow progressively worse over the years, always referred to him as Aldous, both in fact common local Suffolk names.

Not expecting anyone to meet them, the sisters left their baggage behind in the care of the friendly stationmaster and set off to walk the two and a half miles towards their new home in pouring rain but with raised spirits. On the way, Mary recorded, they met their new employee 'Aldous' coming down with a horse and cart to pick up their luggage. He greeted them with the seemingly stony indifference assumed by any countryman in such circumstances and after a short exchange of greetings they left him to go on down to fetch their luggage while they continued on foot to the farm.

They passed the old post mill, which stood on the hill and descended to the village with its triangular green and pump. This provided the sole water supply for the old yellow-washed thatched cottages grouped round the green, including the butcher's shop beneath the walnut tree. It was all extremely picturesque and at this stage the primitive aspects had not impinged on their youthful optimism.

It was only when they had crossed the moat and arrived at their new house that they realised they had no key and all the doors were locked. Short of breaking the windows they were firmly locked out. After two perambulations of the house, through wet nettles, they went to examine the farm buildings and were pleased to meet their old cob Maisie, who had been sent up from Gloucestershire and now greeted them with 'tremulous nostrils and deep-seated emotional whinnies.'

The sound of the cart returning took them back to the house. When they had explained their plight there was 'the suspicion of a smile on Aldous's inscrutable face' and he informed them that the key was to be had from the wife of the second horseman, a Mrs Lloyd. She provided the key and an apology for not having heard they were coming. This they took at its face value, knowing little better at the time. They then returned to the house and helped 'Aldous' to drop off their luggage.

Subsequently Mary wrote:

'Wonderfully large and airy, isn't it?' Eve challenged as we entered the kitchen and were nearly knocked down by the unlived-in smell of dust and damp.'

With the inhibiting presence of 'Aldous' finally removed the two sisters ran like children round the house exploring from room to room eagerly. It seemed the previous owner had allowed two prospective purchasers to camp out in the house while considering the sale. Having sold it more satisfactorily to the Balfour sisters he had then asked them to leave, which they had done 'in high dudgeon.'

As Mary described it, the sight of rooms full of other people's furniture in various stages of packing, dead flowers, unmade beds, and finally in the kitchen sink unwashed dishes moving with rats and mice, which fled at their approach, reduced them after their first quick tour of the house to mutual groans of depression and then to near-hysterical laughter.

Mary noted there was one room with 'somebody's hideous upright piano and a bowl of very dead flowers arranged on top of a fretwork pedestal that shrieked at us from one corner. These horrors without even a carpet or a curtain to accompany them, looked so naked as to be practically indecent . . . We chose the room with the piano to live in for the next few weeks. It had a fairly presentable fireplace, those in all the other rooms, kitchen included, being so much scrap iron. Here we set a blaze going. Put up camp beds, unpacked blankets and after burning the dead flowers began to feel better . . .'

They left their mattresses and bed linen airing in front of the fire, as their old Nannie had insisted they should, and harnessing Maisie into their dog cart set off to find a meal in Stowmarket four and a half miles away. It was dark when they returned, barely able to make out the sides of the road in the cocoon of flickering light cast by the candle light of the dog cart lanterns, and Mary, ever the alarmist, suddenly wondered if by any chance the bedding could have caught fire during their absence and burned the house down. Eve told her sharply not be a fool, but was alarmed by the sight of a bonfire flickering beside the railway line and it was a great relief to both of them to find the house still standing on their return. After stabling their horse and finding the fire had gone out the sisters retired to bed and talked well into the night before dropping off to sleep soundly, disturbed only by the squeaking of rats.

It seems to have been very gradually that the facts of life and living at New Bells began to dawn on them. There was no water supply beyond the moat, which dated from Saxon times and was two thirds mud and one third water. In the Spring the frogs which lived in it penetrated everywhere and even found their way indoors, into cupboards, shoes and other unexpected places. Throughout the Spring and Summer months the dawn and evening chorus of frogs croaking could at times be almost deafening.

The pump in the sink in the kitchen came directly from this source and the only sanitation consisted of a wooden three-seater outside lavatory with a cess-pit which drained back almost directly into their water supply. There was no lighting beyond paraffin lamps and candles. For cooking they discarded the old range and installed an oil-fired stove.

On the farm the cow houses were made of brick, much of it Elizabethan in origin and well worn, hence extremely difficult to keep clean. Sterilisation of milking utensils had to be done over an ordinary copper boiler, heated by coals or wood fires. The farm buildings and the farm itself had both had been considerably neglected for years and they were soon hard at work setting them to rights, but none of these shortcomings seem to have worried them greatly.

One of their earliest family visitors was their younger brother Ral, who had just left Eton and gone up to Trinity College, Cambridge, in October. In December he rode over several times on his newly acquired motor bicycle. Returning to Cambridge from Whittingehame in early January 1920, he was on his way to visit them again and had almost arrived when he fell asleep still riding his machine and crashed. His left shin was severely broken in two places and he spent the next three months in a nursing home in Ipswich before a further period of convalescence at Fisher's Hill[1]. This set back his Cambridge career by a year and naturally proved an added complication to the sisters lives at the time, but they had plenty to occupy them.

One of Mary's first acts was to build several large and heavy hen houses, for amongst her other unusual gifts she was always a very fine carpenter. These hen houses measured twelve by eight feet and seven to the eaves. Although they were secured by corner posts, in the first typical Suffolk gale they still blew over a quite substantial hedge. They were recovered by the united efforts of the entire farm staff and secured with wire cables, but the chickens which had arrived that morning had to be left in their crates all day before being installed in their new houses[2].

In this somewhat haphazard way the two sisters gradually settled down to farming New Bells. The farm staff, under Bob Aldiss as foreman, consisted of the second horseman, Lloyd, whose wife initially helped in the house, but whom they soon found to be a slattern. They also took on George Pitt, who had worked for Eve on the Monmouthshire farm. Another worker was an old man named Eastwill, who lived in one of their cottages with his wife, and, as they began to build up a milking herd, they also employed a couple of dairymaids.

In the house Mary naturally took charge of the domestic side, which was never of much interest to Eve, with a Mrs Spindler as cook-housekeeper and Mrs Lloyd, the second horseman's wife helping her. When their young sister Kathleen was sent to boarding school, at Southwold on the coast nearby, they also acquired their old Nannie, who had reached retirement age with the departure of her last charge, but was happy to live with them and help out in a minor way domestically but particularly in the garden. Despite their acute short-age of working capital they were also able to afford several other women to do odd jobs about the house and garden for wages then were absurdly low and a resident domestic might be had for as little as £25 a year.

In addition they soon took on two close assistants and pupils. The first of these was their mutual friend Beryl Hearnden, known as 'Beb,' who although initially a friend of Mary's, having been a VAD with her, was soon to become Eve's boon companion, latterly indeed to Mary's inward distress. The fourth to join these three was a male, Derry Hawker, son of a neighbour farming at Runton, who came initially as a farm pupil, but stayed on for several years.

This somewhat unlikely foursome remained the principal occupants of New Bells for the full decade of the 20s. Mary, giving way to a natural mysticism, termed them the 'Four Bells' and they seem to have lived together in a remarkably friendly, free and unusually a-sexual relationship.

A whole generation of young men, their own contemporaries, had, of course, been killed during the 1914–18 War and they were all happy that the trauma was over at last. Mary had had her nebulous affair with Oscar, who had died in 1918. Beryl Hearnden had lost the young man she had planned to marry. Eve herself may also have suffered a similar loss, but in any event at this time was in love with agriculture. Derry Hawker was a gangling late-developing adolescent, so that together the four enjoyed a slightly unusual but to them very satisfactory platonic relationship.[3]

The first two years were really primarily settling-in time, when inevitably they failed even to make ends meet, when they grew to know their neighbours, their workmen and their wives, their fields and their stock. The countryside was still a long way from accepting them, for in such conservative circles anyone not born in the county could only expect to be referred to as a 'furriner' or 'incomer' for the next twenty years or so. It is hard for anyone who has not lived in such a closed society to understand how strongly such feelings were and still are held in remote country districts such as this part of Suffolk. However, they managed successfully to sell their milk at top-grade quality locally from the earliest days and duly upgraded their dairy, steadily expanding this side of their activities.

None of this prevented the Four Bells enjoying life to the full. Not unnaturally there was an almost constant stream of friends and relations visiting New Bells and the unconventional household there. Derry's elder brother Vaughan and his sister Bunny were frequent visitors and numerous young men homed-in on New Bells and its somewhat eccentric menage. During the summer months especially Eve and Mary's young brother Ral and undergraduate friends of his from Cambridge frequently came over by motor bicycle and were treated like playful young puppies by Beb and the tolerant elder sisters. Apart from this the Lytton cousins and the Balfour cousins and friends and relations alltook their turns to visit 'the farmers' as they were known in the family. If the house was full they were not above camping in the garden. In summer the moat was used as a bathing pool.

Despite the fact that there was no running water or electricity, and sanitation was primitive in the extreme, everyone seems to have enjoyed themselves in this youthful household and contributed their assistance to the farm, whether feeding pigs, herding sheep, milking, or harvesting. It seems to have been an understood thing that anyone staying must be prepared to help in any and every capacity. It was perhaps the very unexpectedness of life at New Bells which proved amongst its greatest attractions at this time and caused so many people to return despite the obvious discomforts.

An immediate bond the Four Bells had in common was a love of music. Eve was good on the recorder and could also play a moody saxophone, Beb was good on the piano and Mary with the recorder and the ukelele while Derry played the drums. Bunny, Derry's sister, and a rather later addition to the group, played the banjo. In the evenings, after the day's work, they enjoyed playing together and developed a considerable repertoire of popular dance music and jazz.

In 1921, desperate for any solution to help out their parlous financial state, they approached the manager of the Great White Horse in Ipswich with the suggestion that they should play there regularly on Saturday evenings. After hearing them perform he promptly agreed. Since Dickens had stayed there and the inn was associated with the Pickwick Papers, they called their band the Pickwick Dance Club. They soon proved so popular that they were frequently invited to play elsewhere by arrangement.

The Four Bells and their friends also indulged enthusiastically in amateur dramatics, in those days before the advent of either radio or

television a natural way of passing the evening hours. Mary, particularly, was adept at writing plays and producing both props and
costumes. From 1920 they regularly produced a play written by Mary
each year. They even formed an amateur dramatic group, composed
of themselves and their close friends and relations, terming themselves
the Haughley Players.

In addition the Four Bells also dabbled in table turning and
automatic writing with a ouija board. Here again Mary proved a
particularly interesting medium with wide-ranging powers. With her
frail physique and frequent illnesses she really did not pull her weight
as a partner on the farm, but initially at least her artistic abilities
seemed to the others to compensate for this.

Today Mary might have been diagnosed as having a multiple
personality problem possibly stemming from a childhood incident
when her young cousin Oswald back from school crudely revealed the
facts of life to her. This may only have amounted to mild schizo-
phrenia, but she proved to be a medium of absorbing interest to them
all. During the years 1920 to 1924, Derry became adept at putting her
into a 'trance' and the three of them then interpreted her sayings and
writings at great length.

It might be felt today that this absorption was not altogether
desirable, but these were young people in a healthy environment
working hard all day in the open air. It must also be recalled that
Eve and Mary's father Gerald and their uncle A.J.Balfour himself, as
well as their aunt Nora and other members of their family, were
absorbed in similar studies with the Society for Psychical Research.
One side effect appears to have been that as a result of their efforts
Mary overcame her psychological handicap and gradually developed
a new and less retiring personality, although this was not without
difficulties for them all as this new 'Mary' gradually grew stronger and
more assertive.

The farming itself was always under the overall direction of Eve. She
could plough as well as any of the horsemen on the farm. She directed
the cropping and the management of the beasts. When in doubt she
was always the one to whom the others came. Mary, however, was an
excellent carpenter, able to use saw, chisel and hammer with skill and
efficiency at odds with her frail physique.

She was also in charge of the poultry, hens and turkeys and of the
milk and cheese side of the farm. Beb was almost as strong as Eve,
good with horses, animals and also extremely good with humans,

particularly Mary. Her ability to get along with everyone was often important and her tact probably eased their relationships at any times of stress. Derry Hawker appears to have been one of those attractive happy-go-lucky individuals, who managed to be pleasant to everyone and yet surprisingly effective.

In 1921 Lady Betty Balfour wrote a vivid account to her mother of the 'Four Bells' first harvest dinner:

'. . . I will begin by telling about the Harvest dinner which took place on Saturday. Poor Mary woke with an internal chill and could eat no breakfast – bad preparation for a heavy day. Eve also much be-colded. Derry and Eileen (his sister generally known as Bunny) had to go off to attend a local sale and missed the feast. Weather most inconveniently windy. Mary went off to Haughley after breakfast with the milk and brought back an immensely long table top. Long enough for 20 people, which was put on the trestles which hold up Eve's dressing table. She also brought 10 chairs. These all borrowed from the Haughley post office. The table was put at first in the garden but when the flower decorations (Berries and dark leaves) had been thrown down 3 times Mrs Spindler (Mary's housekeeper) decided it must take place in the kitchen. Eve sent us to help move the table. It could only be got in diagonally and so blocked the kitchen entrance from the front door. The visitors had to come in by the back door and the household through the scullery, but here it was warm and comfortable and the table looked awfully nice. An amusing detail was that Lloyd, Eve's carter, lent the carving knife and some of the forks! The party assembled at 2.30, 18 in all:

'Aldous' (Foreman) his wife and seven children! (9)

'Lloyd' (Carter) young wife and 1 child. (3)

'George Pitt' (The man from Eve's Welsh farm) wife, sister and 2 children under 2 (5)

'Eastwill' V. old man who works on the farm, wife too bashful to come (1)

'The two milkmaids' Ella & Lizzie (2)

My part in the affair was nursing the youngest Pitt baby – an 'enormous' boy of 4 months – nearly as big as his sister of 18 months. Luckily he behaved very well. Eve dispensed the drink (Beer and cider – but one of the men took only water.) Kathleen, was in charge of bread and plum pudding! Nanny, Mary and Jeannie (Mrs Spindler's niece) waited and Mrs Spindler carved and at the same time kept up a fire of good natured chaff and talk It was the first time rib joints had been seen at New bells! Roast mutton, Roast Beef, gravy and potatoes – Plum Pudding Blackberry Tart and Apple Tart! All most beautifully cooked in the oil stove! Johnnie Aldous won the prize of greatest consumption – 2 platefuls of beef and potatoes – 2 of plum pudding 1 of Blackberry Tart, 1 of Apple Tart! Mrs Aldous a gentle, sad woman never took a second helping and shared all she had with her youngest baby. I said to her afterwards 'How well the babies behaved. They do 'sometimes' spoil a mother's pleasure!' and she said sadly. 'Yes. I always says there 's no pleasure where a family's concerned.' There spoke the tragedy of the British cottage woman. Cigarettes ended the feast. – and then the table was cleared and the gramaphone brought in. The children ran about outside and the parents played draughts and dominoes – they went away between 5 & 6, extremely happy. Mary forgot her own tea and took Kathleen out in her new pony trap just as tea was ready and was not back for an hour.

That pony trap is a wonderful sight. An old Vet's cart – enormously high 2 wheels – a tiny little seat at top – Nannie upholstered it with an old habit of Nell's. Eve and K and Nan painted it with the only paint on the farm – a bright green. The little Welsh pony (Betty) just gets in between the shafts and goes a jolly pace. Its rather a terror to me and I've implored them not to let Kathleen drive quite alone this year, but it's a huge joy to her.

Fruit picking begins this week. They have a good crop of apples. No pears. Today Eve and Derry and Eileen go to a sale 9 miles off to buy Derry's horses. It's gently raining, but not so cold. Eve has her deep churchyard cough. She is pleased that she sold her barley when she did at the top price – it has gone down now. She sells her pigs on the 28th. Unfortunately there is at the moment a slump in Gloucester Spots. Eve begins to have the 'worried' look of a farmer. Its really rather a harrowing life – and the anxiety has aged Eve. But at anyrate it's a life of unflagging interest. Mary in spite of her one day's illness is looking better than I have ever seen her – her complexion quite free from spots and Eczema and she is very cheerful and adores this place and loves the to and fro of their groups of friends.

Jazz band is practised hard every moment when they are not out or eating. Eve after supper last night looked too tired to play a note. But the others began – Eve dragged herself up to join – and once in the swing they would none of them stop till past 11.

Nannie's garden is wonderful. I have planted her wall flowers out for her and shall take an interest in them forever.

I walked to Bacton church yesterday. (It took me just one hour) and lunched with the Vallelys (local friends of hers) after . . . I pumped her as to what 'the world said about New Bells'. She told me the only two bits of gossip she had ever heard,

1. That Eve is engaged to Derry – Not at all surprising.

That the horse dealer who brought the stallion to Eve's mares nearly had a fit when he found the New Bells farmer was a young girl. He'll get accustomed to that . . .

. . . Nan told me that Aldous (Eve's foreman) told her he thought Eve had broken the back of her difficulties here now and would make the farm a success. This pleased me, but Eve says her anxieties can't be over for another 2 years and that it is just when farms are beginning to pull up that they so often break. However, tho' anxious she is full of hope.'

It was scarcely to be expected that such a shaky venture could make a profit in the first years. It is not in the least surprising that the letters in the early years are full of financial misgivings and over-hopeful estimates, as well as repeated thanks for assistance received from 'beloved father' or 'Aunt Nora.' The Trustees seem to have been very willing to subsidise the farm, but in fact the amounts involved initially do not seem to have been very great.

The farm, however, undoubtedly teetered on the edge of bankruptcy for the first few years. In 1920 their overdraft was £700 and had to be extended to £800 and Eve was forced to ask her father to act as guarantor, the first of many such financial pleas for assistance. In 1921 Mary was writing that they had dispensed with their servants. Mrs Lloyd, the second horseman's wife, who had provided them with the key on their arrival along with profuse apologies for not having cleaned the place had turned out to be a slattern who had clearly known all along that they were coming and simply done nothing about it. Mrs Spindler and their old nannie remained, but Mary was not the first to find that the housework was not all that difficult and that the results were better when she did it herself and saved the wages. It is significant perhaps that Mary naturally took on the housework, not the others.

A succession of visitors, family and friends, came and went, but The Four Bells somehow eked out a precarious living. The principal feature of this period appears to have been their light-heartedness. They were all the products of the 'Twenties'. Light-hearted 'young things' playing jazz and on the one hand running dilapidated antique sports cars and motor bikes, when they could afford it, and on the other riding horses and travelling the roads in ponies and traps when their finances could go no higher.

One of the sayings in the house at this time was 'first up best dressed,' since their clothes were usually left in muddle on the floor when they went to bed and the first up had the choice of what to wear. It would seem that Derry and any other males present were not included in this performance, but both Eve and Beb who normally wore breeches and stockings about the farm, were also sometimes to be seen in trousers. At that time this was regarded as an almost unheard-of garb for a woman and, even if they were only worn on the farm itself, no doubt caused considerable gossip locally.

It was not surprising that Eve sometimes found herself constrained by family and social conventions. An early attempt to go on a motor tour and take Derry to Whittingehame was vetoed promptly by Aunt Alice with some acid comments and poor Lady Betty bore the brunt of it. Vaughan Hawker, Derry's elder brother, wrote on September 16th 1922.

'Dearest Eve,

My sister met your mother at Whittingehame and evidently she does not really like you and D visiting there together on account of all the relations (and specially your aunt Alice) who don't understand the story of adopted brother relationships which we do and your mother does and she feels as it is 'their' house it must be considered. I have written to Derry and I do feel he must give it up. I am afraid I never thought of the gossip side of the question at all. I don't suppose you did either . . . But if my relations had been silly, I know I should have listened and I do so sympathise with your poor mother . . . In haste for post. Yrs ever C.V.Hawker.'

There followed an exchange of several letters and wires between Eve and her mother with Eve arguing that the entire matter was perfectly 'propper' and her mother exasperatedly trying to stress the conventions of the day, and also unwittingly underscoring the rigours of living at Whittingehame under Aunt Alice's eccentric dictatorship. On Sept 14th Lady Betty wrote;

'Darling Beloved

Your letter makes me groan . . . 'Auntie says she will squeeze you in if she possibly can whenever you like to come – She longs to have you . . . but she does 'not' want Derry. She does not know him. or want to know him, he is no relation. This quite apart from the proprieties . . .

Whitt is Whitt, to take or leave and we who really love it accept it as it is and do not attempt to change it. Less now than ever since Auntie is lame, and deaf and blind and hates shocks of all kinds. She has been generous to you beyond measure and she deserves consideration . . . Now as to my feelings. Your tour with Derry may be 'propper' by which strange spelling I suppose you mean 'proper', but it certainly outrages the conventions . . . if you came here together the village and the county would proclaim you engaged or would say you had lost your character . . . Part of the refinement and good manners of life is to accept the conventions of others if you mix with them and not roughly outrage their feelings. At New Bells and Fisher's Hill do as you please and God.

Bless you in all your undertakings, but if you go to the houses of ladies and gentlemen who are kind enough to invite you do as they do. You know how much I hate dressing for dinner. I always do it here . . . If I come here I try to fit in with the rules that have been set up by the owners of the place. If I did not I would stay away . . .'

It seems that Eve then suggested putting Derry up at a local pub in East Linton, for in a further letter her mother wrote: 'The pub in Linton is a fearfully bad plan. The most likely to produce gossip of anything and horribly expensive for Derry. I don't see any way to get him here except quite separately from you as Ral's shooting guest and I am afraid you've queered the pitch for that . . . yr devoted Mum'

Extracts from a letter dated November 24th 1922 from Beryl Hearnden to Lady Betty Balfour give a vivid picture of the farming side of life at this period, mostly concerning the sale of sheep bought earlier in the years as lambs at prices ranging from 45 to 60 shillings each.

'Yesterday Eve and I went to Ipswich to sell a cow and calf and 100 lambs . . . We went in by the 8.50 and travelled in the horsebox. The market was stacked with stock and people . . . Then Spink came up. (A dealer who had previously offered 72/-) He said he'd give Eve 72/6 . . . and pay all the fees . . . So Eve sold them to him and spent the next half hour in agony wondering if she had done the right thing . . . They fetched 73/- and Spink was out of pocket by the time he had paid all the fees. So 'that' was all right . . . The cow fetched £19 and the calf 50/- quite a good price. On the whole a satisfactory business. We went on to the Corn Exchange. Sold the wheat – Yeoman (a popular variety then) – at 23/- a coomb but failed to sell the barley – it still isn't dry.

Eve: 'Infernal nuisance but it can't be helped. Besides the price might rise.' We met Bunnie at Ipswich and sold 2 sacks of Nannie's apples at a v. fair price. Got home at 7 v. weary but quite satisfied.'

She continued:' Eve and I stained 3 floors this morning with permanganate of potash and a broom! Some job too. Her room, Nan's and the little room. Nannie's awfully pleased about it. Actually managed to praise our efforts without saying 'I suppose you think you've done some work.' You must admit a lot for Nan. You bet she'll polish her floor now till you can't stand up on it . . .'

She added an account of the chicken farming:

'Horrible scare on Monday. A fox robbed the hen houses and slew two or three chickens and worst of all – a ghastly business – the white cock was missing. Mary's White Leghorn on whom the future success of the whole show rests. It was a perfectly awful business, but our luck held good for in the evening he returned, a trifle ruffled and chipped, but very truculent and alive. His spurs were all over blood so it looks as if he gave Dan Russell something to go on with. He's been removed to a safer place now . . .'

One of the notable family events which occurred in 1922 was the granting of an earldom to A.J.Balfour in recognition of his services to the nation. The title he chose was the Earl of Balfour of Whittinge-hame. The farming sisters were at this time unaffected by the change, although no doubt their relationship to the newly created Earl was well known locally. Their letter head at this stage read: NEW BELLS FARM, Haughley Suffolk Misses Balfour: Partners E.B.Balfour, M.E.Balfour Stock Breeder, Poultry Stock Breeder, (Smarts Mendels) General Farmer, Dairy Produce and Cheese Maker.

The overall set-up may have been becoming more professional but there was still an extremely haphazard juvenile touch about the whole proceedings. Regular holidays were still taken to Fisher's Hill where they sometimes took part in amateur theatricals along with their Lytton cousins. New Years were still regularly spent at Whittingehame along with their family, particularly their young brother Ral and their young sister Kathleen. Meanwhile the Four Bells continued to struggle on with really considerable success considering that the financial squeeze was once again affecting the whole farming community. The war over the government had not taken long to decide that the farmers must take their chance against foreign competition. The price of corn and of livestock plummeted and the inhabitants of New Bells were forced to economise in every way possible.

Even the fact that their stalwart supporters 'Beb' and 'Derry' as well as their many visitors virtually acted as unpaid labour and chipped in towards all expenses failed to help matters. The farm simply failed to pay its way and each year required further financial backing from the Trustees, Aunt Nora and Gerald. Eve was well aware of the situation although doing her best to produce ever more optimistic prognoses.

In October 1923, perhaps to make up for their disappointment of the previous year, the Four Bells decided on a holiday in Devon. Derry and Beb motored down to Lynton in Derry's little GN cycle car, a popular little runabout of the day. Made by Godfrey Nash with a chain drive to a solid back axle cornering could be difficult at times and it was understandably nicknamed 'the mechanical rodeo.' Nevertheless they joined Mary and Eve for what appears to have been a thoroughly enjoyable, if still unconventional holiday by the standards of the day, mostly spent in the local inns and touring the Devon countryside on horseback and by car. Quite how they managed to leave the farm together is unexplained, presumably 'Aldous' was left in charge, but it appears to have been an enjoyable break for them all.

## NOTES ON CHAPTER FOUR

1. Fisher's Hill:
   Ral also suffered throughout his life from asthma and was always regarded as a weakly child, much spoiled by his elder sisters, although not by his father who regarded him as an academic failure and lost few chances of pointing this out to him. In 1923, however, he distinguished himself by coxing the Cambridge Eight in the boat race, when they lost by only half a length to Oxford in a close finish.

2. new houses:
   Mary happened to be away from the farm that day and heard this saga from Eve on her return. Some years later, recalling this incident, she wrote: 'I remembered . . . how our own house hadn't been ready for us either and how we had to abide for days and days surrounded by crates and ever since then when I have watched newcomers grappling with the hooligan bohemianism which is New Bells, I say to myself, 'Poor things, they are still in the crate stage.'

3. platonic relationship: Eve was to write much later of the 'early New Bells days . . . Before Bunny turned up and Mary's other 'Mary' became such a nuisance.' Looking back, it seemed to her: 'It was a singularly easy and happy intimacy without sex complications or a tinge of jealousy . . . ;' but this period really only lasted the first two years at New Bells. Eve nostalgically recalling those days understandably thought of it as much longer.

# CHAPTER FIVE

# The Farm and The First Novel

## 1924–1926

*'I got my balance sheet out last night and a very depressing business it was. Worse than i had hoped . . .'*

Eve in a letter to her mother.

AT EASTER 1924 the Pickwick Dance Band achieved its greatest triumph. They were booked to play for a week at Sherry's, one of Brighton's leading dance halls. The experience of playing non-stop for ten hours a day, however, proved more than enough for them all. After that they stuck to local engagements. It was, however, probably their share of the profits from this engagement that enabled the sisters to invest in a large ten-year-old Delage open tourer made in 1914, nick-named the Deluge. Derry Hawker, about the same time, bought a 1916 Hispano Suiza open tourer, so that the Four Bells were now fully mechanised.

It was only a few weeks later that the Haughley Players held their 'Play Week.' They staged a Tudor period play with an ambitious cast of twelve characters composed of relatives and friends. Amongst these were Ral and his fiancée, Jean Cooke-Yarborough,[1] whom he had met at a final May Ball just before he went down the previous year. They were cast as the lovers Raleigh and Bess, presumably on the principle that they would not need to act. The play, held in the farm barn, appears to have been an immense success at least as far as the players were concerned. Despite such events, of which she was the focus, Mary was gradually changing in character. Imperceptibly a new personality was emerging chrysalis-like from the old Mary, who had always been intuitive and tactful, but inhibited and taking a background place. The new Mary, brasher and more obtuse, resembling in many ways a teen-ager rather than a woman in her late twenties, was becoming increasingly difficult to live with, especially for those who had known her for years. The situation was difficult in the extreme for those, like Eve, who were treating her as a beloved sister and were, quite understandably, not fully appreciative of the changes that were taking place within her. Had she been seen as an interesting psychological case it might have been much easier for all concerned, but such matters are often only fully appreciated by outsiders and with hindsight.

The entire personality change took a period of some ten years, although largely finished within the first four or five. It was almost inevitable that Eve particularly found it hard to cope with and turned increasingly to the more easily comprehended, supportive and amusing character of her friend Beb Hearnden. This in turn reacted on the changing personality of Mary and hurt her feelings although previously she had been slow to reveal her emotions. A letter to her mother in the year 1924 was a turning point in more ways than one. The farm had reached yet another and almost decisive financial crisis. Mary wrote:

'New Bells; Dec 27 '24

'Beloved Mum,

'Don't think me an awful pig I want to grouse and there's no one but you I can do it to. Please regard this as an overflow, escaping with the express intention of removing the hump. For when one has let out at least half of what one feels it magically ceases to be felt any longer . . .

'You will know by now that we are about £800 down. Eve had hoped for half this. As soon as I knew she hoped for half this I knew it would be double. But what can one do but just sit and let her receive her disappointment. If one warns her of one's own conviction she merely resents your power after to say 'I told you so' even tho' you don't say it. Yet it is awful to see her disappointment and it is still worse that one can't share it. Here comes my grouse.

'I'm not easily a hurtable person, but I can't cure myself of this particular sore. I've kidded myself about it for four years, but I'm unable to do it any longer. The first year we came here Eve promised to teach me farm accounts so that we could do them together and that first season I did help and 'loved' it. Not because I love accounts – who does? but because they were mine as well as hers and it was a way as sharing success and failure. Then bit by bit this didn't happen any longer and it was the same with all her plans about the farm. I ought of course to have pushed. But I don't push easily . . . above all where Eve's concerned. I did once say something and her answer stopped all my efforts in that direction for ages. She said 'I don't need any help now. I've got Beb.' She didn't mean it in any unkind way, Iknow that. I knew it at the time. But the mischief was done. I was hurt. It hurt like hell. She meant, of course, that I need not put myself out any longer to help when I had so much of my own to do. But you see that wasn't exactly how I looked at it . . . It's all damn silly I know, but there it is.

'The result is I never know without a great deal of pumping how things really are. The farm seems to belong to Eve and Beb. The difficulties they encounter are theirs and not mine at all. It is 'we' and 'you' when they talk about it in my hearing . . . I feel sure that Eve is quite unconscious that she doesn't include me. But she doesn't. She thinks of it very definitely as her farm. This is extremely natural from one point of view. She governs the major portion of it and it is right for her to take the credit, but there is no doubt . . . it could have been very much more 'our' farm . . .

'Eve doesn't really love sharing, whereas I adore it. We are both a little unreasonable in each case. That's all. I can't talk of this to Beb because it's so difficult not to make it look as if I grudge her position, which heaven knows I don't at all. If she hadn't been here and been a bridge between Eve and me countless numbers of times I simply don't like to think what might have happened . . . Please believe me I feel better already. I do. Devoted Mary.'

By the same post came a letter from Eve which was a good deal shorter and as usual put first things first. It read;

'Darling Mum,

'I got my balance sheet out last night and a very depressing business it was. Worse than I had hoped yet cheering in a few aspects viz: Profit on cattle £193. On milk £22 Sheep £30 and poultry (in spite of all the bad luck) £9. Also astonishing thing is £30 profit on Barley. Also the car has only cost just over 2d a mile to run. But in spite of all this and in spite of the fact also that to Merchants and Tradesmen we owe £500 less than we did this time last year we still show a deficit of £800 the same as last year.

'If we deducted living expenses, Rates and Tithe, interest on loan depreciation and dead stock and the use of the car we have just made ends meet. One has got to make such huge profits on the things that do pay to pay for this sort of thing.

'If people say at Whitt will you ever make it pay I can only answer I don't know – but at least let me try one more year at least.

'Enough of depressing things I dreamed about it all last night and have a foul headache and it is our party day. Wonderful Xmas box from Fisher's Hill . . . I will write properly later . . .

'I must stop. There is such a lot to do today. Bestest Love Devoted Eve'

Of course, as anyone connected with farming will readily understand, some figures relating to stock and crops can be very easily assessed in almost opposing terms and this was a time of depression in the farming world. Her mother, however, was clear in her own mind as to what to do after receiving these letters from her daughters while visiting Whittingehame. She wrote to her husband Gerald, still at Fisher's Hill, firmly enclosing both letters and for once marking her letter:

'Private

'My own darling . . . I must write to you 'in strict confidence' about two New Bells letters I got today. Read Mary's first and Eve's after and show them both to Nora. Never let on to the farmers that you have seen them, but I send them because I think both you and Nora can help in a sad situation.

'I think when you have your clear up talk with Eve over the accounts that you should say quite sternly to Eve that this terrible over drawing can't go on – If you once more save them this year they must manage to balance next year – that you note that Mary's department – in spite of having been starved of capital has always managed (even in the most unlucky seasons) to show a balance – and that you feel Mary should be taken into very complete partnership over all farm affairs and her advice asked over everything. Also that instead of this hectic brain racking account making once a year the farm accounts should be brought up to date every month and that Mary and Eve together might give one day a month to the purpose.

'Eve ought not to have been so hopelessly out in her reckoning as she is! Believed she had balanced! and £800 out!! It is staggering. However I am not hopeless that things will not get better and I do hope the whole family need not hear of the present state of things. I am 'quite' sure that Eve is utterly unconscious of having treated Mary badly and that Beb also has tried to bring them together and not separate them – and loves them equally – But it is a 'little' like the Auntie Nunkie situation – Eve doesn't find Mary fundamentally an easy person to confide in But she has got some day or other to be shaken into realising how she 'ought' to behave to Mary.

'Mary's letter is horribly saddening, but I am glad she wrote it and think good may come of it if you and Nora deal helpfully with the situation . . . Yr loving Betty.

'Two things I must add:

1. I believe Eve has such unbounded faith in Mary as an artist and creator that she wants to spare her as much of the normal work of the farm as possible.

2. That the £800 is not all want of balance this year but also debts from last year.'

There can be little doubt that anything Betty recommended to her husband in family matters was likely to be duly followed. Gerald might lead his own life sexually at times, but in matters connected with the family he usually did what his wife told him to do. In this case his inclinations were probably towards his wife's advice in any event and once again the farm was subsidised.

This was to be a significant turning-point, for the following year (1925) they were at least paying their overheads with their pupils and the milk cheque each week. The milk round was now beginning to prove profitable, and they were building up a good-looking herd, but even so they were still heavily in debt. Nevertheless, during 1925 they spent then very considerable sum of £20 on a new-fangled wireless set. This resulted in a letter from Betty, tactfully conveying word of criticisms she had heard.

'Fisher's Hill: May 8 1925. Darling Eve,

'In the watches of the night I heard voices say about your wireless 'Why do the Farmers spend £20 on a luxury when they have to borrow money right and left which they can't pay? Is it honest? In a police court it would not look well. I hadn't thought of this before. Geoff and Derry are sharing but the same thing applies to them. In the night I answered thus; 'A Farmer's life is very wearing, ceaselessly anxious and worrying – so most farmers grow hard and inhuman. If you are to keep up the spirit of joy and hope and love in life you must have some relaxation that lifts your thoughts and imagination above the despair of bad weather, low prices, animal diseases etc etc. If this wireless keeps you from cinemas and theatres it is cheap. If it adds to your knowledge and love of good music it is profitable. Is that a good answer? I want the best to face the family with also I like the thought that your farm people will share this luxury. I'm in an awful money depression myself. Have spent a good £400 more this year than I should. Must try to be mean and not spend. It's a crime to spend what you haven't got, so I'm a criminal . . . Devoted Mum'

Despite the hint contained in this letter, inevitably, the Four Bells found it necessary to take occasional breaks from the daily grind on the farm. In February Ral and Jean had been married at Puttenham, near Guildford in Surrey. Eve and Mary had managed to attend the wedding, spending the night at Fisher's Hill. In September Eve and the others decided on an ambitious journey via Blackpool, Carlisle and the Lake District to Redcliff, the house on Whittingehame estate where the newly-married couple had set up home. They took both cars and Eve noted;

'Got to Redcliff on the afternoon of the fourth day. Great fun except for the day through Cumberland when it poured in torrents. I prefer the lakes on a post card myself.'

It was a short break, but an enjoyable one. The first of many visits made by Eve to Ral and Jean in Scotland over the years to come, while they in return usually managed an annual visit to New Bells. During the rest of 1925 further desperate efforts to earn a living included Eve and Beb co-operating in writing a detective novel.

Eve it transpired was good at constructing a plot, although always an outrageous speller, like most of her family. Beb Hearnden on the other hand was good at dialogue and readily enough constructed this around Eve's sometimes very sketchy plot. Rather as in a game of 'Consequences' the novel developed in this somewhat haphazard way. They were close to completing it by April of 1926.

It is perhaps significant of the changing personality of Mary as well as the changing circumstances at New Bells that from 1920 to 1926 they had annually performed a play, but the 1926 play appears to have been the last. The arrival of the radio, the time taken up with writing and many other outside considerations, may have been contributory factors, but there is little doubt that the relationship between the sisters was changing considerably during this period and the end of the plays in which she played such a prominent role is indicative of this.

Eve was not alone in finding the 'new' Mary more than a little trying. Beb also found her attitudes incomprehensible at times. Since Mary was still frequently ill with colds and was in charge of the poultry and household management rather than deeply involved in the work on the farm itself they probably saw very little of each other.

They really only met at mealtimes and in the evening when the farm workers were tired and had little patience for Mary's whims. On the whole this merely aggravated the situation, but in the circumstances little else could have been expected.

Early in 1926, however, the political situation became ugly and in May 1926 boiled over in the National Strike. Just how this affected the lives of everyone even in the remote district of Suffolk can be gauged by one of Eve's letters to her mother. She wrote around May 4th-12th:

'The following three stories are nice;

1. A bus taking passengers from Ipswich to Woodbridge having deposited its load was boarded by strikers who demanded a joy ride. 'Certainly I'll take you for a ride, if you like,' said the driver. He then locked the door on them and drove them all to the Police Station.

2. A lorry carrying eggs from Norwich to London and driven by a woman was stopped by strikers. She told them to clear the way. They refused. 'Well I'm going on,' she said and she did. 'And she broke two of their legs and one of their shoulders,' said Aldous who told me the story. 'They won't stop her again,' he added with glee.

3. The 3rd story is the best. Our milk train was held up at the Stowmarket level crossing gates. The gates were lined with strikers and when the stoker dismounted to open them they refused to let him. The driver then got down. 'Aren't you going to let me open them?'he asked. 'No,' they said. 'I think you 'will',' he said. 'I'm coming through anyway.' and he returned to his engine and started up. Before he reached the gates the strikers opened them themselves!!!

'Our local 'Robert' (affectionate term for policeman, derived from Sir Robert Peel who formed the first police force, known as 'Peelers' or 'Roberts.') has returned from recent disturbances in Ipswich with his head in bandages.

'A large number of the silk factory and manure factory workers have had to be paid off owing to lack of supplies.

'This will add to local trouble no doubt, but on the whole this district is as peaceful and good-humoured as reported everywhere.

'The Station Clerk is very good value. He is making a collection of all the summonses to strike that he has received. He exhibits them with pride. One is a 3/8d telegram. The day before yesterday's train crew was a very amusing one. All university boys. The cleanest stoker I've ever seen in Oxford bags.

'Yesterday's lot were cheery too. but a different type. The train had a van reserved for 4 tons of pork from the Elmswell bacon factory. The lorry hadn't arrived so the train had to wait for it. When it did Maisie (the Welsh cob) came in very handy helping to unload with the cart. We all worked like navvies but it took us a good 1/2 hour to unload so that the train was an hour late much to the disappointment of the amateur guards who were so proud of themselves for having got the train running to time.

'I have not been called up as yet tho' I was going to get a job unloading groceries at Stowmarket today. I wrote to Ipswich and offered my services there and have been referred to the transport officer at Bury. Much love, Eve.'

Two of the Four Bells, Beryl Hearnden and Derry Hawker, were in London. Beb wrote to Lady Betty on the 12th of May;

'. . . since last Wednesday I have been working at the Chiswick L.G.O.C depot feeding bus men. A full-time job. We have all been doing about ten hours a day in that canteen and yesterday weserved 18,000 meals. It seems almost incredible but we were certainly hard at it. 'Bus drivers' conductors, mechanics, policemen and 'specials' they are all volunteers except for the regular 'Roberts'. They are a very cheery crowd and I've run into many people I know. All the Universities seem to be either bus drivers or specials. Derry and Geoff are both in the police. Geoff at Marylebone and Derry in the Flying Squad. The 'Gang' usually collect in my rooms about midnight to have buns and hot drinks before they go out on patrol. We are all very dirty, rather tired but enjoying life enormously . . .'

Astonishingly enough despite these interruptions the novel was finally completed the following month in June 1926. They then sent it to a publisher named Christian. He took a very cautious if encouraging approach as described by Eve in a letter to her mother:

'New Bells June 13th 1926:

Darling Mum.

Two days ago I had a letter from Christian – he said – I have read your novel with considerable enjoyment. It is certainly a very well written book though the construction could be improved in places. The chief fault to my mind is its great and I think unnecessary length. There is too much dialogue (Very good and natural of its kind) which holds up the action. If you will be in London soon I would like to see you and talk it over with you. I will hold the Ms until I hear from you.

'Knowing I could get a lift back with Ral on Saturday afternoon I telegraphed and got an appointment for Beb and self at 11.30 Saturday morning and went up on Friday night.

'Briefly summarised his criticisms of the book itself were:

'For' Very well written good dialogue, atmosphere,

'Against! Too long, wants tightening up – too melodramatic and improbable . . . Now why I asked you to come and see me was because I wanted to know what you were like and what chance there was of you going on writing. I never hunt for good new books but I do hunt for good new authors.'

'Then he asked how we collaborated and when we told him said' Good collaboration of that sort is very rare and I believe you've got it. I think you have the makings of a very strong combination. The technique of Detective Story writing is mainly a matter of practice.

Us; Do you think we'll get it with practice?

He: I do. In fact having read your first book I should say that you have broken the back of your apprenticeship.

I asked him if he thought it was worth offering if we shortened it by 10,000 words and tightened up the action.

He: Are you prepared to do that?

Us. Yes.

He; Well will you show it to me again when you have done that before you show it elsewhere?

Us: Yes,

He: Then if you don't succeed in placing it will you give me the first offer of your next book? Of course if you place this you usually have to contract with whoever took it for the first offer of your next.

'I promised this then asked if Hodder & Stoughton would be a good firm to offer it to? He looked very glum and then said sourly 'You couldn't do better ' He obviously does not want to lose touch with us and is most anxious to get a chance to get our next book which he appears to think he will want to publish. In fact he practically said so, which was very flattering. He obviously does not think he can make money with our first one but wants to stop us going elsewhere so that he can get the 2nd one.

'His whole face beamed when Beb said 'I am not sure we hadn't better shelve this and get on with the next.'

'As a matter of fact what we have decided is to shorten and reconstruct this one and then while he sees it again, start with the next.(We have had the outlines thought out some time.) We'll decide about the first one after Christian's second opinion, but we shall probably try it elsewhere if he won't take it.

'It's all very exciting and he kept us a whole hour which was complimentary in itself. He obviously quite genuinely thought we had a future.'

They went ahead with the revision as quickly as possible and on June 29th Beb wrote to Lady Betty:

'. . . I expect you have heard all about the adventures of 'The Paper Chase.' We have now cut out 7,000 words and are really pleased with the result. It has improved it in construction and tightened up the action considerably. I hope Christian will agree with us about it. Anyway it has just gone off to him again and now we wait to see what he says. In the meantime a man I know has taken the original unaltered copy and is getting a criticism for us from a friend of his, who works for Macmillans. I'm all for knowing what several people think and I believe Macmillans are a very good firm. Of course now we've cut it we felt that nobody could dream of accepting the un-cut copy. It 'has' been fun doing this 'shocker' and I am frightfully looking forward to starting the next one.

'Friday is lamb sale day. Eve's had to get up about 4 a.m to go with the 'Woollies' to Stowmarket. I'm going to take the Car over later. I hope they fetch a decent price. They look awfully nice. All the stock are looking first rate just now. The new pupil – Rachel – comes Wednesday . . . .'

In July Eve, Beb, Mary and a young pupil, David Jensen[2], took the opportunity of travelling up to Leith by boat from Hermitage Wharf in London aboard the Royal Fusilier. Beb noted;

'It was great fun. Baking hot and the sea like a mill-pond. Eve and I made friends with 'Jock' a sailor, and the result was a concert party held on the hatch above the Foc'sle, during the Sunday dog-watch . . .'

During this fortnight's visit to Scotland they spent most of their time sailing on the Forth in Ral's 18 foot gaff-rigged dinghy at North Berwick and crewing on his newly acquired converted cutter Lady Bird, sailing round the Bass Rock. They enjoyed themselves so much that towards the end of the fortnight they discussed plans for charter-ing a yacht for a North Sea crossing the following year. Finally, after this brief, but enjoyable stay at Redcliff with Ral and Jean, who now had a son, Gerald, they returned south again on another boat, the Royal Scot. This was to be the first of many sailing holidays.

At this stage their old Fourth Bell, Derry Hawker, finally left to set up in a farm of his own and marry a girl called Robin. In October of 1926, however, the group at New Bells welcomed a newcomer, Kathleen Carnley[3]. Born in Yorkshire in 1888,and thus some ten years older than Eve, she had been almost the first woman to be accepted as an agricultural student at what was then the Midland College. During the 1914–18 War she had been employed to run a travelling cheese school, teaching farmers' wives to make cheese.

She had just returned from a two-year working holiday in New England and was introduced by a mutual friend to Lady Betty Balfour at Fisher's Hill. They liked each other on sight. Lady Betty insisted that she came to meet Eve and Mary for the weekend. Since there was something of a crisis in the milking parlour at the time she stayed on and within a week or two had become an indispensable part of the farm known to everyone by her initials K.C., a nickname she had acquired in the U.S.A.

Meanwhile the optimism of the amateur authors shone through all their correspondence on the subject of their joint work. Surprisingly, however, it proved to be justified. It was too much to expect that the publisher they first approached would agree to take it, but it was not long before they found a home for it. The novel was eventually sent to Hodder and Stoughton, who provisionally accepted it on the understanding that a further seven thousand words would be cut. In common with most would-be authors they had produced a magnum opus of inordinate length and the cutting proved a major obstacle, but eventually the work was completed. The publishers issued the following advance publicity prior to publication:

'Hodder & Stoughton have an amusing story to tell with regard to the Ms of a novel entitled 'The Paper Chase,' which they are publishing immediately. The pseudonym of Hearnden Balfour hides the dual personalities of Eve Balfour and Beryl Hearnden, two young ladies who run a farm and who decided to write a detective story together.

'One bright morning Eve set out from the farm, on her motor bike bound for the typist and for a radio authority (for in a wireless chapter they had scattered a largesse of heterodynes and rheostats, which, they felt, needed vetting by an expert). In a cardboard box strapped to her carrier were nine chapters of the novel. She arrived to find exactly one chapter in the box, the flap of which had fallen open on the way. The story sounds funny enough now, but there must have been real tragedy in it for Eve at the time. To re-write eight chapters of a detective story without any notes . . . She went back on her tracks and about a mile from home came on the first missing sheets fluttering in the hedge. She pushed on gathering up her magnum opus from the banks and ditches. And then, half a mile from home, she ran into an

East Anglian blizzard. When the storm had subsided the next pages she collected were almost illegible. There was nothing for it but to go home and spread them out to dry.

'But a feature of English country life is that whatever you say or do is common property within a few hours. and soon the pages began drifting in – in ones and twos – until at last, except for the wireless chapter and one loose sheet, they had all been retrieved. But if the authors had nearly lost the book they had found the title – 'The Paper Chase.'

In November, shortly after publication of the novel, Lady Betty noted: 'Eve had a short but violent and rather alarming illness. Acute abdominal pain with fever. Two local Drs diagnosed it as stone in the kidney and thought she should have it removed by operation. Charles of Ipswich . . . said there was no stone. The pain was due to an inflamed gland . . . He stopped all fats from her diet and she recovered quickly . . .'

This was one of Eve's few illnesses and understandably alarmed her mother. The cure probably owed as much to the success of the Paper Chase as any diet, for, surprisingly, the novel, though suffering from the typical amateur's fault of too many characters, was a success and redressed the balance owing at the bank. For the first time they were in the clear financially. They promptly decided to write another and with thoughts of a fortune even ambitiously looked forward to the sale of film rights. In practice one set of film rights were sold, but no film was ever made.

The novels themselves stand comparison with similar products of their era extremely well and are not only well plotted, but have a sound dialogue. They may be shallow affairs by some present-day standards, admittedly, but they were never intended to be taken seriously. In that they started Eve on a literary career of a sort and at least gave her an initiation into the disciplines of writing and some of the problems of dealing with publishers they were a major step forward.

NOTES ON CHAPTER FIVE

1. Jean Cooke-Yarborough: youngest of Canon and Mrs Cooke-Yarborough's five daughters. Brought up at Romsey Abbey in Kent, she was in many ways very like her mother-in-law to-be, Lady Betty Balfour. They took an immediate liking for each other. Lady Betty's mantle as letter-writer and family archivist was to pass to

her. Outwardly unassuming she was a woman of remarkable inner strength of character and will, which Lady Betty soon appreciated, noting only two years later (in 1926) 'Few women that I have met have possessed Jean's iron self-control.' Amongst her many writings is included 'Discord in Four Bells,' a bulky Mss on Mary's changing personalities. She also produced remarkably penetrating pen-portraits of many of the Balfour family.

2. David Jensen, a 17 year old farm pupil, with whom Mary was violently in love. By this time Mary's personality was changing so markedly that they had all begun to notice it. The 'second Mary's' mooning after a youngster almost half her age was indicative of the change. On their return south, however, David Jensen took a job as a merchant seaman and went off to New Zealand, thus it seemed ending the affair.

3. Kathleen Carnley. Typically Yorkshire with great strength of character and mind, she was an admirable foil for Eve throughout their long association, always prepared to disagree with Eve's more dogmatic assertions. Although slimly built she was physically strong and seldom ill. Her nickname was probably a play on her initials and the currently popular song 'Casey Jones'.

11. Beb and Eve sitting outside Newbells in 1925 with Mary (characteristically) almost out of the picture.

12 and 13. The Milking side: The mid-1920s contrasted with the mid-1930s hygienic waxed-paper milk containers.

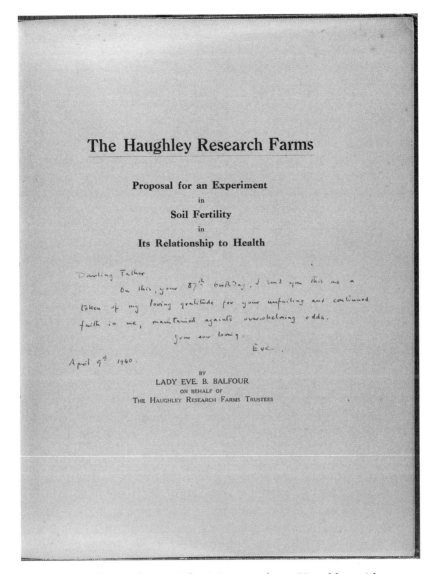

## The Haughley Research Farms

**Proposal for an Experiment**

in

**Soil Fertility**

in

**Its Relationship to Health**

*Darling Father,*
*On this, your 87th birthday, I send you this as a token of my loving gratitude for your unfailing and continued faith in me, maintained against overwhelming odds.*
*Your ever loving*
*Eve.*

*April 9th 1940.*

BY
LADY EVE. B. BALFOUR
ON BEHALF OF
THE HAUGHLEY RESEARCH FARMS TRUSTEES

14. *Also Backcover:* The Monograph on Haughley with
Inscription by Eve to her father.

89

# CHAPTER SIX

# Writing & Farming

## 1927–1929

*'I did rather an interesting manurial experiment the other day . . .'*

Eve in a letter to her father.

COMMENTS BY THE family were varied, as might have been expected. Aunt Frances Balfour wrote to Lady Betty; 'London April 1927: 'I have been rung up twice today for you and yours. First the 'Sphere' wanting to get at Eve and wanting her Telephone No and a photo. I explained their residence in the country and gave the address. I was waiting on Evelyn (Rayleigh) and took up The Paper Chase. A humiliating work when one considers it is written by a descendant of Bulwer Lytton. Why anyone should think vulgar slang and dreary pages of talk between ill-educated people worth putting into print I cannot understand. Arthur (A.J.Balfour)[1] came into the room and I opened fire on the book. He said he did not intend to read it as detective stories never interested him, which appeased me. Did you notice a huge puff of it and its authors in the Daily Mail? An interview with Eve. Also an advertisment of it in The Sunday Times. If advertisment makes a book sell I think they had a good deal,. It seems to me that they might have adorned the name and not sullied it. However I could not make out the story and was so disgusted . . . that I shan't look at it again. I gave Eliza a lecture in style when I came home . . .'

Lady Betty Balfour in reply rashly said that most of Lady Frances' criticisms might equally be applied to Dickens. Lady Frances answered:

'Oswald (her son) says 'Leave her alone' when I spoke of your audacity in speaking of The Paper Chase in the same way as Dickens!

'. . . I am not really conversant with Dickens as we were always discouraged from reading him (I find my father recommending Dombey & Son to his sister in the '40s.)

Oswald . . . spoke of Sam Weller's language. 'But Sam Weller was a great character. He was not just a mannequin created to bear the burden of public house language. He 'lives'. His language is just an incident in a portrait . . . I heard Auntie Alice say 'The story is not original.' Many a great character in fiction used bad or illiterate language but from all I hear there is not a character in this book, just a set of people picked out of the pot house. Is it worth writing? Is it literature? Can it do good to a living soul? Does it not merely add to the rubbish heap of books? . . . Better to occupy their days in selling good milk than in defiling the 'Springs of English'. If the book depicted anything but vulgar language, any character, however bad, I should say nothing, but this! All that the descendant of a great literary name can toss to the public.

'I have heard of one of my friends asking for it at the library. Frances (Dugdale) says that I make her want to read it . . .'

Lady Betty noted in her copy of this letter; 'Selling good milk' alas did not pay!' The Paper Chase. however, brought the authors in £300 which helped to pay some of their farming debts. Other relations who liked 'thrillers' were less severe.

After reading her Aunt Frances's views Eve wrote to her mother:

'Aunt Frances too gloriously up to expectations. Look here we have a scheme. Somehow or other we want that letter to go to the papers, preferably the Daily Mail, as we could put Dixon (a journalist friend) wise as to its coming.

'I'm afraid one cannot send it without permission, but if you were wily enough and said you thought the opinion of the older generation who knew what literature was ought to be made known or words to that effect that you could persuade her to send it . . . Mary read it to Vernon Mackenzie (a Canadian friend, professor, critic and journalist) who nearly wept over the opportunity. Said if we published it the book would be made. It would add thousands to our sales . . . After all why shouldn't we all derive some benefit from her vitriolic tongue?'

Nora Sidgwick predictably took a very different view and wrote to Eve:

'Just a line to say I have read your novel and admire it greatly. I am not a connoisseur of detective novels (Lady Betty inserted; 'But she was')), but of those I have read and remember Paper Chase strikes me as one of the best. The interest issue carries you on all through and almost everything that happens is plausibly and consistently explained (plausibly I mean within the bounds of an impossible story) except I think the presence of a man behind the study curtains to knock down Jonah when they are all about to proceed down the secret passage. Perhaps that is explained and I somehow overlooked it and I have not had the opportunity to look it up. But it seems to involve Lord Fairleigh having a second confidential servant besides Osborne, knowing the secret of the passage who is produced for that occasion only.

'The story is very ingenious and very well written. I congratulate you heartily. And the serious scenes, as well the adventurous ones, are well done. I shall look forward to the next . . .

A.J.Balfour wrote to Eve in April:

'A thousand thanks for 'The Paper Chase' I am sure I shall like it and hope it will prove to be only the first of a long and brilliant series of stories written by H-B published (and paid for) by H & S. I note with pleasure the steady improvement which marks the character of the Family Literature. It began in 1879 at a terribly low level with Philosophic Doubt' and it developed through the scientific mono-graphs of your Uncle Frank. It then showed signs of the Higher Life in odds and ends of Biography, Travel and Theology. It has now blossomed into the only kind of writing worth bothering about – that namely which gives much pleasure and no instruction! All my congratulations to you and your 'collaborator' to whom I am writing under what is officially described as a 'Separate cover'.

In April 1927 Beb was writing to Lady Betty:

'April 29th 1927;

'We've just got some reviews, extraordinarily nice ones. One fellow even says there's nothing wildly improbable about the book. We laughed a bit at that.'

'Last night Vernon Mackenzie and I went through the Ms of the new book (The Enterprising Burglar) at least the first 132 chapters of it and argued and thrashed at it till midnight. Vernon slanged it unmercifully but every criticism he makes is amazingly constructive . . . He had a good many pleasant things to say about it too. And all said in his own incredible mixture of English American . . . There seems to be a chance of my being offered a job on an American

Magazine. It's all very much in the air, but it's a wonderful castle in the air . . .'

In June 1927 Ral, still only a rather immature 25 year-old, alarmed the older members of his family by proposing a sailing trip across the North Sea to Norway in a chartered sixty-foot yawl complete with skipper, mate and cabin boy, but crewed by himself and Jean, Eve, Mary and Beb, along with a rowing friend of his from Cambridge.

Pamela Lytton wrote from Knebworth to Lady Betty:

'Darling Betty,

'Are you and Gerald really satisfied over the holiday plan of Ral's. I have seen Ral's letter . . . with a description of the boat and the accomodation! I do implore you to ask some experienced sailor his opinion . . . I cannot help feeling very anxious . . . Can you make some enquiries as to their safety . . . .'

Eventually, at his mother's instigation, Ral was persuaded to take along an older and experienced member of the family, his cousin Alison's husband, known as 'The Savage,'[2] to oversee the proceedings. Since the chartered skipper only had one eye and had served as a naval cook during the war these precautions seemed entirely justified.

However the holiday proved an immense success. Ral wrote that Eve 'was nick-named 'The Silent One' for her voice, which was frequently used, carried further than any other member of the ship's company . . . On the morning of the fourth day, the Silent One being on watch, everyone on deck and below was aware that land had been sighted . . .'

On June 15th Eve herself wrote from Norway:

'In spite of the weather being so cold and so often wet we are enjoying ourselves frightfully. I have fallen in love with the country and the people. When we put in at a little village for the night the inhabitants gather round and we have a concert. We singing English and Scots songs and they singing Norwegian ones . . . This is the most wonderful holiday. I have not felt so well since before my illness last November . . .'

In a letter to Betty Balfour at the end of the cruise 'The Savage' wrote; 'July 3rd '27;

'Dear Aunt Betty,

'Let me get in first with my letter on a very successful trip, which in the end provided them all with sufficiently realistic thrills to justify everything (They were nearly wrecked on the Bass Rock in a fog) I shan't burden you with details . . . I gathered my descriptions of events . . . were too bald for words . . . The fact remains that there never was a better or more amusing ships' company to sail with . . . Love Savage.

It was, it is almost needless to say, Eve's rousing shout of 'Breakers ahead' which saved them piling onto the rocks as they nosed their way through a thick fog into the Firth of Forth.

Notwithstanding this narrow escape, however, they all enjoyed this holiday greatly and it was to be the first of many that Eve shared with Ral and Jean, crewing on various yachts.

Eve, ever optimistic, wrote to her mother about this time:

'The milk round has jumped up again to pre-Easter level which is satisfactory. Nearly twenty new customers in the last months. Things are going all right but will be difficult until after harvest as I have had bad luck with Cows bought when I was short of milk last Xmas. Two have gone wrong and been a dead loss and a 3rd has had to be slaughtered under the TB Act, a total loss of over £60 which has hit me very hard just now. But the farm 'is' paying now and if I can make £150 to £200 between now and harvest out of book and odd sales we shall be able after harvest to pay all tradesmen everything we owe, a wonderful position to be in and will mean that we shall have pulled up £500 over and above expenses in 9 months. If the Bank will then let us have the O.D for another year we shall really be on our feet. Next month is going to be the hardest of all, a lot of payments fall due then also half yearly bank charges . . .'

Towards the end of 1927 Eve and Beb produced their second novel, which was published in 1928 by Hodder & Stoughton with the title The Enterprising Burglar. It contained some of the same characters as in the first novel, in particular the detective inspector and the 'now retired' gentleman burglar. It suffered from many of the faults of the first novel, it was too long, too prolix and complex. It had however fewer characters and perhaps tighter plotting. Like the first it seems to have sold well enough and was translated into at least two languages.

On January 2nd 1928 Mary wrote:

'My darling Father

'This is to wish you and therefore indirectly ourselves – a happy new year. We 'could do with it I reckon' as they say here . . . Eve will tell you all the practical points of the case – our position at the moment, and our hopes and fears for the future. Both these seem more acute than last year . . . In one way it appears more necessary than ever to stop while the stopping is good, before we lose more of your money;

yet against that those ellusive prospects we have been chasing so long seem nearer fruition. It is, of course, for you to decide, but I just want to say this – if by any possible means we can raise enough money to enable us to carry on for still one more year I am very keen to do so, everything in me revolts against giving up.

'We are tired, both of us, Eve more than me for she has borne the brunt of the responsibility, but I am sure she feels the same . . .'

On June 22nd of 1928 Eve wrote:

'Darling Father,

'I am so looking forward to your visit. I do hope the weather will be fine. There has not been enough rain to do much harm to the hay as yet, but so little sunshine that it is very slow making. We hope to get it in cock to-morrow if it keeps fine.

'I did rather an interesting manurial experiment the other day. When the cows came off one or our new meadows after eating it bare I dressed 5 acres of it with 1 cwt nitrate of lime per acre. The cows returned 3 weeks later and with only feed from the strip that was manured the yield of milk went up 5 gallons in 36 hours. I have ordered more nitrate of lime to dress the whole of that field next time they come off and next year I must try to dress all the meadows. I have proved it'll pay hands down to do so. Only wish I could afford to do more this year. But it is very impressive isn't it?

'I have done quite a good cow deal this week. Sold a couple of old cows and bought 4 beauties. Two young cows and 2 hiefers due in Oct. They will improve the look of the herd very much.

'I am really very incouraged by the way the Ipswich round is developing. It does really look as tho' the company was going to be quite a big thing in the future.

'Experience has taught me not to be optimistic, but things 'do' look better than ever before, apart from which there is a general tendency in farming circles to be rather more cheerful and hopeful so perhaps the worst is really past at last.

'Do hope you will be able to bring good news of mother. It is simply beastly her being ill. Devoted Eve'

This brought a reply from her mother at Fisher's Hill dated June 25th;

'Scene my bed room.

'Nunk sitting in a chair by my bed one side. Father standing upright on the other side. Aunt Nora leaning over the foot murmuring that the gong 'had' gone and no one attending to her.

'Father reading 'your' letter. Nunk deeply interested in the manurial experiment.

'Nunk; 'Now tell me what prevents her manuring all her fields now with this lime, is it cash or is it labour?

'Father: Oh I have no doubt it's cash.

'Nunk; Now really can't I supply that?

'Chorus from all of us': 'No! Nunk you can't.'

'Father; You don't know old man what I have done for them already this year in the cash line.

'Nunk. I know, I know (I am sure he doesn't) that's why I thought I might do it.

'Father. No, no. You haven't got the money and after all we can't run the farm for Eve. She's got to do it herself and I believe she will, but these facts are impressive aren't they?

'Nunk; 'Very.'

'Gorgeous weather for your hay over the week end. Hope it lasts over your father's visit. Loving Mum.'

During the same month in 1928, however, Mary revived her affair with their ex-pupil turned merchant seaman, David Jensen. She went with him to visit her brother Ral and sister-in-law Jean in Scotland. There she indulged in a star-crossed lover's scene which left Ral and Jean somewhat bewildered.

Jean wrote to Eve;

'We were convinced she had never really loved David at all. However she thinks she has and the ecstasy of renunciation is taking its place . . .'

In July there was a public presentation of a Rolls Royce to A.J.Balfour and Lady Betty wrote to Eve:

F.Hill July 31st.

Darling Eve at last a moment to write and send you these papers. Keep them till I come . . .

July 25th. The Prince's speech at the B.Academy dinner and Nunky's reply.

The Personal article on leading Article Page

It is written by D.D.[3] and I think 'very' good . . .

July 26th The account of the Presentation of the Rolls Royce. Baldwin's speech 'quite' delightful Nunk's reply v. moving . . .'

In October Eve was disappointed when her third novel was turned down by Hodder & Stoughton's reader; She sent a copy of the criticism to her mother who wrote back;

'Fisher's Hill. Oct 19th 28:

'Dear Darling Eve . . . It was angelic of you to copy Hodder's reader's opinion . . . it must have been bitterly disappointing for you . . . Have you another story in your heads ready to go on with? and isn't it an awful effort to begin again? I thoroughly enjoyed re-reading The Burglar and Father thinks it is an improvement on The Paper Chase . . . Wonder how it is selling. I've asked for it steadily at all Railway Station book stalls and never got it yet . . .'

On November 1st Eve wrote to her father:

'Darling Father,

'. . . I loved your letter. I can't tell you what pleasure it gives me that you enjoyed 'The Burglar' We are already hard at work on the next. I think, and hope I am right, that we have profited by the criticism of the 3rd to the extent of doing what the publishers like. Its such fun to be at work on another that I no longer have any feeling of disappointment . . . Its a vice writing, once it grips you no amount of discouragement can stop you!

'About your question re finances. The greater part of that £200 odd represents capital either in the form of amassed stock or manures for which I hope to see a return later. A little of it represents loss. During the weeks when I had two cows ill my returns were not meeting my expences. I'll let you have details in due course.

'Yes. £500 at the end of the year will meet all urgent needs or interest. But tho' I quite see that this is not the best time to sell shares I did so hope that I could raise the money that way and not come on you any more. But, of course, I'll do what ever you advise about that.

I am in the middle of threshing. My wheat has come out as well as I expected But I wish the price was better . . . Best love Eve. P.S. Note that I have dated this!'

It is fairly clear that already by this stage K.C's down-to-earth influence had begun to have a considerable effect on the New Bells menage. Undoubtedly the improvement on the milking side owed a good deal to her work and background dairying experience. Furthermore she had spent two years in the United States from 1924 to 1926 working her way from New England to California and back, taking any jobs available on the way and earning her living as well as paying for her journey. On one occasion she answered an advertisment for 'Cook, Christian, White.' At her interview, when asked if she could cook, she replied 'No', but still got the job. Such stories undoubtedly must have had their effect on Mary as well as Eve.

In November either Mary's 'new' personality demanded expression, or her second star-crossed love affair drove her into action. Anyway she wrote two consecutive letters to her father in November, having decided to leave New Bells at least temporarily and go off to the United States and try to make her living as a journalist.

'Nov 12:

'. . . I want to go away from New Bells for a bit, say 6 months or possibly even a year. I think if Eve and I were to separate for a little the change would be wholesome for both ourselves and New Bells.

'I have always imagined it would be Eve – at anyrate to start with – who would take a change, for certainly it is she who most deserves it and I think she had every intention of doing so as soon as it was justifiable. Since, however, the 3rd Novel has been turned down she does not see any immediate prospect of going herself, and therefore after a great deal of thought and consideration I have decided that I ought to go . . .

'Up till now the chief obstacle seemed to be the lack of means . . . This obstacle, however, has been gloriously removed by Uncle Vic, who has most generously offered to give me £50 which is all I should have had to raise. These are my proposed plans. I think of going to America in January – in fact I have provisionally booked a passage in a cheap line that has a boat sailing on Jan 25th. The fare is £20 plus £1.15 head tax (because I am not an American citizen) £20 I propose putting into a bank in New York as a reserve and for the rest earning my own living while I am there. It appears not only possible but comparatively easy to get jobs that I could undertake which would pay quite well and at the same time give me opportunity to write; for that is what I want to do more than anything else in the world and if I could get a start I feel I might really earn something for New Bells worth more than anything I have earned for her yet . . .'

This was followed by a further letter on Nov 15th when she analysed the sisters' relationship and her share in the partnership quite ruthlessly:

'. . . there is no one I could ever contemplate as a partner except Eve . . . but . . . our partnership as it stands at present should not be allowed to go on . . . No one is exactly to blame for what has happened . . . It was right of you to regard Eve as the business head to whom all money communications should be addressed. The fault . . . is the outcome of our relationship ever since childhood . . . It was unconscious on both sides . . .'

Eve's thoughts were already turning to more serious matters. Incensed by the way in which the wealthy brewers were stifling the market for home-grown barley Eve wrote at length in 1929 on the subject trying to expose the situation. The article remained unpublished, for no trade magazine could afford to risk publication and her writing style was still very immature. Her mother kept it with a note attached. 'Sent me by Eve 1929. Not suitable for letter collection but too interesting to destroy.'

Some of her comments, however, remain of interest since they indicate the way her thoughts were turning in the matter of crop growing and health. Her style unfortunately was still more like that of a university essay than slick journalism, but significantly her first paragraph ran:

'In past times beers in this country were brewed from British barley malt and hops and British beer was renowned for its excellence. Today the percentage of British malt used is very small and in many cases adulterated with beans, maize and sugar with the result that, in a great many doctors' opinions, beer which was once a wholesome drink is now not only useless, but in some cases injurious to the system . . .'

Eve went on to try to expose the 'ring' of brewers who were responsible for rigging the market price of barley and by importing cheap foreign barley keeping the price artificially low to the detriment of the home producers. Unfortunately her writing style was still turgid and her facts were poorly presented. She still had a lot to learn about presenting her case effectively.

She was determined to try to get her beloved 'Nunkie' to take an interest in the issue if possible, but he was becoming too old and feeble to take an active interest and despite her mother's help they eventually failed to get a campaign under way. The preparation, however, showed that she was becoming politically sensitive and ready to take strong action in what she regarded as a just cause.

On the 2nd of July 1929 Eve and Beb trained to Scarborough to join Ral and Jean and a friend, Vic Dawson,[4] on board Ral's new yacht Grey Goose. This was a 28 foot ex-Forth Pilot boat, cutter rigged, with 2 cots forward in the Fo'cstle and a central saloon with 2 settees and 2 folding beds, with the engine room aft along with the sail lockers. The accomodation was sketchy to say the least.

They sailed for Holland on the 5th, reaching it within forty eight hours. Beb, like anyone who ever sailed with Jean, was amazed by her ability to conjure up hot drinks and hot meals at all hours in all conditions.[5] They visited Amsterdam and Leyden, using the network of canals. At one point Beb described herself, Eve and Vic out for a walk:

'Vic's grey flannels had a large rent in the knee . . . Eve and I were in khaki duck trousers, mine all spotted with grease, due to cooking sausages while under way . . . We all had salt-stained blue blazers, dirty sandshoes, Dutch yachting caps and no socks. And so we started out much amused with each other. Eve and I endeavouring to imitate Vic's nautical roll . . . The Dutch girls turned round to look at us and smiled archly and Vic said;'My lads this is a dangerous town. We must stick together.'

On the 24th they sailed for Harwich and arrived around noon the following day. They then sailed up the Orwell and stuck on a mudbank within sight of Ipswich on a falling tide. In this fashion they eventually returned to New Bells again after another yachting holiday.

Fired by these sailing expeditions Eve bought a dinghy which she kept at Ipswich. This was a source of some amusement to her friends as a brief description shows: 'Eve has got her boat and a dream of long standing has been realised at last . . . She is a dinghy. I've seen a good many sailing dinghies but never one like Eve's. This is perhaps because she was a dinghy first and a sailing dinghy later; years later. In fact she only became a sailing dinghy when Eve bought her and fitted her out with a suit of sails and a centre board. Before that she belonged to a barge . . . However she floats and she sails, after a fashion . . .'

Later in 1929 Eve was making a determined effort to upgrade the farm and overcome the problem of the moat, their only water supply, running dry in hot summers, by drilling an artesian well.

On September 12th she wrote:

'Darling Father,

'I have sold my wheat at this week's top quotation i.e 43/6 per quarter, but of course it is a pretty rotten price. This will mean 'just' under £150 for wheat and my barley when I thrash it even at 40/- per quarter ought o be another áá150 so that I shall realise my estimate of £300 for corn. I shall not thrash the barley till next month.

'Delighted that Peco news still remains good[6]. Under what heading, if at all, are shares quoted in the Times. I have not been able to find them.

'The water scheme is getting on a bit better. The bore hole is now 52–54 feet deep. Sometime I will get for you the exact extent of the varying stratas a detailed account of which Tompkins keeps, but they have been thro' yellow clay. blue clay, a bed of flints a strip of sand, more blue clay narrow strip of chalk (about a foot wide) more clay and flints and now they are in sand again. Whenever they strike a bed of flints it takes them about a day to do 5 inches. In clay or sand they do about 5 feet per day.

'There is 30 foot of water in the hole and they are pretty confident that they have struck the 1st spring. If so that is about exactly at Tompkins estimated depth of 50 feet. We cannot test it, however or get any out for use until his bore-hole pump arrives. Which I hope it will do this week. In the mean time we are carting some from the pump in Haughley village and still getting a little out of the house pond, but this is now so dirty that I am terrified of the cattle getting ill thro' drinking it.

'As soon as the pump gets here we ought to be able to get enough water out of the hole every few days to keep us going while they finish the boring.

'Until we can get an adequate supply the milk yield is bound to suffer even if health doesn't. There is still no sign of rain which suits me perfectly except for the cattle.

'Best love, Eve.'

Mary was still abroad for she noted; P.S. I enclose the latest Mary letter which please give to mother and asked her to bring it with her.

This letter was soon followed by another from Lady Betty,who wrote:

'New Bells. Monday:

'Darling . . . K and I arrived in time for supper last night. Beb met us at Ipswich and brought us in her car. Quite cool here, but all dry as a bone.

'Well – As you know they had almost 20 foot of water by the time they reached 60 feet. Then they got thro' into a layer of sand and all the water disappeared. Beb says Tompkins says the well is haunted; never known one behave so oddly. He hears mysterious noises in it. Aldous says they are the black men talking the other side of the earth. Eve says Tompkins not the least disturbed by the disappearance of the water and she thinks it may be a good sign, but it means they must go on to 100 feet to get the permanent supply. They do about 20 feet a week. She thinks they will not have finished drilling till the end of 'next' week. Then it will take another fortnight before pump and wheel are fixed up. In the meantime its more and more difficult to give the cows water. The pond gets more and more stirred up and they won't drink it till they get desperate with thirst and much time has to be taken from other work carrying buckets.

'I realised it might save the temporary situation if Eve could hire an outside man and horse and cart to bring the necessary water from another farm. She can do this for £2 a week and I have told her I will pay for this! Don't be angry.

'Except for this water shortage all well . . . your loving Betty.'

By December Eve had several fresh plans afoot. Some idea of her ever-optimistic financial calculations may be gauged from a letter she wrote to her father just before Christmas;

'Dec 23 29.

'Darling Father,

'I simply haven't had a moment to do figures yet. But I want to tell you of an idea I have had. You see everyone wants a day off just before Xmas to go into Ipswich and I have been doing everybody's work in turn since I got back. Then I have had a lot of Xmas business to see to too, and parcels to send off. The worst of the rush will be over by Xmas day and I hope to work out the figures that day.

'My idea is twofold really. The 1st part I feel sure is feasable and the 2nd is only a suggestion. I have a 6 acre field that is a very rich deep soil and clean. The idea is to turn this field into a market garden and work up a vegetable round, sending into the Stowmarket three times a week and supplying our milk customers with vegetables.

'Scheme 1 which I feel sure would work, To start with only 3 acres. Lawrence to take charge of this department which he will be able to do now that Mar is home It could be done with practically no extra labour except a little at hoeing time. We have already a cart and cob that could do the delivery and we could sell at retail prices. I worked out the returns from this taking average crops and prices and comes to £280 a year on the 3 acres. I made Lawrence go over the figures with me and he agreed that they were reasonable. He is a 1st class man for the job and very keen. As our market grew would absorb the other 3 acres by putting it down to soft fruit. This scheme could be started at once without extra capital and our deliveries could start with the first early spring vegetables.

'Scheme No II This summer a young man, an Oxford graduate now a schoolmaster called Hollingsworth came to see me (He is a friend of one of our Ipswich customers) He . . . wanted to invest £500 in the farm or in the milk Co, if there was room for him to work . . . I explained that so far we hadn't got a living for two and there certainly wasn't one for 3 . . . that I couldn't agree to his sinking capital in our concern while things were in the rocky state they are . . . He said it was very good of me to put it to him like that! But that he did not expect a return from his money for a few years and was willing to work hard and to take the risk.

'I said well I wasn't and he went away very disappointed and asking me to let him know if I changed my mind. It now seems to me a possibility . . . That . . . it might be practical to take him on as a partner in the market garden department. Allowing him to buy his partnership by loan of £500. Using £100 to put the other 3 acres straight away into soft fruit and using the £400 to meet some of our liabilities. He would not expect interest of profit for the first year I think, tho' we should have to board and lodge him. If you approve of this idea at all I would suggest that he got interest on his loan after the 1st year at 5% and 1/3rd of the profits in the market garden and that for that first year we boarded and lodged him here.

'In a few years time if the thing went well his share might easily be £2000 without the interest and he could live comfortably in a cottage for that . . .

'If you think te plan a possible one let me know at once and I will try to get in touch with him before I come to Fisher's Hill and discuss it with him. If he likes the idea and is able to come into it right away, then if the bank will continue the extra £200 the loan would meet the other necessities . . . and would tide us over till my milk receipts get big again and Mar's earnings start coming in.

'Then I think it is quite possible Mr Hawker would wait 3 months for his interest this year and perhaps Aunt Nora would do the same. From the New year onwards things will pick up here without Mar's earnings and there is a very good chance indeed of her doing well.

'Let me have your views. I long to know what the brokers said at the Peco meeting. I'll write you again on Xmas day. All Xmas wishes to all at F.H. My small presents when I come. Devoted Eve.'

It is clear from the above descriptions that within a decade the Balfour sisters, if at times in rather uneasy harness, had settled down to farming in East Anglia. Rocky though their finances still were they were beginning at last to make ends meet, depending largely on the milking side, since during the depression any other form of farming was totally unprofitable. Eve's optimism remained undiminished, but things were slowly changing at New Bells, quite apart from Mary's personality. The halcyon period of the 'Four Bells' had ended. Derry had now left though Beb, always a stalwart friend and standby, remained. K.C had arrived on the scene as a friend and supervisor and accordingly the dairying side of the New Bells farm was steadily growing more efficient. Eve herself had begun to mature and her writing style was improving with practice. With her energy and outgoing personality she was already unconsciously looking for a challenge beyond the narrow confines of the farm.

## NOTES ON CHAPTER SIX

1. A.J.Balfour's own well known book A Defence of Philosophic Doubt published in 1879 was well received at the time, making his reputation as a speculative thinker. His brother Frank's monographs were highly esteemed. His sister's 1200 Miles in a Covered Wagon was the other book to which he referred.

2. The Savage: Colonel A.H.Milne, R.A.M.C. Aged at this time about forty and an experienced sailor he was sufficiently old to reassure the elder members of the family and young enough to enjoy the proceedings and get on well with all concerned. He died comparatively young some five years later.

3. D.D. Ettie, Lady Desborough, known affectionately as D.D. The widow of the Earl of Desborough, an old friend and colleague of A.J.Balfour. She was a close friend of the family and lived in the cottage adjacent to Fisher's Hill.

4. Victor Dawson. The mate on the chartered yawl. A keen yachtsman, with a master's certificate, and sales manager of a printing-ink company. A Scot with a sardonic sense of humour. He owned a 28 footer, the Dolphin, which sometimes sailed with Grey Goose.

5. all conditions. 'I don't know how she did it but every time we changed watches she was there with food and hot drinks . . . Never a word about her own difficulties, which . . . were . . . pretty grim. Vic said; 'There's not a man in a hundred could have carried on as Jean has done this trip. She's fine!'

6. Peco. This was the company formed to exploit the extraction of peat as a fuel, in which A.J.Balfour and his brother Gerald both invested heavily. It always seemed about to make their fortune, but sadly never achieved the success its promoters promised.

CHAPTER SEVEN

# The Search for a Cause

## The Tithe War 1929–1933

*'Our Queen, our Star, Lead on, we follow with acclaim, Lead us to war!'*

The 'Fighting Song' on the Tithe War, by LEX, addressed to Eve.

A T THE END OF 1929 A.J.Balfour was at Fisher's Hill and Lady Betty Balfour recorded;

'A unique family gathering gathered at Christmas and New Year of 1929–30 to make A.J.B feel that though he could not go to Whitt the family could come to him.'

Baffy Dugdale (his biographer) and her daughter Frances were there for Christmas. Ruth and Nell left their families at Balbirnie and came south. Jean and Ral came from Redcliff. Mary and Eve from New Bells. Mary just home from America . . . Oswald came for part of the time and Joan and Auntie from London where she was Christmasing with Aunt Evelyn Rayleigh . . .'

'The day after Christmas BB (Lady Betty Balfour) was carried off to the nursing home for an acute appendicitis operation. The affection shown to BB as well as to the 2 Nunkies was a revelation to her and brought her deep and grateful joy . . .'

Jean, Ral's wife, wrote to her on 1st January from the cottage at Fisher's Hill;' . . . I want to give you a picture of our cottage life . . . The first day was very damp . . . but we were all so happy and relieved about you that we just laughed and made a peat fire in the sitting room and enjoyed seeing Mary and all her stories of America. She looks so well and buoyant and seems happy and at ease and so full of quick understanding and tact and of most thrillingly interesting talk upon her adventures that one can just watch the whole family taking in this new Mary with enormous delight. Talks about the New Bells situation in the cottage have been very happy too. I can't tell you how full the cottage appears to be with 4 people of no mean size and all their luggage. The sitting room seems transformed into a sort of cocktail bar (I wonder what D.D. (Lady Desborough) would say) with rows of bottles – gin . . . etc . . . all neatly placed on face towels for we take the greatest care not to spoil any of D.D's pretty things . . . at 10.30 (we) have one vast and mighty boiling bath . . . and then all hop into it one after the other . . . as Ral remarked last night 'How shocked some people would be to see this mixed bathing!' This is all such fun . . . especially to be with Mary and Eve, and the four of us have such good talks sitting up every night till into next morning . . . and then lying late next morning . . .'

After this brief holiday they returned to reality. In a letter from New Bells dated Jan 9th 1930 Mary wrote:

'The well man has been . . . He has several schemes for making the pipe laying and general arrangement for the water much cheaper than we thought possible. He seems against a windmill under present circs . . . (In the margin is inserted; One was put in spite of him.)

On January 12th she wrote more typically:

'Our children's party was a great success. Over 40 people in our old timbered dining room I felt as if we were entertaining a county full of retainers (and with this feeling flashed another' No wonder we can't make this farm pay.)

'Paddy Magill (an Irish friend of Beb Hearnden's) turned up just right to be Father Christmas and the snow turned up just right too – for half an hour before Father Christmas was due The children adored him and Mary Lawrence was thrilled by his saying he had not forgotten her letter and had brought her the engine she wanted.(We found a letter on the table left by her . . . the night we gave the men their Christmas hampers . . . Solemnly Eve left an answer saying Father Christmas would bring an engine for Mary) . . . These Christmas parties make me realise how long we have been here. So many of those who were children when we first came here are grown men and women . . .'

Mary went to London on March 6th to see her literary agent about some stories resulting from her tour which she hoped to get published and had a final meeting with her merchant seaman friend.[1] On March 18th back at the farm once more Mary wrote to her mother:

'. . . a horrible scare. One of the cows went down with a violent lung hemmorhage and died in a few minutes. We telephoned to the vet. The scare was lest it might prove to be Anthrax The vet feared it might be at first. But he had his microscope with him and was able to assure us it was 'not' anthrax. If it has been it would have practically ruined us as we should not have been able to sell milk for 3 weeks. Luckily it is one of the less good cows. Still she was giving 3 gallons a day and her loss is a great bore . . . , (Their young sister Kathleen still at St. Felix School at Southwold on the coast) had some riding at New Bells and she, Eve and Mary Norman played delicious flute and clarinet things in the evening . . .'

On March 19th the inevitable happened and A.J.Balfour, the much loved 'Nunkie,' who had been in poor health at Fisher's Hill for some time, gradually faded away. Mary wrote:

'. . . Eve and I heard the news from Ruth about half an hour ago. I was so glad we were together. It is easy to be glad for him . . . No pain, no long weeks of unconsciousness – perfect peace at the end with the knowledge of great love all round him . . .'

He was buried at his beloved Whittingehame in the family grave-yard next to the old Tower. On his death he was succeeded as 2nd Earl of Balfour, by his brother Gerald, father of Ruth, Eleanor, Mary, Eve, Ral and Kathleen. They accordingly all acceded to courtesy titles as the children of an Earl, Ral became Viscount Traprain and Eve became the Lady Evelyn Balfour. Unfortunately A.J.Balfour's death made no change to their lives financially, for at best his shaky investment portfolio barely covered his debts. Then just seven days after his death came the Wall Street crash of 1930, followed by a world-wide slump in share prices. Always unwise investors, in their latter years unfortunately he and his brother Gerald had been per-suaded to invest heavily in a firm called Peco, which purported to use peat as a source of cheap power.

The central figure in what amounted to a confidence trick was a vastly oversized Dane named Testrupp. His argument that as peat was 90% water all that was needed was to squeeze 20% of the water out to gain a clear 30% more peat for cheap fuel had the obvious flaw that comparisons of percentages in such cases are misleading, which any ex-chancellor of the exchequer should have recognised. Had A.J.Bal-four invested as heavily in oil the results would have been very different. As it was his brother Gerald was also very badly affected and the estate ended £70,000 in debt, a vast sum at the time. If Eve and Mary received little or nothing in the way of legacies, there was one side effect. In the still class-ridden thirties a title had a certain social significance and impact.

Eve was now into her thirties. Thanks to the two novels completed and numerous foreign rights sold, although the farm was not making a profit, the sisters were making ends meet. It may be surmised that no small part of this was due to the influence of K.C., who seems to have largely transformed the milking side. Eve was also now writing articles successfully and thanks to the encouragement of her journalist friend and co-author Beb Hearnden she had regular features appearing in magazines such as Farmer & Stockbreeder and other outlets.

Life was neither all fun and games, nor altogether desperate, but Eve was getting down to being a serious farmer and her journalistic efforts were improving. Her writing was becoming more professional and slicker, as shown by the following article Eve wrote on the farm's annual Christmas dinner. It makes an interesting comparison with the scene depicted by her mother in the previous chapter at the start of the sisters' farming career:

'Whatever the calendar may say, Christmas day on an English farm is the longest day in the year. At anyrate for the boss . . . It starts earlier, ends later, and is more strenuous than any other. It starts in the dark, snatching a cup of tea in a lamp-lit kitchen, buttoning a leather coat to the chin and setting out across the yard swinging a hurricane lantern, to feed the horses, mix food for the pigs and start cleaning the cows before the men arrive. The sheds are warm in comparison to the bitter chill outdoors and the animals blink at you in a surprised sort of way. Soon after that the men arrive. You hear the slow countryman's treads, crackling on ice, or more likely squelching through mud. They are earlier than usual, too, but you have beaten them to it. They are pleased and endeavour to disguise their pleasure by asking after your insomnia.

Milking starts and the rounds-men come out to get their vans going. There's a good deal of chaff flying between the dairy and the sheds. The sun is coming up and it begins to feel more like Christmas day and less like a dash to the North Pole, but the big Chevrolet seems disinclined to start and the cowman suggests kicking her in the radiator or alternately hiring a barrow. The milk is bottled and loaded into the vans and the rounds-men drive off exhorted by every one to hustle and not be late for dinner. On ordinary days they don't get back until 1 but today they must make all their deliveries before 1. The dairy-maid has a shrewd suspicion that they won't wait for many empties and that the dairy will look like a second hand glass factory tomorrow, but what's the odds. It's Christmas.

Then come the usual chores. Stalls to clean out, pigs to feed, hay to cart, meal to be mixed, horses to groom and turn out. Everyone lends a hand and by 12.30 the work is done. The men go home to dinner and the farmhouse gang get ready for their own meal. Ten people sit round the long table today. Two owners, four 'living-in' hands, two guests, and two servants . . . Just before one the vans roar up the lane. Several people go out to help them unload. The rounds-men are accused of eating mince-pies in every house and admit it cheerfully. The vans are parked and the whole gang troops indoors. One notices that the handouts have not affected the rounds-men's appetites to any noticeable extent. The turkey comes in, there is the usual struggle to light the brandy on the pudding and as usual someone drops a spent match into the sauce. But it all tastes very good.

After dinner there is a blessed interval, spent in happy coma round a vast open fire . . . But at 3 work starts again. Someone says a cow should have been invented that doesn't have to be milked on Christmas day, but we all go out except the rounds-men, who have to add up their books. As we leave one distraught soul yells:'17 1/2 pints at 3 1/2d?' We say 'No thank you' and shut the door. After all we have our own troubles.

By 5 the work is done and the real Christmas begins. At 6 the party begins to assemble. All the men with their wives and children come to tea. It is a cheerful meal. Life on a farm is a friendly and intimate affair. There are jokes against everyone and they are retailed rapturously. And through all the talk and laughter the children sit and eat . . .

After tea there is a Christmas tree and a bran tub. Then they play games. They spin the trencher and play Postman's Knock' . . . The party goes on until about 10, but it always ends with everyone dancing Sir Roger de Coverley down the length of the big room. Then here are many good nights, the childrens' pockets are bulging with toys and oranges and so at last to bed . . .'

Mary's year in the United States supporting herself by journalism had done her a great deal of good. She now wrote another play and the same members who made up the yachting crews on their periodic trips across the North Sea also made up the cast. The Haughley Players, many of whom had performed Mary's plays up to 1926, were all regular visitors to New Bells and most of them had also crewed on the various yachts owned by Ral. The whole thing was very light-hearted.

Ral and his wife Jean were prominent amongst those involved along with Beb Hearnden, Vic Dawson, Bunny and the familiar hangers-on, known in the language of the twenties as 'The Gang'.

In July 1930 the play 'The Firebug' was favourably reviewed in the local paper. The review read: 'In the Barn Theatre at Haughley Green, an ordinary farm building converted for amateur theatricals, 'The Firebug' an original play by Lady Mary Balfour was presented last evening and it will be repeated tonight and tomorrow . . . Altogether . . . a play of considerable possibility . . .'

It is significant, however, that this was the last of these plays. From this time onwards life was geared towards more practical farming. Regular yachting expeditions each year were fitted in if possible and soon after the play had been performed there was another such expedition to Holland. In turn Ral and Jean and their growing family were annual summer visitors in the school holidays, but the pace of life was quickening and the farming side was becoming all important.

Although Mary had returned revitalised from the United States, Eve badly needed an outlet for her superabundant energy. She was a human dynamo in need of a cause to support and this came her way with her introduction to the Suffolk Tithe-payers Association. The aims of this Association, along with many similar bodies in other counties, were to gather all tithe-payers together to organise a united protest against the injustice of this enforced payment and draw attention to the iniquities of the system, especially the ways in which it adversely affected farmers during a period of severe depression in the industry and the manner it was being enforced.

This Association had been formed in 1931 by a Mr. Mobbs, a Mr Turner and a Mr Butler. These three very contrasting characters were well described by Beb Hearnden thus:

'Mobbs is a leader . . . He has that indefinable quality . . . a quick smile and ready sympathy. He'll stand up to anyone and he's always ready for a 'knock down blow' . . . He knows how to talk to the Aldous's of this world and he's perfectly sure of himself, mentally, socially and physically.

'Matthew Turner is a born 'Power-behind-the-Throne. He's a little man and he doesn't like rough stuff . . . He speaks very precisely . . . Turner doesn't like anyone much, but he appreciates subtlety. He'll use anyone who is apt to be useful. He doesn't talk much, but he listens . . . Mobbs tells you, Turner gives you a hint. They back each other admirably . . .

P.J.Butler is a Quaker . . . the best sort of Quaker, for he never condemns other people. He doesn't smoke or drink but sees no reason why other people should not. It is their affair. I can't imagine him losing his temper . . . I wonder how he first came into touch with Mobbs and Turner . . .'

Such a formidable combination quickly saw the advantage of having a titled lady farmer in their ranks and here it must have seemed to Eve was just the sort of cause for which she was unconsciously in search. Along with her friends, especially the able reporter Beb Hearnden, she threw herself into the fray. Soon they were organising support for farmers penalised for non-payment and preparing a barrage of press releases and information booklets. Eve herself was ever in the forefront, where her title and youth caught the imagination of the journalists.

The whole business of tithe-paying was, of course, an anachronism stemming from the payments due to the church by agricultural landowners and dating back to the 16th century when they were instituted after the Reformation. Historically they went even further back as an adaptation of the payments made to the Catholic church by all churchgoers prior to the Reformation. During the 19th century there had been a series of Parliamentary Acts gradually abolishing or reducing the power of the Church to charge tithes until only the land-owning farmers were charged tithes by an Act of 1891 and this in turn was amended by a so-called stabilising Act of 1925 at a rate established in the boom years of post-war farming, which the farmers, squeezed on all sides in the slump years of the late twenties and thirties claimed with good reason was manifestly unfair.

One casualty of the farming slump in 1930 was their next-door neighbour in the 80–acre Walnut Tree Farm. Eve was able to buy the farm at the foreclosed price of five shillings an acre. Kathleen Carnley, KC, then introduced Eve to a friend of her's, Miss Alice Debenham. The latter had started to train as a doctor, but for health reasons had been advised to take up an open air life as a farmer. Although she had farmed successfully, running her brother's farms in Dorset during the war, she was by this time crippled with arthritis. She agreed to buy Walnut Tree farm from Eve, on the understanding that Eve would farm it in conjunction with New Bells. The arrangement was one that depended on mutual trust and understanding and they were soon to become close friends. Meanwhile Eve's immediate financial problems were eased.

In late December of 1931 Eve and her old friend Beb Hearnden set off for the U.S.A on a month's visit, having a very stormy crossing of the Atlantic. They both clearly thoroughly enjoyed themselves and in early 1932 once again co-operated on a novel. The thriller contained the same detective inspector and the 'retired' gentleman-burglar as the two previous novels. Rather slicker than the previous novels 'Anything Might Happen' was published in 1933 by Hodder & Stoughton. This, although quite successful, was her last attempt at fiction, for during the next year or two her efforts were concentrated in more serious spheres and from then on her life took an altogether more earnest bent.

In 1932 and 1933 Eve and the Suffolk Tithe-payers organisation came out in open defiance of the system. They arranged a network of informers and resistance in the countryside, which was universally against the iniquitous and antiquated system. Inevitably Eve was persuaded to refuse to pay and her cattle were impounded in April 1932. The iniquitous part of such proceedings was that despite offers to compound for the tithe demand by paying a certain amount, say half, the amount of goods impounded was invariably worth well above the sum required. At a forced sale these goods then went for knock-down prices to outsiders prepared to buy cheaply and risk unpopularity with the area concerned, for the country areas would boycott the sales. The whole thing was thus a vicious circle with neither side gaining, but each refusing to give way.

In May they took part in an organised resistance against a tithe seizure on Delvyns Farm in Gestingthorpe. A very good account of the proceedings was given by Beb Hearnden:

'We heard the news from M.T. (Matthew Turner, Vice-Chairman of the Suffolk Tithe-payers' Association) at 10.15 or thereabouts. Eve came down and told me about it then fled back to the house to make the necessary arrangements for work to be done in her absence, while I got gas and water into the Buick . . . and we got to Gestingthorpe in 35 minutes. 26 miles.

The farm is at the top of a hill beyond the village. We saw a crowd of men standing outside the gates, a couple of policemen, two cars and a lorry . . . I pulled up and we got out, and then the men in the road started cheering . . . Gestingthorpe is just over the border in Essex and they were cheering the first Suffolk contingent . . . Several men told us the news . . . the bailiff had arrived about 10 with the buyer and a solicitor's clerk. The buyer was from Swansea, name of Meurig Jones

. . . They had arrived . . . to take the impounded implements, but had been stopped by a gang of farmers and men . . . there had been words on both sides . . . some bad eggs had been thrown. They were now in the barn . . . with Mr Krailing, secretary of the Halstead T.A., trying to come to terms . . .

Then Mrs Gardiner came to greet us. A woman of about 45 . . . her husband was killed in the war . . . We went to the barn . . . In front was a hay baler with one wheel off . . . This useful obstacle blocked the entrance most effectively . . . Only one man at a time could get between it and the wall to the barn doors . . . as many men as could squeeze in were standing there listening to the argument in the barn . . . Five or six more had climbed on the hay-baler, a gallery view . . . The crowd made way for us to go and look. The buyer . . . was very pale and his eyes were never still . . . he was scared stiff. The solicitor's clerk was covered with egg yolk and chaff and he looked pretty green too . . . The tithe goes to the rector, Greening . . . The living is worth over £900 a year. Greening is a Welshman and bought the living ten years ago . . . No-one had a good word to say for him . . . The police arrived – about a dozen of them – and tried to open the doors . . . At last the police got one door open and there was some shoving and the mutter of the crowd began to get angry . . . the tension was growing fast . . . I . . . found Eve. She was as worried as I was and agreed something ought to be done at once . . . Eve said with a rueful grin. 'It isn't 'my' farm. It isn't even my county.' . . . As we talked we could hear the sound of the crowd altering. Eve got up on the baler and I followed.

The sergeant was saying: 'You let these men go!'

Eve shouted 'But will they go?

It was a brainwave. There was a sudden silence. The sergeant stopped heaving at the door and looked up. There was hope in his face.

'Will they promise to go and not come back?' said Eve. 'If they will I think we would all agree to let them go.'

The men in the barn shouted approval. The struggling ceased . . .

'Let me in and I'll ask 'em myself,' said the sergeant.

'No you don't,' said a large farmer, 'Speak to 'em from there.'

'Come up on the baler, sergeant' said we and laughed. He laughed too and heaved himself up beside Eve and myself. The crowd clapped and laughed . . .

'You two there,' said the sergeant in a voice like a fog-horn. 'Will you guarantee to leave the place and not return?' . . . Some of the police took Jones and the clerk out. Four stood by the doors and the Sergeant said; 'Take their names as they come out.' . . . By the time the last name was taken the prisoners had got well away and the police were on very good terms with the crowd . . .'

Such actions distinguished Eve as among the natural leaders of the Tithe protests. In 1933 she published a 22–page booklet, priced at 3d (All Profits . . . to the Suffolk Tithe-payers' Association) which ran to a second edition, entitled:

'What Is All This About Tithe?' by Lady Eve Balfour.'

This very comprehensive and well-laid-out little booklet owed something, but by no means all, to the aid of Messrs Mobbs, Turner and Butler, also Beb Hearnden, all of which was duly acknowledged in the foreword. There followed a brief history of the Tithe, The Farmer's Viewpoint, The Tithe-Owners View, The Tithe-payers Association, The Effect of Seizures on Farmer and Church, The Odds against the Farmer, A Suggested Solution and various appendices. Appendix 4 read:

'Extract from: The Daily Herald: July 11th 1933:

'Farmers in all parts of the country have been mystified by the activities of a newly-formed company which has become in the last few months an unexpected factor in the tithe war. This company registered as General Dealers, Ltd., with offices in First Avenue House, High Holborn, London W.C., has two shareholders – solicitor's clerks – who have each subscribed £1. The chairman of directors is Major Thornton Millar, a retired army officer. None of the directors owns shares. General Dealers Ltd has entered the market for agricultural products and live-stock distrained upon for tithe dues and so affected the policy of passive resistance adopted by the farmer-landowners.'

'Tithe owners themselves are disallowed by law from buying distrained goods, but General Dealers Ltd. are now tendering for goods. When the tender is accepted as it generally is the company sends men in motor lorries to seize the goods. 'Obviously the actions of the company are such as to benefit the tithe-owners and one can scarcely believe that it should have been formed quite fortuitously,' said Mr Reginald Primrose, of Messrs Deacon & Co., solicitors to the company, yesterday.

'Within the last few weeks General Dealers Ltd., has been concerned in the seizure of distrained goods at farms in Cornwall, Gloucester, Denbighshire, Kent and East Anglia.'

This was a fairly damning account of the activities of this firm clearly set up by the Tithe-owners to counter the nation-wide country boycott of the sale of goods distrained for non«payment of tithes, but Appendix 6 rammed the point home even further. This read:

'Some examples of irregularities in tithe collection:

Mrs Waspe: of Kingshall, Suffolk: Implements which have always been privileged as being tools of husbandry were taken by Kings College, Cambridge. They were left impounded for six months. General Dealers Ltd., then collected and entered the farm without notification to the owners, smashing the gates to effect their entrance . . .

Mr Clark of Hundon Suffolk: General Dealers Ltd collected cattle seized by Jesus College, Cambridge. They took several animals that had not been impounded and were therefore not in the custody of the Court. They broke fences and drove other cattle off the farm. The owner was not informed and knew nothing of it until after the lorries had left.

Lady Eve Balfour of Haughley Suffolk. Eight cows (which like implements are privileged) valued at £168 seized for a £105 claim in April 1933. Tithe owner Dr Triplett's Charity. These cows remained impounded until July when General Dealers Ltd., collected. As usual they raided at dawn, supported by unemployed men armed with cudgels and over forty policemen. They smashed gates under police protection; no warrant was shown, even on request; the cows were over-crowded into two small lorries with considerable cruelty. Police picketed roads leading to the farm and attempted to turn back cars proceeding in that direction.'

This went a long way towards consolidating her position as what would now be termed a protest leader. Her actions even inspired a seven-stanza 'Fighting Song of the Southern Farmers' which was printed in the southern papers, dated 28th August 1933, and 'inscribed to Lady Eve Balfour.' If nothing else this showed the strength of feeling the whole problem inspired. This 'Fighting Song' on the Tithe War by 'LEX' ended in somewhat high-flown terms;

'Then, Lady of the lovely name
Which even now is one with fame.
A sword a trumpet and a flame;
Our Queen, our Star,
Lead on, we follow with acclaim,
Lead us – to war!

The papers carried a great deal of news on the Tithe War as it was termed at this time. In this respect Eve and her journalist friends proved a formidable force, gaining publicity in the most unlikely places. For instance TIME Magazine for August 14th 1933 printed an article critical of the Tithes and wrote, somewhat to Eve's embarrassment:

'Last week for the first time an aristocrat popped up among England's tithe-embattled farmers. Horsy and determined Lady Evelyn Balfour is a niece of the late great Lord Balfour . . . Last week pretty Lady Evelyn was among a crowd of more than 100 Essex and Sussex farmers who set upon a bailiff. After rescuing the bailiff police charged Lady Evelyn and 36 farmers with 'unlawful assembly'. In Castle Hedingham court she protested that she had been trying to stop the riot. With the whole countryside smouldering indignation the court adjourned until after harvest time . . .'

In November 1933 Eve along with 35 other defendants was charged with 'unlawful assembly' as a result of the day's events. Eventually the case against her and 28 other defendants was dismissed and they were discharged. With over 1500 cases outstanding in East Anglia and several thousand elsewhere in the country the law was rapidly being brought into disrepute by such scenes and it soon became evident that a Royal Commission was required. It also became clear that when it arose she would be expected to present the Tithe-payers case.

Towards the end of November Eve was disturbed by the headway that the blackshirt movement of Sir Oswald Mosely appeared to be making in the countryside and she even contemplated at one time trying to get a new political party on the move. She wrote:

'My work on the tithe question has for some time led my thoughts in a political direction and the ideas that have been turning round in my mind were finally crystallised by a speech I heard delivered a week or two ago by Oswald Mosley in Ipswich.

I think that a very large section of the community today feel the existing old political principles and the old monetary system inadequate to deal with present day conditions and that if the life and health of the nation is to be restored something new must be found. The Labour party represents international unity of workers and the Conservative party which once represented the countryside now in the main represents international finance and is governed by the Bank of England and the City. Both these parties seem to me to be pursuing their ideals at the expense of the home producer (by which I mean those engaged in industry and agriculture, whether employer or employed.) The home producer may go to the wall if it is better for the wage earner in Central Europe, or if the City can line its pockets in foreign dividends or by juggling with currency fluctuations. I think it is time that the home producers in this widest sense of the word, banded together and demanded a look in,

Now the only party claiming to put forward a policy to uphold the producers' interests is Mosley's party and I think that there is a very grave danger that if his remains the only party with such a policy the whole of rural England will go black-shirt. I view this prospect with alarm ... Cheap foreign food which ruins the English farmer and increases unemployment does not in the long run benefit the urban worker ... The flood of cheap Argentine meat and manufactured foreign goods which undercut our markets only benefit the men who have sent money to the Argentine or invested in foreign finances and their profits consist of money which does not exist, while real wealth ceases to be produced. This is not right.

All these views are held and preached by Mosley and people forget his ghastly methods, his anti-semitism, his intolerance. I want to see a new party emerge that can legislate with the same end in view, but without dictatorship ...'

This burgeoning political scheme, fortunately perhaps, came to nothing, for she was deeply involved in the battle over Tithes, as well as the serious day to day business of earning a living as a farmer. With the encouragement and support of Beb Hearnden journalism increasingly became one of her means of earning money to supplement her income from farming. The business of making a profit from the farm remained a constant struggle as it was for all farmers in those depression years.

NOTE ON CHAPTER SEVEN

1. friend: She wrote to her mother' ... David (Jensen) and I had an absolutely heavenly time yesterday. He took me down into Kent ... We lunched and tea'd at a little old Trust House, The Bull Inn. Then we returned and went to a movie before separating ...'Lady Betty noted in brackets; 'Mary in a further letter said that their topic of conversation at the Bull Inn was Caesar's Commentaries which he had just read. At sea he told her the thing that kept him sane was ... Jane Austen ...' According to Jean they lived together for a week and he then sailed for New Zealand, where he settled down and married.

15. *Also Front Cover:* Portrait of Eve in the late 1940s.

16. The Silver Ghost and Caravan about to set off from New Bells on Tour in 1948.

17. The Soil Association Stand at the Highland Show in the early 1950s. Eve standing on right.

17. New Bells from the air c. 1950.

# CHAPTER EIGHT

# The Haughley Research Farms
## 1934 to April 1940

*'On this your 87th birthday I send you this as a token of my loving gratitude for your unfailing and continued faith in me, maintained againts overwhelming odds.'*

Eve to her father in a copy of her Monograph
on The Haughley Research Farms.

IN MARCH 1934 an article appeared in The Farmer & Stock-breeder. The influence of K.C may be discerned behind the scenes, since it seems unlikely that Mary was responsible for the latest dairying improvements noted, but overall the article gave a very succinct account of the progress made at New Bells over the past fifteen years, as follows:

'The Producer-Retailer's Lot,' by Lady Eve Balfour.

Selling Retail, Like Peace, has its Horrors – How I dealt with the Bottle Problem.'

'How often farmers who moan to me about the trials of the milk producer end by saying 'Of course, 'you' are all right. You retail your milk.' The producer-retailer may not be harassed by the variations of wholesale milk prices, but retailing, like peace, has its own horrors – and having been a producer-retailer for 13 years I can speak on the subject from practical experience. And I made my retailing even more arduous than the ordinary by producing Grade A milk.

In my early days the conditions on my farm were as bad as could be. My water supply was the moat around the house, one third water and two thirds mud. This had to be used for washing everything – sheds, cows and dairy utensils. The cowsheds were brick – and battered brick at that – and were surrounded in winter by good sticky mud which made it impossible to tell the colour of a cow's leg. Having no steamer I had to sterilise my utensils in a 'Heath-Robinson' contraption over an ordinary copper. The copper held moat water too. Even so I produced milk of well over Grade A standard and won a prize in the Suffolk 'Better Milk' competition, my bacterial counts being often as low as 300.

When I found I could produce milk of a good bacterial standard without too much expense I improved my water supply and plant, applied for a Grade A licence and started selling retail. I knew of the advantages of selling retail, but I had a lot to learn about the difficulties!

To start with there is the delivery. This is a machine age and one is apt to regard a machine as a constant thing unaffected by the emotions and vagaries that afflict the human race. A fallacy. Milk delivery vans are frequently temperamental and break down on the very day that you have sworn on your crossed heart to your most cherished customer that her milk shall arrive at 8.15 a.m. Your roundsman bursts into tears and cuts his throat, your customer doesn't get her milk until 9 a.m and by the time you've finished explaining and apologising you feel like the defendant in a successful breach of promise case!

Then about customers – well there are, so to speak, and good humoured. But there is the lady who takes a quart of milk, lets it stand for six hours, pours off the top portion and then mentions sadly that 'there isn't much cream!' There is the cook who mixes Grade A milk with someone else's non-Grade A and then says the keeping quality 'isn't what it used to be.' And of course they all want their milk delivered between 7.30 and 9 a.m., which simply isn't possible with two hundred customers.

There are too, peculiar trials at home. Farmers who slap their milk into churns and send it off by train have no idea of what a retailer's dairy is like when the rounds-men come in. It is a cross between a bargain-basement at Christmas time and a London bus-stop at 5 p.m. If one pint of milk has gone sour the rounds-man curses the dairymaid, the dairymaid passes it on to the cowman, and they all rage furiously together.

I personally keep well out of the way unless appealed to for arbitration! In my time I have done all their jobs and know their trials. The rounds-man has to be bright and civil all day, which is an awful strain. The dairymaid has a job which takes all the prizes (and a bonus) for hard work and discomfort.

Glass bottles were for years the bane of my life. They break on the round; they break in the steriliser; they waste the rounds-man's time waiting for them at backdoors, and they frequently disappear altogether. I am told the half-pint bottles are splendid for bottling fruit and thathe pints make good flower vases!

At one time we were washing 400 bottles a day. My coal bill was a nightmare; we had to get up steam three times a day. In cold weather it was a heart-breaking job. One washed the bottles, stacked them in the steriliser, turned on the steam and kept the temperature at the regulation 212 deg. for twenty minutes. Then one opened the door of the steriliser and as the cold air rushed in gladly the bottles started cracking like machine-guns.

Those glass bottles are now no more than an evil memory. A year ago I started using waxed paper 'bottles'. They were not on the market in the ordinary sense; and it was an experiment, of course, but I never regretted it. At the beginning the construction of the containers was erratic, but at their worst they were easier and cheaper to use than the glass bottles. Within six months, however, I had no fault to find with them.

I knew all along that these containers would be a godsend to the retailer, but I did not realise at first what an improvement they would be for the consumer. Almost all my customers were enthusiastic from the start. They realised that nothing can be cleaner than a non-returnable bottle. Also they were saved the trouble of returning the empties (Incidentally that saves my rounds-man a good hour every morning. You have no idea until you have experienced it how much time is wasted while the cook or housekeeper looks for the empty bottles.)

My best boosters were, of course, the doctors. Members of the medical profession never believe that anyone can sterilise anything efficiently unless it is done in a laboratory. They have reasonable grounds for their suspicions. It takes a very conscientious dairy-hand to get steam up and keep it at the right temperature and for the right length of time seven days a week throughout the year.

For myself I think the paper bottle has solved a great problem for the producer-retailer. There is no expensive outlay in plant as there was for the earlier paper bottles. Ten pounds covers the lot; at least as far as the small producer-retailer is concerned. For the big retailer too the container has an advantage. I contend that it materially reduces distribution costs. And this should allow the distributor to pay the producer a better price without increasing the price to the public.'

It is noticeable how much her journalistic style had improved during the five years since she wrote on the machinations of the brewers, but it is only fair to add that some of her conclusions regarding the manufacture of the paper containers were belied by a correspondence she had with the company manufacturing them in October of 1934, some eight months after her article was published. This letter listed a number of faults in the machinery and it is apparent that Eve was financially involved in the company which ultimately appears to have had to cease operations. Whether she continued to use paper cartons or not, her views on the subject remained well ahead of her time. Her conclusions were perfectly sound and logical and although it may have taken the rest of the century have now become generally accepted.

Apart from contemplating political action, earning her living by farming, running a milk-round, and writing articles, Eve continued to be heavily involved in the struggle against the power of the Church over the question of tithes. Professor Vernon McKenzie, who had proved so helpful over the matter of Eve and Beb's novels, again proved an invaluable ally. He wrote leading front-page articles on 'ENGLAND'S TITHE WAR' recounting Eve's part in it in the VANCOUVER SUN (in September 1934):

'One of the more spectacular raids occurred on the 150 acre farm of Lady Evelyn Balfour at New Bells, Haughley, Suffolk. Lady Eve is no absentee owner. She has had practical experience including years of horny handed toil covering nearly two decades. She is a niece of the famous 'A.J., daughter of the present Lord Balfour and a great grand daughter of Bulwer Lytton. She thus comes by her fighting and forensic abilities honestly. She offered to find, out of capital, 50% of her £535 tithe. This was declined. Addressing a public meeting in Ipswich she told the detailed story of the raid on her farm:

'I became aware of a rumour circulating in the district that I was to be raided next morning. Rumours travel, you know, by 'farm telegraph.' Others heard it and a score or two of my friends and more distant neighbours gathered during the night, not to resist, but to get first hand evidence of methods . . .

'I locked my gates, went on with my work and waited for the attack. On demand I was ready to supply keys and open all gates. I wanted to let the raiders carry on in as legal a fashion as they could, 'Dawn came and soon after five the alarm signal at my gate went off. But no-one demanded a key. A mob of men, about 30 unemployed Londoners and about twenty policemen broke locks with a crowbar and simply overran my land, looking for my herd. They were armed with long sticks and thick cudgels. One had a length of iron piping. Another had a piece of metal which he hurled at one of my heifers and hit my dairymaid . . .

'I asked the bailiff and his assistant for a warrant but they claimed other legal rights and passed responsibility one to the other giving no satisfactory answer . . .

'Eight cows were separated from their fellows and driven towards the lorries with the utmost brutality. One heifer was so knocked about that she later slipped her calf, dead. Can you imagine how I felt having to stand by helpless while men treated my animals like this and under police protection? Eventually the poor beasts were dragged to the lorries and then my crowning horror occurred. General Dealers Ltd. (A notorious firm which had been formed to take on Tithe distraint cases) had brought only two Bedford lorries, 6ft 6 in by 10ft 10 ins . . . My cows were large cross-bred Shorthorns, several heavy in calf. The lorries were quite full after three cows had been dragged into each. It was inconceivable that anyone in his right mind would attempt to force a fourth. I heard one or two policemen protesting, but they could do nothing as of course they were under orders . . .

'Shall I tell you how the loading was done? These raiders dragged a cow's head in, forced her to her knees between two other cows and then about ten men slammed the tailboard up. I can't think why they didn't break her back. When they got the lorry shut the cow's hindquarters were up in the air – and they drove away like that!'

'Today Lady Eve said to me. 'None of us can stand many more incidents of this kind. There is serious trouble coming. Oh it is a damnable business, this tithe. And the method of collection is so often vindictive, punitive and expensive.'

'Her chief cash revenue is from Grade A milk sales. And the bailiff seized her cows!'

Such articles and world-wide publicity had their effect on the government and the decision was taken to set up a Royal Commission, but in the nature of things it was a further year before this actually took place. Finally in January 1935 Eve was summoned before the newly appointed Royal Commission. She spent several hours giving evidence and was examined at some length.

In terms of preparation for later life Eve learned a great deal from this campaign. Press reports of her speeches commented:

'No speaker was so impressive as Lady Eve Balfour. She calmly related all that happened on her dairy farm at Haughley and was insistent on Parliament taking in hand without delay a revision of the 1925 Tithe Act which indisputably bears harshly upon the agricultural community . . .' There can be no doubt on reading the proceedings that her evidence had a powerful effect on the Commission, which decided that the charge was socially divisive in the country, although Tithes were not finally to be abolished for several years.

Although too busy with the Tithe War in 1934 to do more than make her customary visit to Scotland in the New Year, Eve managed to take time off from a hectic farming life in 1935 to crew on her brother's yacht across the North Sea to Sweden. In 1936 they visited Northern Ireland and the West coast of Scotland by way of a change. In 1937 in his newly acquired forty-foot Bermudan-rigged yacht named Dunpelder, capable of sleeping eight on board rather more comfortably than the smaller Grey Goose, they visited to Norway once again. These were pleasant, if energetic, breaks in a very busy life.

in 1938 Eve suddenly discovered flying and with her customary fervour threw herself into this new-found delight. With her experienced rider's hands and clear eye and judgement she was a natural flyer and after a comparatively short period of training on a Tiger Moth at the nearby Ipswich Aero Club she flew solo for the first time in March 1939 and obtained her coveted flying certificate. From then on she was flying whenever she could obtain the money to spare for a plane. In order to pay for this she resorted to her familiar technique of writing about it. She was soon writing about flying and about the state of chaos to be found in the Air Ministry in the 1938/39 years. When the outbreak of war seemed inevitable she at first applied for the task of ferrying planes around the country. This was turned down by the Ministry and despite her protestations they refused to accept her, pointing out quite rightly that she would be needed on her farm.

The later thirties also saw an upturn in farming incomes, although Eve and Mary, now happily reconciled again, were still only just beginning to make ends meet. Encouraged by talks with Alice Debenham, with whom she had become increasingly and deeply involved, Eve began to formulate a whole concept of man and his environment as a single indivisible unit. This was first inspired by reading Lord Lymington's book 'Famine in England' in 1938 and then discovering the research of Sir Albert Howard and Sir Robert McCarrison. The former concluded that the composition of healthy food depended on the fertility of the soil and the latter that the health of man and his beasts was dependent on the composition of their food. Both conclusions are now widely and freely accepted but were then revolutionary in concept. A meeting with Sir Albert Howard in 1938 encouraged and inspired her greatly.

With her mind soaring freely and following these twin chains of thought and correlating them, she came to the conclusion that man, beast, crops and soil were all one and indivisible; that they formed a natural chain each dependent on the others. Today there may seem nothing very startling in this, but it must be appreciated that then it was revolutionary thinking and far ahead of her time. With her background it followed that she was not merely content to think and wonder, but felt the need for action. It seemed to both her and Alice Debenham that a research centre on a farm scale was required urgently to test these theories for the good of mankind.

Already, however, the stresses of impending war were affecting all their lives. In January 1939 Eve and Beb Hearnden took a month's holiday together in the U.S.A, spending some of the time in New York. In view of Eve's plans for New Bells, which she fully supported, Beb Hearnden had finally accepted a post in full-time journalism and taken a flat in London. This was a well-earned holiday together spending some of their earnings from their combined authorship.

On her return, with her customary energy and the full support of Alice Debenham, Eve set about forming a farming research project to test the theories they had evolved between them. They decided it was essential to form a Trust to raise finance for the project. Throughout the rest of 1939 and well into 1940 Eve was involved in a hectic round of discussions and argument in a desperate search for financial backing.

Without Alice Debenham's help and support the project might never have been successful. By donating her farm, by deed of gift in Trust, to the East Suffolk County Council for the purposes of agricultural research, she formed the basis for the Haughley Research Trust. Alice Debenham supported Eve both mentally and morally, as well as financially, in raising money for the venture, but since she was by now totally crippled and not far off dying the bulk of the work fell on Eve.

The outbreak of war in September 1939 seemed to have brought their plans to a standstill, but The Haughley Research Trust had already been formed. Eventually with the invaluable help of the clerk to the East Suffolk County Council, Mr. Cecil Oakes[1] they succeeded, even in wartime, in achieving their aim of turning the two farms into an experimental unit. Largely on his advice, The Haughley Research Trust created a subsidiary farming company, Haughley Research Farms, Ltd. The Trust leased Walnut Tree Farm, which Alice Debenham had given by deed of Trust to the Council, and Eve and Mary leased New Bells to this Company. Eve then became farm manager for the company, which started operations in 1940.

It was agreed between the sisters that Mary was to receive the income from the leased farm. Eve herself was to be paid a minimal wage as organiser. With the two farms as one unit she set about farming the Haughley Research Farms with a group of Trustees. The Foundation Trustees in 1939 were Mr Clement Smith and Mr. Harwood Junr., for the East Suffolk County Council, who were the Custodian Trustees; Mr. Cecil Oakes, (later Sir Cecil) Clerk to the E.S.C.C.; Viscount Traprain, listed as farmer and landowner, who was, of course, Eve's brother; Mr. Leonard Hempson, Estate Agent & Valuer; and Mr. W.H.Richards, a farmer.

As planned by Alice Debenham and Eve the Haughley Experiment was simple, yet very demanding. The research they planned was not being done anywhere else and had in fact never been attempted elsewhere, but clearly had a very considerable importance. The intention was:

1. To compare three different systems of farming on a farm scale,[1] not on small plots of land, allowing for as nearly equal conditions for each as could be managed. The three systems were:

a. Unit A; Organic: farming with humus, including livestock:

b. Unit B: Mixed: farming with artificial fertilisers and livestock: (Both these were in ley units; i.e. Temporary pasture alternating with arable.)

c. Unit C; Stockless: i.e. as commonly practiced, grain and chemical fertilisers, with crop rotation, but no livestock.

2. To continue the experiment over many years, thus being able to compare different generations of plants and animals reared by the different methods.

3. To document in detail and continuously as many varying factors as possible, month by month and year by year.

The Consultants to the Management Committee were listed as:

W.S.Hollis, Esq., Managing Director of the Leckford Estates, Ltd., for General Management and Finance:

Sir Albert Howard C.I.E., for Humus Manufacture and Treatment of Unit A., and

W.Duncan, Esq., I.C.I Representative for Manurial Treatment of Unit B.

As might have been expected by anyone acquainted with her, Eve set up the experiment with rigorous fairness. At this stage in any event she was not identified with any one particular method of farming, although her instincts already inclined her strongly towards humus farming. Her intimate knowledge of each field on the farms enabled her to allocate them to each section absolutely fairly. The choice of sections was indeed approved by a senior member of the staff of the Rothamsted Agricultural Experimental Station, but it was appreciated by all concerned that it would be several years before the experiment could be started fairly since the land had first to be cleared of chemical traces.

In the process of setting the whole scheme in motion, initially with a view to raising finance for the project, Eve wrote a Monograph on the subject. This was by far the most ambitious piece of writing she had so far produced and in itself must have caused her endless hours of work. It must also be remembered that at the same time she was still running the farms and attending numerous meetings in her attempts to translate this new and visionary scheme into action.

Forewords to the Monograph were provided by Sir Robert Hutchison, Bart, M.D., Ll.D., D.Sc., F.R.C.P., President of the Royal College of Physicians and by Viscount Bledisloe G.C.M.G, K.B.E., P.C., Parliamentary Secretary to the Ministry of Agriculture from 1924–28 and President of the Imperial Agricultural Research Conference of 1927, as well as late Chairman of the Committee of Lawes Agricultural Trust (Rothamsted) as well as by the County Palatine of Chester Local Medical and Panel Committee. (It was they who were responsible for financing publication of the Monograph, which had the enthusiastic backing of their Hon. Secretary, Dr. Lionel J. Picton, O.B.E.[2])

After Forewords by Sir Robert Hutchison, Bart., M.D.,LL.D., D.Sc., F.R.C.P. and Viscount Bledisloe, G.C.M.G., K.B.E., P.C., Part One of this Monograph was headed 'Soil Fertility and Health'

Section 1. Was headed: The Medical testament

In this section were:

i. Evidence pointing to a deterioration in Public Health

ii. The McCarrison Experiments[3]

iii. The Deterioration in Foods.

Section 2: was headed: The Howard Experiments[4]

i. Humus and the Indore Process

ii. Results that have been obtained by the Adoption of Humus Farming.

iii. The Mycorrhizal[5] Association aud its Relationships to Humus and Disease Resistance

Section 3: Whole Diets and Ancient Systems of Humus Farming

Section 4. Conclusion.

Section 5 Appendices

Part Two: was entitled: The Haughley Research Farms:

1. A Challenge – And The Need To Answer It.[6]

2. The Proposed Experiment[7]

Privately printed in a limited edition the eight-inches-by-eleven-inches slim volume was an awkward shape to handle. At the end was a map of the farms duly divided into the trial plots. The thirty five thousand words it contained, mostly quotations from various works, were hard reading for anyone who was not deeply involved in the experiment. This was, however, a historic document for with it and the formation of the Haughley Experiment Eve had taken a giant step forward. She was no longer merely a young titled female farmer leading protesters in a national dispute. She had graduated into a visionary at the forefront of a vitally important international crusade with an all-important message for mankind.

Although the war naturally held matters back, a major point secured initially was that the experimental farms were excluded from any regulations regarding the use of fertilisers. Phase One of the Experiment had thus been completed. Throughout the months before and after the declaration of war Eve was primarily engaged in setting her project on an even keel despite the inevitable frustrations and interruptions. It was a curious period with everyone in the reserves being called up and reporting for duty and those who wished to do so volunteering for the various services, or for the A.R.P. ( Air Raid Precautions), or for the W.V.S. (The Womens Voluntary Services). Hundreds of thousands of schoolchildren were evacuated to the country and billeted on country families. Everyone was equipped with gas-masks, which were to be carried everywhere. Everyone was also issued with unfamiliar identity cards, carrying a special number, and with clothing and food coupons, with which they were to be able to buy specific rations of food. Initially, however, there was no real rationing and many stocked up on tinned foods and other necessities which they thought would soon be in short supply. Food hoarding, however, was regarded as anti-social and early on there were campaigns against such practices and against that new emergent economy the 'black market.'

Even deep in the countryside the effects of the war were felt strongly enough, possibly in some ways even more strongly than in the towns. Army camps appeared like mushrooms and new airfields were suddenly built on requisitioned land. Coils of barbed wire suddenly blocked off areas which had previously been accessible to the general public. The all-pervasive presence of the army, on the roads in lorries, in camps and billets, throughout the area was increasingly noticeable.

Petrol rationing was instituted almost at once and for some farmers especially, despite their special ration system, proved a logistical nightmare. Fortunately, like many other farmers, Eve was able to continue without much difficulty with horse power. She had not yet invested in tractors and combines, although her brother Ral, in East Lothian, had been the first in Scotland to introduce combine harvesting as early as 1934. The first winter of the war proved to be a particularly hard one when pipes froze and water supplies were only obtained by boiling snow in coppers. Mary wrote in her diary of the period:

January 26th 1940: . . .'This unusually prolonged winter weather(for this country) makes a queerly suitable background to all the war news. It fits the accounts all too well, leaving one thanking heaven that we are not quite so cold, or so hard pressed, or so persecuted as most other countries.

The men have constructed a very adequate snow plough which keeps our main thoroughfares passable and (I couldn't help feeling) gives the horse that draws it an opportunity to get warm. The water situation is not good as the house well has given out. So it looks like carrying on with rainwater and snow water for kitchen and washing purposes. Privately I and the kitchen couple rejoice in having the copper going with rain water for washing and no more of that vile hard tomato soup and there is something absurdly enjoyable, I find, in packing the hip bath with snow from the cleanest spots I can find and watching this melting – with incredible slowness – standing on top of the copper (the bath, not me!) I have no objections to the use of rainwater for cooking so long as it's boiled and necessity has taught the kitchen folk not to mind, but for drinking water the snow tastes better and Eve has an almost townee's dislike of drinking rain water from a tank in which creepy crawly things have lived, no matter how well strained and boiled – and KC dislikes it because Eve does. I am afraid it doesn't worry me in the slightest as long as it tastes all right, or disguised if it is not. But Bessie gathers the snow now . . . .'

Instead of taking in evacuees in New Bells they had taken in her younger sister Kathleen Oldfield and her two daughters, Eve and Mary's nieces. With these and a married couple to cook for them and look after the house and various pupils they had a full house. K.C. had her own cottage, Oxerfield, at the foot of the lane, close by. They were thus a very close-knit circle.

It is plain, however, that Mary was still the odd one out. Since her personality change in the twenties the sisters had regained very much their old relationship, but, for all her surprising artistic skills, her ability to write plays, to turn out excellent carpentry, and her willingness to attempt almost anything from journalism to filling sacks on the farm or milking, Mary simply had not the physical strength to pull her weight.

There was a natural tendency still for Eve on the one hand to protect her and on the other to ignore her, which naturally grated on Mary herself. It was almost inevitable that she rather resented Eve's friend-ships with others, whether as in the past with Beb Hearnden, or at this stage with K.C., who had replaced Beb Hearnden as Eve's co(-worker around the farm. While admiring her younger sister's strength and energy, which she herself lacked, she also took a slightly sardonic view of many of Eve's activities.

This is very plain from Mary's diary and letters in the first year of the war. She noted early on in December 1939:'Eve's geese are safely installed. Feels so funny to have Eve looking after poultry of any sort. They were let out today for the first time and she and Aldous drove them home tonight – with some difficulty. Soon no doubt they will be waiting at the door of the yard where they are to spend the night. They are white and oh they will be so dirty soon!'

Later in December she wrote to her mother;'Your letter intensely interesting I passed on the . . . pages to Eve and was promptly scolded for telling you she had been ill . . . I am afraid I felt quite impatient. If Eve had her way there'd be hardly anything about New Bells I could tell you! But I suspect in this case she minded the admission – so keen is she to prove her diet is curing her of all ills. Both she and K.C have had colds and K.C. streamers . . . yet (touch wood) so far me not one. Both K.C. and Eve are so funny when I point this out. Refuse to believe it and say caustically it is strange the way I always conveniently forget things . . .'

Tuesday 'Jan: 40; . . . didn't rain so we were able to thrash. I took on John's job – dressed in a Klu Klux Klan mask. It certainly saves an enormous amount of dust going down one's throat. I couldn't either fill the bags as full or tie them astight as Eve likes, but she had to be content with the best I could do – my fingers are sore from the effort – Aydua (a friend) . . . carried chaff bags gallantly, was so stiff at the end of the day we recommended a bath – she had one – but of course the beastly water was like tomato soup, it always is when we offer a bath to guests . . . I thought I had to go into Haughley in the evening for the first of a group of Home Nursing lectures, but to my joy found it was not till next Monday . . . I should go to the Folk Dancing tonight but am going to shirk – can't do both thrashing and dancing and walking unless I have to. Shall have to go on Wednesday as I have a Theatre Centre meeting in the evening . . .

At New Year 1940 Eve managed a short visit to Redcliff with Ral and Jean. Whittingehame House, where she had been brought up, had been turned into a school for refugee Jewish children and Eve gave them a talk while she was there, as a result of which two asked to come to her as pupils. Her brother Ral, who had obtained his Master's Certificate in 1938 as an amateur yachtsman, was hoping to pass his medical in order to join the Navy as an RNVR officer where qualified masters were much in demand. Later (February 12th) Jean wrote to Eve:

'. . . Your lecture was a great success and several said how interesting they found it . . . If you would really like the help the 2 boys – and they are good workers – and if your head is yet above water in April – I am sure they will manage to get to you somehow.

'Ral went off on Wednesday and took almost the whole day to get through the Drs, who eventually passed him, and said . . . he would be wise to get his tonsils removed next month and that he would be at Donibristle for 3 months. After that, when strong, there seems every prospect that he will, if he wants it, get some job on the sea . . . I think the dates for our visit to New Bells will be the beginning of April . . . love from Jean.'

At this stage Eve's monograph had still not been published but there was occasional mention of it in Mary's diary: 'Tuesday 13th Eve and K.C were out all day yesterday doing business in Ipswich and attending a sale where Eve anted to buy two gilts in pig. She got what she wanted and came home pleased. It will involve selling some of her own, but the new pigs will have litters much sooner than hers possibly could, so she will profit sooner. Her magnum opus keeps coming back from the printer in proof and she corrects it as it comes.

Wed: Feb 14th 1940:'This morning Eve was radiant, having had a charming letter from Bledisloe, who 'will' write her a foreword. He is keen for the thing to be published and says he thinks the time is ripe for the scheme. If only someone would pay for publication . . . Still this arctic weather! We are all white again.

She commented somewhat sardonically on Eve and KC's frequent friendly wrangles: 'The cold forms a constant topic between Eve and K.C at breakfast, but they never agree. Eve announces It is much warmer. K.C retorts she has never felt so cold in her life! Or perhaps it is Eve who is positive it is the coldest day we have had and K.C who knows it is not nearly so cold as it was on such and such a day. That is the opening clash. They then both proceed to bring evidence to prove their assertions, thickness of ice (or lack of thickness) on the particular water tubs that supply their needs – or some other argument, each raising the voice and tone higher and louder with each 'proof' put forward. I take care to play no part, but seize the opportunity to look at the papers, which, but for their argument, they would be reading themselves. I am never sure how much they enjoy this daily sparring. I dare say they like it. Perhaps it warms them up.'

It is fairly clear that Mary was increasingly becoming aloof from the farm and a somewhat detached spectator of events, although very busy with work in the village. From her comment on the pamphlet it seems the Chester Medical Panel must have promptly come to the rescue regarding publication once Lord Bledisloe had agreed to write a foreword. Eve's comparatively short monograph outlining the proposed Haughley Experiment was published within the next six weeks.

Mary continued more enthusiastically on March 14th:

'Yesterday Eve showed me Bledisloe's foreword to her great work and I thought it first rate. At first she thought it too long, but I didn't. It made me want to go on and read her pamphlet all over again. I 'am' so glad she has secured it and feel it must help . . . I rather wish Bledisloe had not referred to Eve's paper in the terms he did – 'Booklet' and 'Brochure' etc., but that is just personal prejudice and perhaps no one shares it. These terms suggest to me something slight and trivial and in no way prepare one for the emmense labour that lies behind it. The term 'paper' on the other hand does not suggest either slight or trivial. Very odd. . . .'

She continued;

'The other night Eve turned to, to hurry over her supper with a groan. Surprised, I asked if she had to go out. Yes she had, worse luck. What was it? Sparrow Club, she said with just the hint of a smile, as if to give me leave to ask more, Which of course I did. It appears clubs are being formed all over the country to exterminate sparrows or at least curtail their numbers. I felt Anti-Sparrow Club would be nearer the mark, but no doubt it would soon be shortened to Sparrow Club. Eve as one of our local farmers had been invited to help organise the affair. I suggested she might do a little trade in cats! She agreed but as I feared no one wanted more cats! Each member contributes 5/ and a reward of a 1/2d or 1d (can't remember which has been offered for every sparrow killed and produced. Not hedge sparrows, of course, which do not eat grain.'

Despite her desire to prove herself fit, Mary was still frail and liable to catch any ailments going. Inevitably she went down with flu and wrote;

'. . . My zealous endeavour to conquer my cough by inhaling has brought out an exczema all over my mouth and eyes and I feel leprous this morning! To go out in this weather would make me unrecognisable in a very short time . . . After lunch Eve came up for a moment, big and powerful (she always seems extra so when I am in bed) her arms full of cats and Cobley (her sheep dog) at her heels . . .'

Later she wrote: 'I am feeling anti-cats at the moment. My blitzkrieg flu has left me with an acute sense of smell, especially (like Auntie) for the smells I don't like. The house to me smells like the cat house at the Zoo, only not so clean. I do nothing it seems all day but bail out the cats that leek in here when I don't want them. Sitting down involves lifting a cat off the chair leaving the room involves carrying a cat with you [a] or two cats – or three cats – or four cats and a kitten which is uncatchable. Eating at meals involves suppressing the hungry overtures of at least two cats – on each side. The trick is to shove them over to Eve's place where they will get all the attention they want. Laying meals involves covering all the edibles with covers and cages to protect them until the diners arrive to take command. I also suspect that having so many cats will involve many more pests in the garden because the birds are kept down. But I am not popular when I hint anti-cat propaganda.

It is safer to talk anti-pigeon. The pigeons have destroyed Eve's crop of young cabbages. She says they are far worse all over the country than they have ever been before. She adds they come from Norway.

Feeling this is no explanation I ask why. Eve says nothing beyond making the peculiar noise in her throat which is her own pet way of saying 'That is a stupid question!' I say nothing but privately to myself wish the cats would go hunting the pigeons all day long. It would be such a simple solution . . .'

The research that went into the Monograph of the proposed experiment for the Haughley Research Farms was the basis on which Eve's book, or testament, The Living Soil was to be founded. The monograph was the product of her life's work up to then, but she was still experimenting with humus and compost making herself. She was still forming conclusions as a result of her life as a working farmer and her reading and experiments since then.

Eve's mother, Lady Betty, had broken her leg and was bedridden, but at once grasped the magnitude of the step the monograph represented. She wrote on April 7th:

'Beloved Eve,

'Mary told me nothing about 'the' pamphlet till she was alone in my room and then she said 'I have a surprise for you' and produced it. It was a 'great' thrill. It is very handsomely produced tho' I am a little sorry it is on such a large scale as its a bit difficult to handle and will take such a huge envelope to send out whenever this is allowed. I immediately re-read the forewords and Part II. I was very favourably impressed with the forewords – Bledisloe specially – Makes the reader at once realise what a tremendously worthwhile and important experiment the Haughley research scheme is. Eve if this comes off it will make all that you have gone through these 21 years of struggle – all that Father has sunk at New Bells justified and immensely worth-while. I lay back and thought of all this and gave great sighs of thankfulnes and excitement.

'Not a word to anyone about it (except Nell) (her sister back from Kenya) until Father has received 'his' copy on his birthday 'next' Tuesday. Mind you post 'early' Monday. When he has got 'his' copy can you still spare me mine, or shall I send this back to you? Wasn't AA (Alice Debenham) pleased to see it?

'Mary says your lecture to the WI was a great success the audience intensely interested . . . Your devoted Mum'

Eve sent a copy of the book to her father at Fisher's Hill on April 9th 1940, his 87th birthday. Her mother wrote to Eve:

'Darling Eve,

'At first Father thought he had not heard from you – not realising the mysterious parcel was from you. Then when he joined us for the 1 o'clock news, he said: 'Eve has sent me her book – but no word with it from herself.' I took the book which was in his hand – opened it and found your dedication in your handwriting – and held it up to him. He read it with real emotion. His voice breaking over your touching words and adding; 'Dear Eve' . . .

Eve had written on the inside cover of the copy of the book;

'Darling Father,

'On this your 87th birthday I send you this as a token of my loving gratitude for your unfailing and continued faith in me, maintained againts overwhelming odds.

'Your ever loving, Eve. April 9th 1940.'

The monograph was the product of Eve's farming training combined with the experience she had gained during the previous decade in writing and in practical experiments with compost on her farms. It was as if she had rather late in life completed a doctorate and the booklet represented the thesis for it. The outbreak of the 1939–45 war at this stage merely held up progress temporarily. Her future was already mapped out by Fate and all her training and upbringing had fitted her for the battles in the years ahead.

NOTES ON CHAPTER EIGHT

1. Mr.Cecil Oakes. For 25 years Clerk of East Suffolk County Council, appointed Managing Trustee for the County Council as the Custodian Trustees of the original Trust Deed set up by Miss Alice Debenham, which he was instrumental in seeing through. Subsequently was appointed Chairman of the Haughley Research Farms Ltd., formed when the Council decided that the war prevented them carrying out the terms of the Trust. Later became Sir Cecil Oakes, C.B.E and a Founder member of the Soil Association.

2. Dr. Lionel J. Picton. Hon. Secretary of the County Palatine of Chester Local Medical and Panel Committtee, a group of doctors who in 1939 after 25 years of Health Service concluded in a publication entitled Medical Testament that the health of the average individual had generally deteriorated over that period. His support and encouragement for Eve included backing publication of her monograph. A pioneer of the organic movement and a considerable influence on Eve's thinking

3. McCarrison Experiments. Major General Sir Robert McCarrison, C.I.E., M.D., F.R.C.P., spent many years devoted to medical research in India. As Director of Nutrition research in 1927 he used colonies of rats to test the diets of the Hunza, Pathan and Sikh. He found that when fed on diets similar to people whose physique was good they thrived. When fed on diets similar to those of people of poor physique their health was bad. When fed on the diet of the poorer classes of

England 'they suffered from diseases of the lungs, stomach, intestines and nerves.' These experiments were fully described in Wheel of Health by G.T.Wrench M.D.

4. Howard Experiments: Dr. Howard began experimenting on 75 acres in India in 1905 producing disease-free crops as a result of composting with humus made from the decomposition of animal and plant residues by the Indore process which he developed. i.e. making compost in layers, a process now widely known and accepted.

5. The Mycorrhizal Association: In conjunction with Dr.C.M.Rayner (see p.178) Howard discovered that mycorrhiza, the fungus found in the roots of certain trees, notably pines, and tea plants appeared to transmit the benefits of humus and aided resistance to disease. It was also stimulated by the humus. Howard discovered that cotton, strawberries and numerous other plants formed mycorrhiza naturally. Research at this stage was still developing.

6. A Challenge: This read: '. . . conclusions:

  1. The health of man, beast, plant and soil is one indivisible whole.

  2. Starting with the truly fertile soil, the crops grown on it, the stock fed on those crops, and the humans fed on both, have a standard of health and power of resisting disease and infection, from whatever source greatly in advance of anything ordinarily found in this country.

  3. The fertility of the soil is dependent on the humus, and can only be maintained by keeping the land well aereated and continually replenishing the humus supply. Humus must be properly prepared and must consist of waste products of both vegetable and animal origin in appropriate proportions.

  4. The facts so far known support the theory that Nature's direct link between a fertile soil and the plant is the absorption and literal digestion by the plant roots of the Mycorrhiza Fungus.

  5. If this theory is proved then this link is an essential factor in health.

  Dr. J.L. Picton . . . quotes Sir John Russell, F.R.S. Director of the Rothamsted Experimental Station . . . July 28, 1939:

  'We have searched diligently for evidence that organic manure gives crops of better quality than inorganic fertilisers . . . No difference has yet been found.'

  Dr Picton comments . . .

  'This amounts to a challenge . . . A conclusive experiment is called for . . . say 100 acres or so manured with organic manure and another 100 side by side . . . manured with chemicals. The cropping, of course, to be identical, the stock carried identical . . . It will be a long term test, but ten years is . . . likely to be decisive . . .'

7. The Proposed Experiment: It was originally intended to extend the experiment into feeding the 1,000 or so people of Haughley on wholemeal food grown at New Bells, as in the Peckham Experiment: (see p. 177)'

# CHAPTER NINE

# *The War and* The Living Soil

## April 1940–1943

*'Your reaction to my book is 'most' encouraging, I only hope the reading public will share your views.'*

Eve to Richard de la Mare of Faber.

THE HAUGHLEY RESEARCH FARMS, Ltd. naturally proved something of a headache to the local War Agricultural Committee throughout the war years. The important point was that they were exempted from the wartime regulations and were not forced to use artificial fertiliser.[1] Eve herself, however, like most farmers, was short of staff and was forced to run things frequently with unskilled labour, in particular a succession of pupils of both sexes including some German Jewish refugees. For a lot of the time she relied to a large extent on pupils who knew next to nothing about the land, however willing.

Mary noted in her diary in April 1940:'We no sooner get rid of one German than we acquire another! I had got up in makeshift fashion – trousers over pyjamas, hair still in plaits, when Eve broke into the sitting room where I sat mending linen to say she was just off to pick up the German.

'What German?' Oh, didn't I know? She was getting a pupil, a German who was going to Reading . . . later he turned up . . . Tall, young, fair-haired, Scandinavian type, a professional musician, plays the flute, loves the sea and has spent much time on it . . . He has an attractive soft voice and speaks pretty good English . . .'

Later she noted: 'The police are distinctly interested in our German inmate . . . If he is a Nazi spy it is the best acting I have ever seen . . . I 'can't' believe it isn't genuine. All the same we instinctively keep clear of informative talk when he is in earshot and will continue to do so until we have irrefutable proof of his trustworthiness . . .'

It all predictably proved a false alarm, but was very typical of the period. Even more typical was Mary's description a few days later of a race to catch a train when a pre-war friend now in the army was being taken by Eve to the station. Mary described it thus;

'We took James to catch his train at Needham, going first to see Derry and Robin (Hawker). I went too and did enjoy it. It is a long time since I saw Derry & Robin and a long time since I went anywhere with Eve and a long time since I experienced anything so exciting as our chase for James's train. Eve, characteristically, ran it rather fine and we only had 15 minutes when we left the Hawkers. This was cut even shorter at the level crossing, where we had to wait. The distance to Needham from Derry's house is 5 miles. The train that held us up at the level crossing was going to Needham. We toyed with the idea of shoving James into it but as we toyed the train moved on – slowly passed – and at last the gates were opened. Eve spurted forward, got ahead of the cue of aristocratic looking cars in front of us and let her out for all she was worth.

To appreciate her difficulty fully you must realise the car was an Austin 7 'very much the worse for wear'. Soon we discovered we were making on the train! It reminded me of old days at Whitt, but what a difference between Mill's car and Eve's! Luckily there was hardly any traffic. We arrived with just 1/2 a minute to spare . . . All was well . . . we even had time for a calm farewell . . . Back home to hear we had sunk another German merchantman. Hurrah! All hands saved as usual so we could enjoy the sinking to the full. Eve's sows have pigged – the two she bought a while back and there are piglets and little pigs squeaks once more in her long deserted sheds. Excellent litters 10 each, nice strong youngsters. She is very happy . . .'

Later in April Mary noted; 'Another very busy day, chief items being the (Women's) Institute Meeting, with Eve's talk on Health and Soil Fertility. She had feared being unable to fill 20 minutes. Knowing the vastness of her subject – her interest in it . . . I feared she might talk for hours. I proved nearer right than she did! But she held her audience completely and it was a great success. To me of course, tho' I knew it all it was breathlessly interesting, but I knew by the silence around me that I was not the only spell-bound listener. I have heard too many talks at W.Is and know how often the speaker has to contend with coughing, whispering and even conversation. Eve had none of that . . .'

Shortly afterwards there was a meeting of the Tithe-Payer's Association, but Eve was unable to attend as with a break in the weather she was forced to get on with ploughing. Mary, however went and wrote:

'. . . to the Tithe Meeting, arriving as the minutes had just been passed. I slipped Eve's letter up to the Chairman's table and found a seat. Considering that many farmers must have been in Eve's plight and like her seizing the opportunity offered by a dry day, the room was remarkably full . . . I had to slip out in the end in defiance of eager signs of protest from familiar faces who would have liked a word with Eve's sister . . . Just caught my bus with 3 minutes to spare. . . .'

The first bombs were dropped in the area in May 1940 accidentally by friendly planes returning from a bombing raid. There were rumours of casualties at first then it transpired no-one had been injured. Mary noted; 'A local lady, telling of the occurrence, as eye witness, concluded; 'And you know, the odd thing was, the planes never stopped.'

With the advent of Dunkirk in June and a declaration of National Emergency, which included the overnight formation of the Local Defence Volunteers, later known as the Home Guard, the seriousness of affairs suddenly came home to everyone and all that had gone before seemed suddenly decidedly 'phoney'. The 'real' struggle everyone realised had now at last begun. Mary's diary shows this clearly. First their German pupils were interned in Bury St. Edmunds, although neither of them were really in the least suspect and they appear to have taken it comparatively philosophically. Mary for the first time retired to the Anderson shelter in the garden and noted;

'All day today we have heard the guns. Sometimes near enough to make the windows rattle. I suppose we shall become increasingly familiar with that noise. About two hours – from 4 to 6 – they were very marked, even to my deaf ears . . .

'I slept out for the first time. To the sound of endless droning planes. They come over here in such huge squadrons. Coming and going on the night raids over Germany. We lie in the fork between the Norwich and Cambridge lines. The junction is a landmark for the aeroplanes.' She noted the return of their land girl John Foster who had left them temporarily; 'John is back and the nice English pupil is still here. It was lovely finding John and I heard from her more about the farm in one hour than I should ever have heard from Eve and KC. My two kitchen girls were very welcoming and had much enjoyed their garden work. I said they must look on it as their garden henceforth as well as mine. The two Germans I believe are at Bury in the barracks there. Hans contrived to send Eve a message via the padre who visited the camp . . . I gather he took it philosophically . . .'

She also noted;' . . . The defence volunteers are numerous and terrifyingly keen here. I tremble to think what destruction they may do in an emergency. I only hope they will confine their efforts at illiminating, or liquidating, or whatever it is one is supposed to do to parachutists – to the enemy! Last night apparently the local forces were inspected by a Major General. Old Newton (a neighbouring village) is suffering from swelled head this morning because its detachment was the only one who blocked the road correctly. Haughley lot were not in the running as their job was trench digging – they have been appointed to guard Haughley Station. How fantastic and how loony the whole thing is, yet horribly real. The passing of the Emergency Act was a beautiful illustration of the way we can do it if we like. The Germans will take it as proof we have the wind up, but no matter . . .'

It was around this time that Eve heard one of her favourite wartime Suffolk stories, which she retailed effectively in her deep voice. A home guard sentry was on duty at a cross-roads half asleep, when he heard footsteps approaching. Half remembering his orders he raised his pike, which was all they had been issued with in those early days, and challenged boldly:

'Halt! Who am I?'

Out of the darkness a broad Suffolk voice replied:

'Give 'ee three guesses, lad, an' happen 'ee'll find out!'

Inevitably Eve had numerous war-time jobs, notably that of air-raid warden, enforcing the black-out in the district. This was by no means an easy task in the countryside where milking and animal feeding before dawn or after dusk often led to flagrant breaches of the restrictions as harassed farm hands wandered round with uncovered hurricane lamps. Of course a routine was established in due course, with thick coverings over doors and windows and skylights, but it was not an easy matter to enforce.

In a area surrounded by many airfields, and with numerous troops in the district, the sound of planes during the day and night was to become such a frequent occurrence as not to rate any notice being taken of them unless a dog-fight took place overhead, or a returning bomber was in obvious difficulties. The sound of anti-aircraft batteries, like the sight of searchlights and barrage balloons, was commonplace at the time. In such an area, filled with strategic targets, the importance of enforcing the black-out was considerable.

Having to carry identity cards and gas masks wherever one went were restrictions on everyday life, which soon became accepted by everyone. Crowded trains with little or no distinctions as to first or third class, all equally dirty and the corridors crammed full of troops from any or all of the services slumped on kit-bags or suitcases, were the common hazards of travel. Those civilians left were gradually taking on a uniformly shabby look as rationing began to take effect and clothes were perforce worn until they had to be repaired. Eventually patches and darns became almost fashionable badges of honour in civilian life, worn like medals in the services.

It was in this period that Eve's dog bit a postman and despite the war the due legal process took effect. She was called before the magistrates and duly fined 30 shillings after the postman had exhibited his old uniform trousers with a tear in the leg. However Eve was not one to miss such an opportunity. Having failed to prove that it was the postman's fault, she agreed willingly enough to pay the fine, but noticing the postman was much the same size as herself, she asked the bench if, having paid the fine, she might not be allowed to keep the torn trousers. Somewhat roughly patched, (for sewing, like housework, was never one of her more practised accomplishments) she wore them round the farm for the rest of the war telling the story triumphantly with embellishments.

As the difficulties of farming in wartime with inadequate skilled staff continued, Eve reluctantly had to give up milk production in favour of suckler-reared calves, which could be worked easily enough on the organic and non-organic fields of the Haughley research farm. Here KC proved her worth yet again. Reluctant to do without their own milk supply, she started a small goat herd. This provided enough milk for the local inhabitants of Haughley Green throughout the war. She made her milk round on a bicycle, a feat which was extremely well received.

East Anglia, like Kent and Sussex, was the scene of much aerial combat during the Battle of Britain and much air activity later as massed bomber squadrons passed overhead. Of course for those who had occasion to visit London during these years the scenes of bombing and the sight of old familiar streets in ruins brought the war even closer. Eve's old friend Beb Hearnden was engaged in working part-time for the W.V.S finding homes for bombed-out families during the Blitz and whenever Eve went up to London she stayed with her and witnessed the destruction at first hand. Beb wrote from London in September 1940:

'This has been an astonishing ten days. Most nights I go to bed so tired that only the near bombs and the big Navy guns that run round on trucks can wake me. But I never heard anything like the din. When it first started the whistle and shriek of the big bombs was a bit alarming. Now one's got so fatalistic it doesn't matter very much . . . We average five raids a day and pay no attention to them except to duck under cover when the Hyde Park guns start. (I have a very wholesome respect for shrapnel!) Quite a lot of people go to shelters but I simply haven't got time. Every minute I can spare from the office I have to put in for the W.V.S coping with the people who have been bombed out. We take over empty houses, rig them up with beds, china, kitchen utensils and so on and rush them out food in mobile canteens. It's quite a game . . . I don't think I ever knew what morale was before . . . the women are superb . . . their unselfishness beyond all praise . . . The work of the Civil defence services has been beyond all praise . . . Any night about 10 one can see five or six fires and they are all out before dawn breaks . . . Everyone looks very tired, but quite determined . . .'

Although rationing was increasingly severe there is little doubt that those in the country fared better than those in the towns. Eve was able to provide herself with eggs and with goat's milk as well as fresh vegetables from her thriving kitchen garden. Although kept busy with the farm and her war work she still managed to get away on occasions.

In September Ral wrote from Plymouth where he was then based that he had '. . . moved out of barracks . . . and . . . taken a small flat . . . I get a lodging and food allowance when living out so it is not costing me much more than before . . . I have a small spare room . . . so that if any of the family feel like coming down to visit me I could put them up and of course it would be pure joy to have them. . . .'

This letter was forwarded to Eve by her mother from the Fisher's Hill cottage, where she and her husband had now removed, as the house had been requisitioned as a hospital. Lady Betty added;' Could you possibly go to him, now your harvest is over for a long week end . . . and let me pay your journey. Would it be more than £3? I could manage that and I should like you to go. Could you delegate your A.R.P duties just for those days? . . .'

It seems Eve did manage to get down and furthermore managed to visit friends in the country for she typed the draft of an article on farm life in Devon. She wrote:

'Major General Dunsterville, a much-travelled man, once said that he judged a country by its farming population . . . I should be glad to have England judged by the state of mind of her country folk today and especially her countrywomen. The way they have risen to the occasion compels admiration . . . The war-time farmer must raise crops to feed his animals as well as his fellow citizens . . . The young men are being called up . . . Thousands of girls are joining the land army but farming . . . cannot be learned in a season . . . Extra work for the farmer always means extra work for the farmer's wife . . . Extra stock means more milking, more calves to feed, more chickens to tend. Every farm woman knows this . . . but this war has brought a great many more complications . . . For instance there is the black-out . . . In winter it is dark for both morning and evening milking and if you leave the cowshed door open, because both your hands are full, you hear about it next day from the local air-raid warden . . . and from the men on guard with the anti-aircraft gun across the valley.

'Another new responsibility for the farm woman today is the evacuation scheme . . . However fond you may be of children, seven or eight little 'townees' planted down on your farm do complicate your life . . . I was down in the West Country last week end and saw some of the London children who have been there since the first week of September. They are now entirely acclimatised . . . and say they never want to go back to the city . . . To them England has become a reality, not just a city street . . . You can't learn history in a city street, but two thousand years of English life lie under your hand on an English farm. Ninety nine out of a hundred English people loathe war . . . It is hard to think of anything helpful coming from it, but on that West Country farm I saw a new understanding being born, a link being forged between town and country that may prove of great value . . . there is something in that.'

In August 1940 Alice Debenham had suffered a stroke and was removed to hospital, although in no pain and fully conscious. On her return from her visit south Eve continued, with Alice Debenham's full backing, with the plans to form the company Haughley Research Farms, Ltd. This included making arrangements to lease the farmhouse at New Bells.

With the formation of the Experimental Farm at Haughley Eve and

Mary's old partnership had now come to an end. Both sisters had willingly put their share of the farm into the experiment, but arrangements had to be made for their future. This aspect does not seem to have worried their mother unduly.

On September 26th Lady Betty wrote:

'. . . Re letting New Bells. Nell says all she could get for her house in Ireland – furnished – was 24/- a week. We both doubt if you will get more than £3 if that. Re sale of A.A's furniture. Ours, valued (conservatively) at £2,500 was sold for £95!! I doubt if A A's will fetch more than £100 (There are over 400 lots. It is a 2 day sale, Eve noted).

'You say Trustees (? 4 of them) will as individuals invest £400 each in the Company.' Father asks does that mean each one of the 4 will invest £400 or that jointly they will invest £400 . . . Ral is one . . . can he afford to invest £400? . . . Father's second query is: – will the bank consent to carry on the overdraft. If not won't he be called upon for his guarantee – and if . . . he can't pay what then?

'These are our doubts and queries – but the glorious fact is that before A.A dies (God bless her) the scheme has actually been started and the unbearably heavy burden lifted from your back . . . I am not afraid of you having to live cottage style, instead of farmer style, and on a cottager's income . . . You and K.C, Mary and that dear John will all face that and I hope Bessie (their cook) will be able to stick to you (she did) . . .'

On October 8th Lady Betty wrote again;' . . . I ought to have assumed from what Mary told me . . . that A.A died last Saturday . . . Hope KC will not be worried over her AA executor duties and that AA has been generous to her. My thoughts will be with you at the sale . . .'

Meanwhile it seemed that Ral, still at Plymouth, had belatedly learned of the changes taking place at New Bells. As Trustee for the farm in succession to Nora, who had died in 1936, he wrote to Jean expressing amazement that Eve proposed to lease the farm without consulting him. Jean wrote to her mother-in-law Betty passing on his views. Betty wrote back firmly:

Oct. 17 1940:

. . . Ral could not have been more amazed at Eve not consulting him about her new plans than I was to read this in your letter.

'I gather that the disposition of the 2 houses – New Bells and Walnut Tree – are quite outside 'The Trust' which is only concerned with the land. I am not clear to whom Walnut Tree belongs, but the letting of

New Bells is necessary to give Eve an income. Her £3 salary can't do more than feed and clothe Eve and Mary. The New Bells let would have to pay Eve's farm expenses up to the Trust taking over and I suppose her interest on her debt to the bank.

'But I now send you her original letter which I should like back. I gather the £400 provided by the Trustees does not involve Ral since 2 of the 4 Trustees are paying the whole £400.'

Throughout the whole of 1940 amidst the chaos of wartime Eve had successfully been trying to tie up the last details of the Haughley Research Farms limited company and it is apparent from this letter and subsequent information that she had finally been successful. By the end of 1940 the Haughley Trust had been successfully formed and a Limited Liability Company, The Haughley Research Farms Ltd, had been set up to run them, of which Eve was the principal employee.

By this time Eve had managed to lease the farmhouse at New Bells to an army officer's wife and family. She herself then bought a horse-drawn gypsy caravan which she parked in the garden of Oxerfield Cottage, close by, owned by KC. Her transport varied between an ancient Austin 7 and an old open bull-nosed Morris two-seater.

The grim days of 1941 followed, when it seemed that Germany was triumphant everywhere. The British tightened their belts and stood by to repel invasion. Never had the country been so united. Then in December came Pearl Harbour and the United States of America finally entered the war. During 1942 the entire face of England was transformed. East Anglia especially seemed to become another State of America. Everywhere there were Jeeps and Sherman tanks as well as G.Is and the unfamiliar olive green uniforms.

Chewing gum and nylons became the local currency amongst the young and impressionable East Anglian girls. Overhead, Flying Fortresses displaced the familiar Wellingtons and Halifaxes. The pace of the war suddenly began to quicken and the sleepy East Anglian villages and pubs soon reverberated to the sound of high-powered engines everywhere and to the sound of jazz and Glen Miller.

In 1941 Miss Agnes Debenham, sister of the recently deceased Alice Debenham, had also sought aid in the U.S.A. Attempting faithfully to fulfill her sister's aims and wishes, with which she was in entire agreement, she had sent a copy of Eve's monograph to a publishing friend in the U.S., asking for his assistance. Frank Morley, who had been a neighbour of hers in Surrey, was a director of Harcourt, Brace

& Co of Madison Avenue well known American publishers. They often worked in conjunction with Faber & Faber in Britain.

In a letter dated February 4th 1942, Frank Morley wrote to C.W.Stewart of Faber & Faber, then at 24 Russell Square:

'. . . You may remember that towards the end of last year I mentioned Miss Debenham of Little Hobs, Lingfield, Surrey and said that she wanted some advice about a monograph on the Haughley Research Farms. In your letter to me of December 3rd, you said you wouldn't mind hearing about this . . . Here is the problem. Miss Debenham was one of our most respected neighbours in Surrey. Her eldest sister who died a year or so ago was very interested in farming. She made over her property at Haughley to the Suffolk County Council for agricultural research and in spite of various difficulties good progress was made. The manager of the Haughley Research Farms, Lady Eve Balfour, wrote a monograph on the experiment (which was an experiment in soil fertility in relationship to health) which I have read. It is, I think, an important monograph, but originally it was privately printed and there are now scarcely any copies left. In order to extend the research work and to raise money for operations on a larger scale, Lady Eve wishes to reprint the monograph and is anxious to re-write part of it.

Miss Debenham is prepared to help financially but cannot speak certainly while in ignorance of what sum would be required. I am suggesting to her that she send you a copy of the existing monograph with a notation as to the extent to which it might be revised; and that you would be able to give her an idea of the cost of publication. It seems to me something that with a subsidy from Miss Debenham you might wish to issue.

That is at least the hope in which I raise the matter. If then you hear from Miss Debenham, you will know what it is all about; or if you don't hear it might be a courtesy very much appreciated if you could drop her a line to ask whether it is still in her mind.

Yours ever. Frank.'

It was in February 1942 that Lady Betty, who had never really recovered from her broken leg, finally died, aged 78. Eve was able to get up to Scotland for the funeral and for a while her sister Mary remained with their father at Lady Eleanor's Cottage in Whittinge-hame, before Nell took over. Mary then took a job working in the tail sections of the wooden Mosquito bombers, which were so small that the average male carpenter was unable to work inside them.

On the 19th of March C.W.Stewart of Faber & Faber wrote back to Frank Morley.

'Dear Frank,

Many thanks for your two letters dated February 4th. I have received from Miss Debenham a copy of the monograph on the Haughley Research farms with a letter to say that Lady Eve Balfour will send us details of the changes she proposes should be made in the reprint; we are then to discuss publication and the terms for it. It looks our kind of book . . . Kind regards . . .'

Frank Morley also wrote to Miss Debenham suggesting she sent a copy of the monograph to Faber & Faber with a view to obtaining 'an estimate for the publication of a revised edition. 'She duly wrote to them as he had suggested on March 15th, adding: 'I am unable to tell you . . . the extent of the necessary revisions, though I have reason to believe these may have increased considerably since I wrote to Mr Morley last September . . .'

In the circumstances it is not surprising that Faber replied almost by return of post on 17th March saying; 'We shall be very pleased to consider publication and look forward to hearing from Lady Eve Balfour about the changes there would be in a new edition . . .' Thus, once more, in 1942, Eve was involved with publishers.

On March 22nd she wrote to C.W.Stewart at Faber:

'Dear Sir,

'Miss A.E.Debenham has sent me the correspondence between herself and Mr Francis Morley also a copy of her letter to you on the subject of my pamphlet . . . If you think it is the kind of thing in which Faber & Faber might be interested I would like an opportunity to discuss its revision with you.

'My idea was to write it for a wider public than I had in mind originally, cutting out some of the technical stuff and enlarging on the wider implications of the subject . . .

'My object would be to turn out a readable booklet which I hope would sell enough copies to pay for publication, though I realise of course that a guarantee would probably be necessary . . .

'Yours very truly . . .'

Events then moved very swiftly, as Richard de la Mare of Faber & Faber took a hand. On 26th of March he wrote to Eve:

'Dear Lady Eve Balfour,

'I am writing to say that my firm would be very pleased to undertake publication for your little book about the experiment that is to be undertaken by the Haughley Research Farms. I have read the original pamphlet with the greatest interest and should very much like to have an opportunity of discussing the project with you in detail. If it is your intention to come up to London to discuss the matter with us would you be good enough to let us know when . . . we can arrange a meeting? . . .

'I find the whole subject of your experiment of absorbing interest – it fits in well with other things that seem to me of fundamental importance. I had read a certain amount before but I certainly want to know more. And I have little doubt that there will be many other people who feel as I do about the whole subject . . . Yours sincerely.'

On April 5th Eve replied:

'Dear Mr. de la Mare,

'Please forgive the delay in answering your letter, which I was more than delighted to get. I have had a hectically busy week and have not had one moment till today, Sunday, for any correspondence.

'I need hardly say what pleasure your letter gave me (quite apart from the prospect it holds out of realising my ambition of publishing a version of my pamphlet), for I feel so strongly on the fundamental importance to the future of mankind of a proper attitude to the land, that I glow every time I meet some one who shares my views! My pet dream is to see the Ministries of Health, Food and Agriculture merged into one . . . The earliest date that I could get up to town would be around . . . April 19th . . . yours sincerely

With her manifold war work, running the farms short-handed, Eve had little time for writing and revision. For much of 1942, however, she kept hard at work on the monograph, expanding it and improving it beyond recognition. As she noted in the preface to The Living Soil her friends assured her she was doing the impossible, 'trying to write a book for both the specialist and the layman.' It was her success in achieving this which made the book the classic of its day. The Contents page[2] indicated the difference between this publication and her previous monograph on which it was based. The latter was a booklet of 53 pages. This was a book of 250 pages.

Whereas the monograph was a collection of extracts from other people's works, the new work contained many of her own ideas and reflections. It still contained considerable excerpts from the works of Howard, McCarrison and others, which she used skilfully to make her points. That many of her comments were little more than paragraph or so long made little difference. This was a book where her enthusiasm for the subject, even for the very mundane process of making compost, shone through like a beacon. She gave little or no proof of many qualified assertions, but in many ways the book was a testament of faith rather than a scientific treatise. As such it was received triumphantly by the reading public. It is impossible to precis the entire contents of the book, but one excerpt included at the end of this chapter may give an example of the style.[3]

It will be gathered from this and the contents page that Eve was not far out when she wrote to Richard de la Mare that it was 'the most remarkable 12/6 penny production on record!' She was certainly right when she added; 'You are doing me proud.' On the other hand she had put in an immense amount of work in extremely trying conditions and as will be seen from the contents page, compared with her previous monograph, she had transformed it almost out of all recognition. That she may have argued cogently from the general to the particular and back, and presented her case both with a delightful personal touch and occasionally blinding the reader with science is by the way. This was the forerunner of many 'popular' books on farming and science and still remains that rare thing a readable classic. It should be appreciated, however, that Eve's primary aim in writing the book, as in writing the monograph, was to arouse interest in and raise money for the Haughley Experiment.

Inevitably it all took longer than she had anticipated. Every spare moment of 1942 was fully taken up with re-writing. The revised Ms was finally delivered at the very end of the year and on 14th January 1943 Richard de la Mare wrote:

'Dear Lady Eve,

I have now sent your Ms off to the printers for an estimate . . . I have now read all except the very last chapters of the book and there is nothing in it that I have not enjoyed reading or thought worth while keeping in, if we can possibly manage it . . . I am not expecting it be very long before I shall be able to tell you whether or not it will be necessary to make any cuts.

With all good wishes . . .'

Eve replied on Jan 25th:

'Dear Mr de la Mare,

I am so sorry not have answered your letter before. I have had a frightfully rushed week . . . Your reaction to my book is 'most' encouraging, I only hope the reading public will share your views.

About the title . . . I still feel we haven't hit on the right one yet . . .

Something like Soil & The Citizen or Health, Soil & Citizen or simply The Living Soil' . . . By the time the proofs are ready I expect the right solution will have turned up . . . If I have to shorten please let me know approximately how many words you want cut out. Yours sincerely'

Richard de la Mare replied at length:

'Dear Lady Eve,

'Thank you so much for your letter of January 25th . . . Of your latest suggestions our own preference is for The Living Soil . . .

'I have now received our printer's estimate of the length . . . If the 12/6 price is to be possible I'm afraid it will mean that you will have to reduce the length . . . by round about 37,000 words out of a total . . . of 157,000 words. I'm afraid this is going to be an annoying additional task for you, but I am hoping you won't find it too difficult, because my own feeling is that you can do it . . . by summarizing in your own words some of those very long extracts you have . . . of other people . . . for I cannot help feeling that some . . . are really rather too long . . .

'Now with regard to terms for publication: we are quite prepared to take the whole risk ourselves for it is a book we shall be happy and proud to have on our list and what we suggest is that we should pay you a 10% royalty on the published price of all copies sold with an advance payment of £40 to be made on publication on account of that royalty. I should like to have been able to offer better royalties, but the truth is that there is going to be rather a narrow margin on this book on account of its considerable length and the desirability of keeping the price down . . .

'We shall be ready to go right ahead with the production of the book just as soon as the Ms comes back to us . . .'

To this very generous letter Eve replied on February 2nd;

'Dear Mr de la Mare

'Many thanks for your letter and the returned Ms. I'll get down to the revisions right away and let you have it back just as soon as I can.

'I consider your proposed terms perfectly satisfactory, not to say generous under the circumstances . . .

'I had no idea the book was quite so long! I will aim at getting it down to 100,000 which is 20,000 words less than your limit and will mean taking out 57,000 . . .'

On February 13th after a further exchange of letters Eve wrote;

'Dear Mr de la Mare,

'Many thanks for your letter. I did not mean that it was difficult to decide where the cuts must come. I really meant the actual cutting was difficult. I always find adequate precis writing difficult. I am getting on though. I have just about reached your target. I may not succeed in quite reaching mine, but I'll do my best . . . I thought I would perhaps bring the Ms up in person on Monday March 1 . . . Yours sincerely,

By May 24th she had received the page proofs. Most of June was taken up with captions and illustrations and providing the index. By August the book was in print and arrangements were being made for advance copies to be sent out to selected names and addresses around the world. Finally on August 30th Eve wrote:

'Dear Mr de la Mare,

'An advance copy of the book has just arrived and I write post haste to tell you how much I like the look of the finished article and how pleased I am with the quality of paper, printing and photographic reproduction.

'Have you noticed though, the rather unfortunate mistake in Plate V p 79? The 'control;' in the top plate has been left out. I am puzzled as to how this can have happened for as you can see by the enclosed it was quite correct at proof stage. 'Apart from this – many congratulations on a remarkable wartime production. In haste, your ever . . .'

It was decided eventually to print an errata slip and correct later impressions, as Lord Teviot was scheduled to ask a question on humus in the House in early October. Eve wrote;' . . . it would be a good plan if the book was available before the whole question is discussed in Parliament . . .' By 28th October de la Mare was writing:

'Dear Lady Eve,

'I am sure you will be glad to hear that we find it necessary to reprint The Living Soil. Sales have been very good as I always felt confident they would be and clearly we must go ahead with a reprint without further delay. What I am wondering is whether you have discovered any misprints that need correction before the reprint is put in hand . . .'

Eve replied promptly by return of post on October 30th;

'Dear Mr de la Mare,

'Your letter 'was' a pleasant surprise, I will send you a list of corrections on Monday without fail. There are only about half a dozen minor misprints, but I am most anxious to add a short paragraph or two . . . When Mycelium taken from my compost heaps was grown in a laboratory media beside cultures of B.Coli and also in two cases beside Staphilococcus the fungus inhibited the bacteria. You can see this opens up an extremely important new line of research . . . I will try to put it in the least inconvenient way from the printer's point of view . . . In any case I shall be in London some time next month and would much like to come and show you some of the letters I have had, if you can spare the time. In haste.

P.S I forgot to say how very pleased I am for your sake (apart from other considerations) that the book is selling well, because you have been so sporting about it all.'

NOTES ON CHAPTER NINE

1. artificial fertiliser. On the contrary, there were frequent supplies of sewage from Stowmarket in the Spring and the ensuing appalling smell permeating throughout the surrounding countryside was the cause of considerable local grumbling and complaint.
2. Contents Page:

Introduction

I Preliminary Survey

'Soil erosion. Nature of Soil. Law of return. The case outlined.

II Medical Evidence

'The Medical testament. Decline in health. McCarrison

Experiments. Orr's Experiment. Primary cause of disease. Papworth

McMillan Nursery School. Mount Pleasant.

III Humus

'Deterioration in food. deterioration in animal health.

Deterioration in plant food. Leibig Theory. Decline in fertility'

'The Law of return'. Definition of Humus. Humus Manufacture. Indore process. Sheet composting. Compost v muck. Howard's Experiments.

IV Direct Evidence

'Mycorrhizal Association. Soil Ecology. In search of a starting point. Rayner Experiments'. The complexity of compost action. Compost v equivalent salts. Mycorrhizal responses.

Inoculation experiments. Conclusions. Lawson's Cypress

V Circumstantial Evidence

'Facts proved at Wareham. Wider application. A new light.

Mycorrhizal Association in crop plants. A report on cotton. Function of Mycorrhiza. Neilson-Jones investigation. Toxicity in soil. Soil aeration. The fungus in cultivated soils. Cellulose decomposition. Indirect effect of compost action. Fungus nutrition. Soil fertility and the fungus.

VI Indications

1 Plants

'Plant diseases. Results of compost treatment. Parasite larvae. Predaceous fungi. Soil ecology. Earthworms. Insect parasites.

2 Animals

'Animal feeding experiments. Vitamin B. Dr. Rowland. Soil-less culture. Sir

John Russell. Satisfying quality of humus grown food. Foot-and=mouth. Rabbits. Scour in pigs. Baker and Martin. Animal preference. Palatability, 'Fertility' bread. 'Quality'

3 Man

'Human feeding experiments. Africa. England. New Zealand' Singapore. Personal experience. results in Cheshire.

VII Whole Diets

'Health. Wholeness. Fragmentation. Hunza. Value of skin. Hunza diet. Hunza farming. Hunza to-day. Faroe Islanders. Icelanders. An experiment in Denmark. Polar Eskimoes'. Tristan da Cunha. North American Indian. Rural China. The common factor.

VIII Haughley Research Trust

'Need for proof. Pioneering and the individual. Alice Debenham. Need for a clear-cut issue. The Problem. The Programme. The Programme interrupted. Haughley Research Farms Ltd. Dangers of delay. In your hands.

IX Facing the Implications' Revolution in Outlook. Practical first steps. Repercussions of soil erosion'. Switching labour. Humus mines. Utilisation of town wastes. Cost of farm composting. Machinery as labour. Necessity for mixed farming. Rural housing. The Pollitt Plan. Fertility stored' in vegetation. The value of weeds. Agriculture a service. Interests of town and country do not conflict. Education. Need for control. Public v private ownership.

X Postcript

Appendix to Chapter VIII

'Trustees of the Haughley Research Trust. Directors of Haughley Research farms Ltd. Extract from the first annual report to shareholders. Extracts from the second annual report to shareholders

Technical references

Bibliography

Glossary

Index

3. style: Chapter VI; Indications: 1. Plants . . . Para 3.

In Chapter 1, I gave a summary of the far-reaching claims made by many advocates of humus farming. Let me remind you what these are. That if the fertility of the soil is built up with adequate supplies of humus, crops do not suffer from diseases and do not require poison sprays to control parasites; that animals fed on these plants develop a high degree of disease resistance, and that man, nurtured with such plants and animals can reach a high standard of health, and a power of resisting disease and infection, from whatever cause, greatly in advance of anything ordinarily found In this country.

19. Oxerfield: KC's Cottage near New Bells in the 1950s.

20. Eve dressed for the weather on her brother Ral's yacht
Dunpelder off the Norwegian coast 1953.

21. Eve & KC on tour in the 1950s.

22. Eve at her desk in the New Bell's office with Ali on her shoulder c.1950.

# CHAPTER TEN

# The Soil Association & Haughley

## 1943–1953

'. . . a National Association has recently been formed for . . . all those interested in the inter-relationship of the health of soil, plant, animal and man . . .'

extract from a passage inserted in the 7th edition of The Living Soil

OWING TO VARIOUS printing delays due to bombing and shortages, almost inevitable in wartime, the 2nd imprint of The Living Soil was not available before the end of 1943. Eve spent Christmas and New Year at Whittingehame, where her father, now approaching ninety, was living in the cottage beside Redcliff being looked after by Nell, returned from Kenya. Her brother Ral had by this time left the Navy, having been called back to civilian life as Chairman of the Scottish Coal Board, so that she was able to enjoy a family reunion with a considerable part of her family.

She was at this time extremely gratified by the heavy and con-gratulatory mail she had been receiving. On her return south she wrote, on January 14th 1944, to Richard de la Mare's secretary with notes on various corrections to be made and added; 'Please tell Mr de La Mare that I am still getting floods of appreciative letters. The latest an air-graph from Basuto Land! All, including the last, are from strangers.'

Amongst the early letters she received was one from a Mr. Charles Murray[1], which she found particularly inspiring. They subsequently became involved in a lengthy correspondence in which he suggested that she should set up 'a clearing house for information.' There were many other interesting correspondents at this period, several of whom urged a similar course.

On February 27th she wrote to de la Mare mentioning a letter she had from an American G.I who had worked on the Ohio Earthworm Farms:

'Dear Mr de la Mare,

'I have had another letter from the American soldier who used to work for Dr. Oliver.[2] It is rather an interesting one, and as you said you would like to get in touch with him I send it to you . . .

'Lord Teviot has asked me to ask you to let him know the moment the second edition is available. I believe he wants to send it to China and India . . .

I am 'still' getting several letters a week from readers!'

Some review quotations made good reading:

'Enlightening . . . convincing' George Murray. Daily Mail.

'An arresting book; The Scotsman

'Will go far in persuading the doubters. Cavalcade,

'I should like to see it in the hands of very doctor and every farmer and every member of the National Gardener's Guild . . . The country cannot afford 'not to buy it.' Editor. Guild Gardener.

'A remarkable book . . . In it is given for the first time, at anyrate in our country, the evidence of the indications which go cumulatively to prove something is very wrong with our present methods. The Earl of Portsmouth in the House of Lords. Oct 26 43.'

On March 18th Eve wrote;

'Dear Mr de la Mare,

'Many thanks for your letter. I too am delighted the book is on sale again and I am longing to see the second edition. When are my copies coming? . . . Without wishing to seem impatient could you just make sure that they have not been forgotten . . . The enclosed cheque comes from a serving sailor, Lt L.E.L.Silla RNVR to pay for 9 copies of The Living Soil to be sent to prisoners of war. He is a Kenya farmer in peace time. If it is possible for the Red X to arrange this and the book could be sent against my account . . . I would like to add £5 and so send 24 copies . . . Would it be possible for you to send a sample copy to the Red X and ask their opinion . . .'

Unfortunately on April 10th a letter arrived from the Red X;' Thank you for your copy of The Living Soil with the list of doubtful passages. We are afraid that these definitely preclude the despatch of the book to Prisoners of War. It is most unfortunate . . . but we have already had to reject some . . . books because of a few sentences . . .'

Mention on page 13 of 'the Nazi conquest of Europe' and 'Europe in revolt against the tyrant;' on page 194 'should be anti-Nazi . . .'and on page 199; 'It took the rape of Europe to make us fully alive to the Nazi menace' were perhaps understandably too much for the German censors.

By May the 3rd edition of The Living Soil was at the printers and both Eve and Richard de la Mare were confidently discussing their plans for the fourth editions. Congratulatory letters were pouring in from all round the world, including the Antipodes, both direct to Eve and to the publishers' office. Translations were being suggested and urged into numerous different languages.

With the Allied invasion of Normandy and the sudden drastic emptying of East Anglia of troops it must have seemed to everyone in the country that the end of the war could not be far away. This was certainly Eve's feeling as may be seen from her correspondence with the publishers concerning sending books to POW camps, which was still proving a problem.

In September the publishers had overcome the objection of the German censors to delivering the book to prisoners of war. Some copies had already been sent uncensored in any way. However the publishers had agreed with the Red Cross on a satisfactory way of 'excising' the offending sentences. Eve wrote to Richard de la Mare's secretary;

'Sep 7.44. Dear Miss King, It is frightfully good of you and Miss Mathieson to offer to delete the offending passages for the copies of my book to the P.O.W. 'As you will see the censor uses the word 'excised' but don't you think that in view of the fact that at least one copy of the book has already reached a POW camp uncut in any way and that the war may well be over before the books even reach Germany that blacking out with Indian ink would do as well so as not to interfere with the text on the other side . . .

The reply on the 8th September was firm;

'Dear Lady Eve,

'Thank you for your letter of September 7th and for the copy of your book with the marked paragraphs. I have discussed with Mr de la Mare the question of what method to use in 'excising' and we agreed that, although, as you say, the war may well be over before the books reach Germany, yet they may object to the use of Indian ink on the ground that it is removable; so in the circumstances we are proposing to cut out the offending bits and then type out the passages on the back of them and paste them in again, so that there will be no interruption on the following pages. . . .'

Clearly Eve had not been infected by the general malaise of creeping bureaucracy, which was gradually affecting many of the British as they accepted long queues, form-filling and increasing control of their lives as a natural part of existence in order to win the war. It is difficult today to realise how much this had become a part of life in wartime Britain. Shortages were accepted philosophically and anything that was regarded as necessary by petty bureaucracy was accepted without protest. The British had unwittingly come a long way down the road to servitude in fighting dictatorship.

Eve was at this time engaged in a series of broadcast talks on compost and farming, which were widely appreciated. Faber declined to publish them in book form. They suggested, however, that they might consider a simplified form of The Living Soil for younger readers, but not while the sales continued so well.

Meanwhile as a result of her correspondence with the G.I who had worked on an earth worm farm with Dr. Oliver, Eve herself was engaged on correspondence with a Miss Leasure of the California Earthworm Farms regarding earth worms, with the aim of arranging the import by air of a small consignment of earthworm egg capsules. Since the importation of almost anything but essential goods was prohibited her chances of importing earthworms in any form at first seemed negligible.

In October preparations for the 4th imprint of the Living Soil were begun and Eve was asked to send in any further corrections. She wrote back with her characteristic spelling: 'The great majority are of an extremely minor catagory . . . In addition . . . I have added a short 'Forword' . . .' By the end of the month Richard de la Mare was writing: 'The book is still selling very well and I have no doubt that before very long we shall be writing to you about a fifth imprint.'

In March 1945 her efforts regarding the import of earthworms at last proved successful. Astonishingly enough a small consignment of earthworm egg-capsules from the Californian Earthworms Farms was sent across the Atlantic. They were transported by air in an American airforce bomber direct to East Anglia, from where they were delivered by Jeep to Eve at New Bells.

On the 9th of April 1945 personal tragedy struck. Her father, Gerald, 2nd Earl of Balfour, died. At the age of 91 this was not unexpected, but nonetheless it was a personal blow. Her brother Ral thus succeeded to the title as 3rd Earl. Another more unexpected death at this time was that of her Scottish correspondent Charles Murray, whose letters, along with those of others, had inspired the concept of forming a group of like-minded enthusiasts, which was now taking shape. Eve was already making plans to gather interested parties together to form what became The Soil Association.

With the reprint of the 4th edition finally produced in early 1945, before the end of April she was told that a fifth edition was planned. By this time she was also acting as reader and advisor for Faber and Richard de la Mare obviously depended on her advice.

She wrote on 2nd May 1945;

'Dear Mr de la Mare,

How staggering! I had quite made up my mind that the fourth edition would exhaust the demand. I don't intend to make any major alterations . . . I have come across another little book lately that I think well worth while. It is a New Zealand publication, but I should imagine you could easily arrange for publication if you thought this desirable . . . I . . . took the opportunity of glancing at Sykes Ms[3]. In its present form I fear its message may go unheard through his blowing of his own trumpet! He will have to be made to tone this down a bit I feel. Incidentally this would be one way of cutting the Ms . . . Ever Yours'

Having regard to the comment Eve had made on Friend Sykes's Ms. it is not unamusing that on 18th May Richard de la Mare wrote;

'Dear Lady Eve,

Friend Sykes happened to come in and see me this morning and while he was with me he made a suggestion for a small omission from your own book for future editions. He told me that in his speeches he had been heckled on two or three occasions by someone who quoted the paragraph on page 127 about your farm cat. The point the heckler 'tried' to make was that if this was the best you can do by way of evidence, it doesn't amount to very much! I am not sure there is not just a little point to the criticism and that the example might not perhaps by some people be described as trivial. However I leave it entirely to you and pass on the suggestion for what it was worth, and I am sure it was made with the best intentions. Of course I won't do anything unless you give me definite instructions. Yours ever . . .'(Eve did not appear to take the hint. It will have been gathered that she was fond of cats.)

The end of the war in Europe on May 8th brought celebrations throughout Britain, but the war in the Far East was still continuing and was to do so for a further year. Although there was widespread rejoicing throughout Britain the people as a whole were exhausted after the four years of total war during one and a half of which they had stood alone against the triumphant might of Germany. Now that it was all over they just wanted to return to the old 'pre-war' days, but of course those had gone for ever. The returning servicemen found the new Britain of austerity and even tighter rationing a dreary place indeed.

At this time, however, encouraged by the wide public support and nearly five hundred enthusiastic letters she had received, many suggesting that some form of clearing-house for information should be established, Eve circulated over a hundred and twenty five of those who had written to her and were outstanding in various fields. As she wrote later, it was not an easy task, since they had to represent 'not only . . . farming, gardening, medicine, social science, sanitary engineering, the biological sciences, milling, baking, retailing and merely consuming – but also all the different shades of opinion within each of these groups . . . The common ground of opinion which unites them all is . . .

1. The concept of the soil as a living entity.

2. Recognition that human activities must conform to Nature's fixed biological laws if they are not to end in self-destruction.

3. Desire to promote research to interpret more fully what these laws are and how they work.

4. A determination to resist attempts to discard these laws, when they are known, from whatever quarter and with whatever motives such attempts are made.

5. The belief that this can be best achieved by using all possible means to disseminate information concerning proved knowledge in this way to expose exploitation, particularly the exploitation of ignorance.'

Eve could of course rely on her New Bells old reliables, KC, and Beb Hearnden, but she also received enormous help and advice from the founders of the Peckham Health Centre[4], Dr. G.Scott Williamson[5] and Dr. Innes Pearse[6] and their manager C.Donald Wilson[7]. In the end they circulated over 125 people and she eventually gathered together over sixty from all walks of life 'doctors, dentists, biologists, social scientists, cultivators of all the organic schools of thought and members of all political parties.' Notable amongst these was Mrs Elizabeth Murray, widow of her enthusiastic correspondent, Charles Murray.

On June 12th 1945 this first meeting of over 60 Founder members of what came to be known as The Soil Association was called, with Eve herself in the chair. There was no real agenda, since the meeting was called to discuss views and ideas, but an initial sum of money was raised. More importantly a Founders Committee was elected. The task of this steering committee was to incorporate the views that had been expressed at the meeting in the 'Aims and Objects' of a new society and produce a constitution. This was an extremely difficult task with so many diverse elements holding opposing views and the Committee met almost monthly for nearly a year before a constitution could be presented to the members and approved. During that year the first General Election since the war was held and a Socialist Government was given a vast majority by the votes of serving and ex-service voters, many voting for the first time. The country, however, was worn out by four years of war. A long struggle to regain anything like normal living lay ahead.

By November of 1945 a sixth edition of The Living Soil was proposed by the publishers in a characteristic letter;

'20th November 1945: Dear Lady Eve,

We are in the pleasing position of having to put in hand yet another reprint of The Living Soil. Have you any correction

This brought an equally characteristic reply;

'Dear Miss King, 24th November, 1945.

How astonishing! I shan't make any . . . major alterations this time . . . I am going to slip in a paragraph somewhere giving an announcement about the formation of the Soil Association . . .'

Eve then suggested an insert which read in part:

'. . . readers will be interested to learn that, as a result of public demand . . . , a National Association has recently been formed for the threefold purpose of gathering together all those interested in the inter-relationship of the health of soil, plant, animal and man, of building up a large body of 'informed' public opinion and of establishing a research fund and sponsoring research.

The Haughley Research Trust will work in the closest co-operation with this new Society . . . Full particulars . . . can be obtained from: – The Honorary Secretary. Soil Association, 8F Hyde Park Mansions, Marylebone Rd, London N.W.1.

Eve as the founder of both the newly formed Soil Association and of the Haughley Research Trust was, of course, heavily involved. Neither venture would have become reality without her vision and determination. It is also fair to say that Beb Hearnden's support and advice, along with that of KC, was invaluable to her at this time, just as Alice Debenham's had been in the earlier stages.

In February 1946 an approach from the Mazaryk University of Czechoslovakia suggested a translation of The Living Soil. The American edition by this time was also well under way. In addition a Swedish translation had already been arranged. More were to come. All this involved frequent visits to London.

It was on one such occasion that a niece of Eve's met her in London for tea at Browns Hotel. Eve appeared in a very dashing and fashionable hat and her niece commented on it.

'Yes,' replied Eve, with a broad grin, her voice resounding round the hushed lounge. 'I've had it over twenty years. It was very fashionable when I bought it, then it went through a very bad period, but now it's come into its' own again.'

They went on to the Mayfair flat of another aunt, Eve's sister-in-law, for cocktails. Amid the fashionably dressed crush Eve was expounding the advantages of running pigs and geese together on the same ground. There was one of those sudden hushes and her voice rang out clearly, vibrant with enthusiasm;

'You see they eat each other's dung. They love it! Like cake!'

Now aged 48, Eve was at the height of her powers. Basically trained as a farmer, covering general agriculture in the widest sense, she was also well-versed in public speaking, able to deal with audience questions and hecklers with equanimity, and furthermore she had an invaluable training as a journalist. Few people could have been better qualified to take over the initial organisation and promotion of the newly formed Soil Association.

Eve did, however, have an unfortunate failing, of which she herself soon became conscious. Although a good organiser and able to deal with committees, she was the first to acknowledge she was not a good chairman. She tended to talk too much, joining in the general discussions and as a result could not keep the meetings in order. Eve may often have been dogmatic, but she was never bigoted. She was also, usually, aware of her own faults and prepared to accept them and even laugh at them. She always had that saving grace, which is by no means common.

After much discussion, the Soil Association was finally registered and in November 1946 the inaugural meeting was held. The President, appointed by the meeting, was Eve herself. The Vice-President was

Lord Teviot. (It is significant that within a year the positions were changed and Lord Teviot had taken over as President while Eve had become Organising Secretary, a role much more suited to her talents and one she was to fill successfully for many years to come.) Familiar names amongst others on the first Council were, Richard de la Mare, and Miss B. Hearnden. Amongst the Panel of Experts appointed were Eve herself (ex-officio) Dr. G.Scott Williamson, Chairman, Dr. Lionel Picton, (Secretary of the Chester Medical Committee), L.F.Easterbrook (agricultural journalist), Dr. M.C.Rayner[8] and Friend Sykes. Over £1,600 was raised at this first meeting to set the Association into action. It was then formed into a Limited Company, with C.Donald Wilson as Hon. Secretary.

The objects were condensed into three main sentences:

1. To bring together all those working for a fuller understanding of the vital relationship between soil, plant animal and man.

2. To initiate, co-ordinate and assist research in this field

3. To collect and distribute the knowledge gained so as to create a body of informed public opinion.

During 1946 the East Suffolk County Council became increasingly conscious that the Experimental Farms were liable to prove an economic millstone. Each of the sections was being run as a small independent farm, which inevitably increased costs. Following the formation of the Soil Association an obvious course seemed open to both parties. In 1947 with the willing agreement of the County Council the Soil Association was persuaded to take over the Experimental Farms. These in turn were formed into another Limited Company, in order to ensure that the Soil Association did not find them a financial burden. They were re-formed as The Haughley Research Farms, Ltd.

It was thus 1948 before the second phase of the Haughley research project could begin and the farms could be set up to run successfully on the proposed experimental lines. During the war all that could be done was keep the three sections separate and free from fertilisers. Now, under the chairmanship of Dr. Scott Williamson, a small group of organic farmers and scientists set about organising the three sections that had been planned.

This phase lasted roughly from 1948 to 1952, by which time each section had been set up and was equipped with an agreed livestock policy and rotational plan.

Helen Zipperlen, who as Helen Murray was closely involved at the time, wrote later: 'It was agreed that the three sections, Organic, Mixed and Stockless, were to be each, as far as possible, closed systems, as originally planned. In other words seed from each system was re-sown, to find out the effect of the system on genetic health. All wastes (straw, manure, etc.) were returned to their own section. Only the organic section ran on its own, importing nothing except some seaweed meal as mineral supplement for the animals, which they took ad-lib. (How much they took each day was in itself a revealing indicator of the field they were grazing, etc.) Mixed, carried its flocks and herds, but added imports of chemical fertilisers and pesticides according to 'good farming practice.' Stockless, however, imported all its own chemical fertilisers, pesticides. This made the organic section unique. It could not at the same time be a demonstration 'how-to' organic farm, most of which import material for compost and often other items such as feed as well. The cost of such research, however, is considerable, even when conducted with the minimum facilities.'

From 1947 onwards Eve's life began to move into high gear. Her role as Organising Secretary of the newly formed Soil Association was a post which covered a multitude of tasks. To begin with she organised the overall management of the Experimental Farms. Secondly she acted as public relations promoter and publicity organiser for the Association. She also oversaw the training of farm pupils and contributed to the quarterly magazine, which was entitled 'Mother Earth,' as well as a hundred and one other miscellaneous tasks.

From this time onwards she became involved in an annual series of promotional stands at the main agricultural shows on behalf of the Soil Association. With the ever-present KC at her side she toured the shows annually in a 1928 Rolls Royce Silver ghost with a large caravan body mounted on the chassis and with a large trailer in tow. This remarkable machine was to be seen regularly at all the major shows throughout the country. On one occasion while driving up Shap Fell in Cumberland in top gear at a steady fifty miles an hour they were surprised to see everyone waving to them, but put it down to their stately conveyance. It was only on arrival at their destination that they discovered that the window of the Elsan (the non-flush lavatory) had been open and they were trailing yards and yards of toilet paper behind them.

At this stage she was living at Oxerfield Cottage with KC and New Bells was being used by the Farm Manager or by sundry other resident staff. Walnut Tree Manor was early converted into a residential home for visitors to the Haughley Farms. In those days New Bells was still fairly primitive, despite the fact that the Balfour sisters had occupied it for thirty years. Its charm lay in its Elizabethan beams and crazy angles internally, in its situation and its age. It was charming but draughty and still somewhat undeveloped by any standards, although there was by then indoor sanitation.

The moat still had its population of frogs, which croaked a chorus at dawn and dusk and found their way indoors into all sorts of unexpected places. The oak tree mentioned in the Domesday Book still stood in front of the farm buildings. The farm, by modern standards, was far from trim and neat. Suffolk mud is sticky stuff and in those days hedges trimmed by amateurs easily got out of hand. After years of unskilled wartime labour this was a widespread state of affairs. On the other hand the fields were well tended and the experimental areas all carefully planned and marked.

Oxerfield Cottage with Eve's creosoted gypsy caravan close beside it, was somewhat different. A two-bedroom plasterboard and corrugated roofed bungalow with sitting room, bathroom and lean-to kitchen it was in many ways more comfortable than Newbells. Although the small bungalow was wired for electricity and had a bath, it was only equipped with Elsans. In the spirit of true scientific enquiry there was one for Eve who was alkaline and one for KC who was acid. Their twin compost heaps were carefully segregated and the results checked when used in their garden. The cottage was also close to bulging with the combined possessions of both Eve and KC. An outhouse which they used as a repository for anything not immediately required was so full that it was extremely difficult to shut the door.

The cottage also had its inevitable cat population. The mother was a mighty hunter called Ali who regularly produced a rabbit each day. In those days of meat rationing this was not be rejected even by vegetarians such as Eve. Apart from that the vegetable garden produced more than enough to feed two people. To look after matters in their absence KC and Eve usually arranged for a tenant to stay in the cottage during their tours.

Eve was deeply committed to making the Haughley Research Farms operate successfully, as well as the continuous task of spreading the Soil Association message. With a head office in London her visits there became an almost weekly occurrence and she was in the habit of spending the night in Marylebone, near the Soil Association office at the flat of her old friend Beb Hearnden, now organising secretary of 'The Association of Countrywomen of the World.'. Visits to London were usually by train, but her normal transport, apart from the stately station wagon converted from a Silver Ghost, was a surprisingly frisky two-seater bull-nosed Morris.

Eve's old foreman and friend, Bob Aldiss, continued to supervise the Experimental farms. Along with a severely reduced staff and various pupils, they contrived to keep the farms running on a shoestring. Eve's stentorian voice could often be heard sounding across the fields as she started a conversation from a hundred yards or so away. On one occasion Bob and a pupil were in a gateway watching another pupil making a hash of backing a tractor through it. Eve appeared from the other end of the field and started giving advice in a formidable bellow.

'Missus will murmur so,' Bob remarked, shaking his head.

Two of her pupils in this period are particularly worthy of note. One was John Marland, who was briefly a pupil of Eve's after leaving the army in 1946. He married Cynthia Hamilton, who was then working temporarily at Walnut Tree Farm House as the cook. After agricultural college at Cirencester he returned to farm 300 acres at Brazier's Hall at nearby Creeting St. Peter, just the other side of Stowmarket from Haughley. He served on the Soil Association Council from 1951 to 1962 and he and his family remained lifelong friends and supporters of Eve.

The other notable pupil of this period was Helen Murray, from Easter Ross, who went on to study agriculture at the Edinburgh East of Scotland College of Agriculture. Daughter of Charles Murray and Mrs Elizabeth Murray, a Founder member who served on the Council of the Soil Association for many years, she too went on to become a Council member, serving from 1955 to 1964, and Eve hoped she would take on the Haughley Research project. She deputised at New Bells for Eve in her absence, but subsequently married and moved to the United States, where she became a director of the well-known Camp Hill Village Trust. Both she and her mother remained amongst Eve's lifelong friends and supporters.

In 1949 the first of the Haughley week-ends was instituted. These were guided tours of the experimental farms led either by Eve herself, or by various Council members. Any members who wished could book in at the Walnut Tree Manor where they were provided with organically grown food and wholemeal bread. There they would be shown a film and a lecture on the Soil Association aims and aspects of the work being done. The next day they would be taken on a guided tour of the farm. This might well be followed by another film in the evening.

From this time forward and throughout the fifties the pace of life for Eve began to quicken even more. Part of each year was spent on the regular round of the Agricultural shows. This was usually followed by an area tour of members, which would be written up in the journal 'Mother Earth'. Regular lectures and film shows demonstrating the aims and objects of the Soil Association to recruit new members were also a constant feature of her life. Another was visiting members whenever possible, and stimulating interest in the aims of the Association by lectures and seminars.

There were regular weekly meetings in London at the Soil Association headquarters to discuss plans for the experimental farms and report progress to fellow Council members. An overnight stop with Beb Hearnden would be followed by a train journey back to Haughley. Then a quick tour of the farm and preparation for a lecture, or further reports would follow. Somehow she also managed to fit in an almost continuous series of lectures delivered at anything from village halls to Agricultural Colleges, where she was frequently heckled by a hostile audience, although well able to hold her own. It was a gruelling schedule to keep up throughout the year. In a way the trips she made visiting members at home or abroad on lecture tours propagating the Soil Association message were almost a relaxation, testing though they too often were.

Eve had by this time become a highly competent photographer and to this she now added a cine-camera, with which she was also adept. Whenever visiting members she would take a photographic record and very often such records were incorporated subsequently in lectures, using slides or cine-camera shots to illustrate her points. As Organising Secretary and initially almost the only paid employee of the Soil Association she had a very full time job. Her faithful standby KC accompanied her as unpaid help and organiser. When Eve lectured KC was there to work the cine-projector or slides. Afterwards she would be handing out leaflets and advising those who wished to become members on to how to go about it. Her unobtrusive presence was an enormous help to Eve.

When it came to setting up the stands at Shows a great deal of work was involved. The caravan and trailer had to be driven to the site. Then the task of erecting the tent and setting up the tent followed.

Although local volunteers might be there to help, the knowledge of what to put where and how to get the job done most efficiently combined with overall direction usually fell on Eve and KC.

After a lengthy drive to the showground, as anyone who has ever done so will testify, the job of putting up a tent can often be something of a nightmare. Windy conditions and soil baked hard as concrete, or, worse still, liquid mud and driving rain when the tent pegs will not take hold and everything is a mass of wet canvas, can make this a fiendish job. Manning a stand for several days in all weathers and being the target of searching and often hostile questions from sceptical members of the public is no easy task. To do the rounds of the show circuit year after year can be wearing in the extreme, Yet Eve and KC seemed to thrive on it.

As the Soil Association attracted more members the business of helping at such shows could to some extent be delegated to local branch members. There was never, however, any way in which the actual hard work of getting there, erecting the stand and manning it during the show could be avoided. By 1950 they had enrolled 3,000 members and the Association were successfully making ends meet, if only just.

During 1950 apart from her usual tour of the Agricultural shows, Eve also made a journey to the Channel Islands, where she visited the members and lectured successfully. Towards the end of the year, however, a good deal of time was spent organising a prospective tour for 1951 round the U.S.A. Arrangements for this had been proposed for some time, but it required a good deal of preparation. Lectures, film shows, and a complete itinerary, had to be planned. This did not stop her making her customary journey to Scotland for New Year.

In April 1951 Eve joined the Mauretania at Southampton and crossed the Atlantic to arrive in New York on the 25th. There she was met by a friend, who put her New York flat at Eve's disposal and with typical U.S. hospitality acted as her unofficial secretary while she was on tour, taking any telephone calls and passing them on whenever necessary. Amongst those in New York who greeted her warmly were Devin A.Garrity, President of the Devin-Adair book publishing company, running 'The Farmer's Book Club, who were publishing another edition of The Living Soil in the U.S.A.

On the 26th of April, after three days' preparation in New York she flew to Los Angeles and after a 12–hour trip through a dust storm in one of the worst gales for several years arrived to face a battery of press cameras. That evening she met Dr. Albrecht head of the Soils Department of the University of Missouri. She showed the film produced by the Soil Association, 'The Cycle of Life' and in return was shown Dr Albrecht's film 'The Other Side of the Fence,' concerning the effects of mineral deficiencies, of which she was given a copy.

On May 1st she gave a speech to the Academy of Applied Nutrition and again showed the Soil Association film. This was followed on the 2nd by several radio broadcasts, starting with a live breakfast-time interview and continuing all day. Unlike the lectures these were unpaid, but provided good publicity.

The next day she flew early in the morning to Oakland across the bay from San Francisco where she was shown over the Compost Corporation of America's plant by its organiser Dr. Pfeiffer. where 25% of the city's garbage was turned into compost. On her return to Los Angeles on May 4th she gave further lectures, followed on the 5th by a visit to the Champion brothers' healthy organically- composted orange groves which were surrounded by dying groves of oranges that had relied on sprays to survive.

After numerous further lectures and visits on May 6th she flew to Chicago. Here she saw the composting plant at the Stockyards. This was followed three days later by a flight to Iowa, where she stayed with the Treichler family. She had first met Bill Treichler as an air-gunner in the U.S.Air Force stationed near Haughley during the war and he was the second American citizen to become a member of the Soil Association. This was followed by further lectures and visits to farms, eventually returning to New York on 14th May.

A lunch and speech at the Colony Club was successful in raising new members. Further important speaking engagements followed and she made numerous influential friends and contacts, notable amongst them Dr Paul Sears, head of the Conservation department at Yale, where she was asked to speak. She next flew to Virginia where she had to face the Blacksburg Agricultural College and State Experimental Station, the centre of orthodoxy, addressing both staff and students and holding her own. A tour of a compost plant at Stephen's City was something of a relaxation by contrast, before going on to Pennsylvania for further broadcasts.

After a visit to Princeton, she continued on to Philadelphia and more broadcasts and lectures where she was a guest of Mr. J.L. Rodale, publisher of Organic Gardening, and Organic Farming.

Further lectures, broadcasts and visits followed before her return to New York on June 2nd. The next seven days continued on the same hectic schedule, including a visit to Buffalo and to Niagara Falls on the Canadian side. Finally she returned to New York by June 7th, where she was given a farewell dinner, meeting amongst others the Lawrence Rockefellers, with finally a 4 a.m end to the day at the Colony Club. This was followed by an 8 a.m start and further final interviews before returning to the Mauretania and a long sleep.

During the six week tour she had travelled several thousand miles, mostly by plane, given 18 lectures, 15 broadcasts and numerous interviews to the press. She earned $500 more than her total expenses in fees for the Soil Association as well as enrolling 48 new members and laying the foundations for a second visit with hosts in every State in the U.S.A. For a whirlwind tour of this nature it was a remarkable feat and her experiences had broadened her horizons, making her conscious of new and challenging problems arising from Mankind's misuse of the environment and the even greater need for her message to be broadcast on a global scale.

On her return she went almost immediately into the usual hectic tour of the agricultural shows with KC. When that was finished there was an even larger than usual correspondence to answer, a considerable amount of it as a result of her U.S tour with suggestions for a repeat performance. By September the Devin-Adair Company in New York were making plans for selling another printing of The Living Soil to their Farmer's Book Club. Their publicity hand-out[9] was enthusiastic.

Meanwhile the financial situation of the Soil Association burdened with the costs of the Haughley Research farms had reached crisis point. To save the Association, the stock and equipment were advertised for sale in September. At the last moment the Earl of Strafford stepped in and bought the farms, allowing the Association a year's grace rent-free to form a foundation to run the project.

Dr. Reginald F.Milton, B.Sc.,PH.D.,[10] an extremely distinguished biochemist, who had worked with Dr. Scott Williamson took charge of the analytical work at Haughley from late 1951 onwards. Working on a shoestring, along with Eve, or when she was away and busy elsewhere, with her dedicated pupils, every record was painstakingly transcribed. Phase three of the Haughley Experiment had begun, almost as an act of faith, with no certainty as to how long it would last.

One of the pupils involved in those early days with Dr. Milton recalled how he impressed on her the absolutely unique research which was being done, not only the obvious weights, yields and financial picture, but the monthly variations in the chemical constituents of soils and plants, without any additions or human interference. After his day's work in the fields each month he would return to eat with the pupils and on one occasion he said: 'If what I am finding is true, I have to re-learn all my basic training in bio-chemistry.' Basically he was discovering that the laws of 'life' differ from the laws of 'chemistry'. Such opinions expressed by a consultant of international fame and integrity impressed her beyond measure. Yet it was always a question of where the financial support was to be found to keep going.

In December 1951 the Soil Association issued a 16–page pamphlet largely written and composed by Eve entitled 'The Future of the Haughley Research Farm Project.' This gave an outline of plans to found a Trust to take over the research farms, which had once again become a financial burden threatening the continuance of the Soil Association itself. The sum it aimed at raising was £71,000, but the response was slow, merely enough to keep it going on a temporary basis.

The following year, 1952, after their usual round of the agricultural shows Eve managed to fit in a sailing trip across the North Sea to Denmark crewing on her brother Ral's forty-foot sailing yacht, Dunpelder. It was all good fun, even though by this time aged nearly fifty-five such expeditions, involving keeping watch from 2–4 a.m. in squally conditions, were by no means as easy to cope with as they had been before the war.

Later that year in the Autumn in addition to a tour of Lancashire, she and KC crossed the English channel in a more orthodox fashion and made a tour of the Dordogne, starting at Lot. Eve was particularly struck by the condition of the cows and wrote: 'The breed of the district is indistinguishable from the English Red Sussex cattle . . . All the cows I saw were in splendid condition and I was told that their working life averages 25 years. Throughout this they regularly breed one calf a year, milk, plough, haul and do all the other field operations. The milk is exceedingly rich . . . There seems to be no anxiety about foot-and-mouth in the district.'

Eve noted; 'Summarising my impressions of our French trip from the point of view of the work of the Soil Association I felt there was a very fertile field in France for mutual co-operation, but no satisfactorily close association can take place . . . until we are in a position to establish subsidiary headquarters . . . and circulate members . . . in their own language.'

Somehow or other Eve also managed to prepare a memorandum concerning 'The Ecological Research Foundation.' This was the body she proposed to form to raise the requisite finance to run the Haughley project. In this pamphlet the objects of the Haughley Research Experiment were outlined and various methods of financing it proposed. That December Eve's office at New Bells, a converted nissen hut, caught fire, probably as a result of a wiring fault. Although the cause was never known. She wrote to her sister-in-law, Jean: '

December 12th. New Bells;

'Darling Jean,

'Yes, I am coming on the 30th by 2 p.m. from Kings X and getting out at Dunbar and Mary is coming with me, but . . . there will be no film show . . . Last Sunday evening my entire office and everything in it was completely destroyed by fire. How it started is still a complete mystery, The immense amount of valuable equipment, dictaphone, film projectors, cameras, typewriters, etc and my desk and other office furniture are, I hope and believe, fully covered by insurance, but the things that mattered most were without money value and irreplaceable. Documents of all kinds, farm records, research records (only some of these are in duplicate) letters, past and present, private papers, account books, personal treasures, 'all' my photographs . . . All my coloured slides, all my films . . . not least of the trials this fire has caused is the immense amount of extra work. I had practically finished rough drafts of several important reports (several weeks work) which had to be done before I sail for America. Now they will have to be done again and this time without references and notes. I have had to cancel as many engagements as I can, including the Shetland Islands on January 10th, but I shall only cut short my time at Whitt by one day. I shall have to go to Glentanar on Monday 5th (instead of the 7th) and then catch the night train south from Edinburgh after giving my lecture there on the 6th.

Both my and KC's passports were burnt and all that paraphernalia has to be gone through again and my wartime savings certificates in a cash box in a steel deed box, in a steel cupboard were completely destroyed, which will give you an idea of the heat of the fire. Even metal objects are hardly recognisable and everything else charcoal . . .

Lots worse things have happened of course and don't think I am down hearted, but it has for the moment disrupted my normal life and I do 'mind' the disappointment to you all over the films. Love to all Eve'

Apart from explaining why there was a considerable gap in Eve's correspondence dating from before 1937 right up to 1952, this also gives a very clear impression of her resilience in the face of a blow which would have had most people reeling. She appeared as undisturbed as ever at New Year in Scotland, merely apologising for having lost the film records of the various members of the family. After her brief respite at New Year to see in 1953 with her relations in Scotland she set off on her hectic round of lectures once more.

NOTES ON CHAPTER TEN

1. Charles Murray: landowner and farmer in Easter Ross. During the war was closely associated with Dr. Scott-Williamson and the Peckham Experiment (see below). He was amongst the first to write to Eve after the publication of the first edition of The Living Soil. She greatly valued the correspondence she had with him, although they never met before his unexpected early death in 1945 and the letters were subsequently destroyed in an office fire in 1952. His daughter Helen was one of Eve's earliest pupils at Haughley in 1946 and his widow, Mrs. Elizabeth Murray, was a Founder member of the Soil Association.

2. Dr. G.S.Oliver of Texas: wrote a 3 volume book: Our Friend the Earthworm. A breeder of earthworms on a large scale for farmers, he claimed:

   1. Darwin found that on average English soil, eathworms brought to the surface about ten tons of castings per acre.

   2. The estimated numbers . . . per acre in the soils of Rothamsted Experimental Station . . . are . . . roughly a. 0.5. million on unmanured land. b. 2.75 millions on farmyard manured land. c. 8.6 millions on grassland.

   3. Earthworms render soil permeable to rain thus checking erosion.

   4. They mix organic matter thoroughly throughout the soil and prevent . . . sour pastures.

   5. Earthworms are excellent sub-soilers . . .

   6. Earthworms perform equally useful work on the compost heap – abundance of them is a sure sign that the process is going well, just as their eventual withdrawal in the normal way is an indication that the compost is ready for use . . .

3. Sykes Ms: Friend Sykes Author of Humus & The Farmer. the Ms referred to in the letter. He also wrote later Food, Farming and the Future. In 1959 he also wrote Modern Humus Farming. A Founder Member of the Soil Association and on the Council for many years. Eve's comments were, however, fully justified.

4. Peckham Health Centre: or Pioneer Health Centre: or Peckham Experiment: Founded in 1935 to study the health of the family as a unit and eventually

involved 3,911 individuals of both sexes, in 1,206 families, investigating all aspects of nutrition, exercise and life as a whole, providing food from their own organic farm. Had their own gymnasium, swimming pool and social club. The aim was to study the 'living' structure of society and health rather than disease. It was re-opened in 1946 after being turned into a Munitions Factory during the war.

5. Dr. G.Scott-Williamson, M.C., M.D.: one of the founders along with his assistant and collaborator Dr. Innes Pearse of the well-known Pioneer Health Centre at Peckham, in London, known more widely as The Peckham Experiment. A Founder Member of the Soil Association. With Dr. Innes Pearse author of Science, Synthesis and Sanity, published in 1965, an exposition of the philosophy which inspired the Experiment.

6. Dr. Innes H.Pearse; She qualified in 1916 at the London Hospital and became Dr. Scott Williamson's research assistant at the Royal College of Surgeons and St. Bartholomew's Hospital, Ten year's experience of one of the first Infant Welfare Centres impressed on her the need for full and continuous contact with the family, which led to the Peckham Experiment. The organic farm attached to it stressed the importance of diet. Also a Founder member of the Soil Association.

7. C.Donald Wilson: Born in 1900. Spent nine years as works chemist in Sheffield after graduating at Cambridge. Joined Pioneer Health Centre at Peckham before 1939 War. Became Manager during the war and was still acting as such while assisting Eve for three months prior to Founders Meeting of Soil Association in 1945. Then Hon. Sec. to Founder's Committee until 1950. Became Development irector for Soil Association in 1956 and lived at Haughley until his death in the 1970s.

8. Dr. M.C.Rayner. Author of Problems in Tree Nutrition and Trees and Toadstools. A Cambridge botanist of high standing, noted for her investigations into the role of mycorrhiza in healthy plant growth. A long standing friend and correspondent of Eve's and a Founder Member of the Soil Association, died 1949.

9. Publicity hand-out: 'Eleven printings of this remarkable book have been sold in England since it was first published in 1943. It is now established as a world-famous scientific classic in soil biology and fertility relationship. 'My subject,' 'says the author, who is both a practical down-to-earth farmer and a highly trained student of soil research, 'is food, which concerns everyone, it is health, which concerns everyone; it is the soil, which concerns everyone, even if he does not realise it – and it is the history of certain recent scientific research linking these three vital subjects.

'The author recently completed a most successful tour of this country having lectured to doctors and dentists, farmers large and small, scientists and thousands of plain ordinary folk.

'A second American edition of her book has just been revised to cover conditions in the U.S. and it should prove a welcome addition to your permanent agricultural library . . .'

10. Reginald F. Milton, B.Sc., Ph.D, FRIC, worked with Dr. Scott Williamson in the late 1920s. Became an independent consultant in 1937. In charge of the Medical Research Council's Dept. of Industrial Medicine during the war. Returned to private practice as distinguished bio-chemist in 1945. Started work at Haughley in 1951 and continued until the end of the Experiment in 1970.

# CHAPTER ELEVEN

# *The Haughley Experiment & Travel*

## 1953–1969

*'I have never had any 'personal' ambitions about Haughley or the Soil Association and if I had they would be totally unimportant . . .'*

Eve, in answer to a letter after a Council Meeting of the Soil Association

IN SPRING OF 1953 Eve and KC set off again for the United States. This trip was an ambitious one by any standards and indeed most of the Americans shown her proposed itinerary were totally horrified and announced firmly that it could not be done. It involved a marathon journey across the entire width of the United States and back again covering an amazing 9,600 miles.

Having made her exploratory journey alone in 1951 and made contact with numerous people and places she wished to visit, Eve was determined to try and take them all in at one go. She was convinced that it was only by driving that she would be free to take the route she wished. Yet if she was to do so she required a companion to whom she could chat, who was both reliable and amusing and also one with whom she could totally relax. KC, her friend of 25 years' standing, seemed the perfect choice.

She wrote; 'It was quickly obvious that there were likely to be more invitations to lecture than I could fulfil and the problem of hospitality was solved beyond my wildest dreams. I have the great advantage of membership in three international societies. The first, of course, is the Soil Association . . . Next is my membership of A.C.W.W (Associated Countrywomen of the World). This is the international body to which all national farm or village women's organisations the world over are affiliated . . . Last, but not least, I am a member of the London Club of

Altrusa International Inc. This is the first executive and professional women's service club and was started in America in 1917. There is now a club in almost every town and city throughout the United States, and when neither the Soil Association nor A.C.W.W could offer hospitality Altrusa could and did . . .'

She wrote later; 'Now that it is over and has been a success in every respect, I will confess that I think it would be unwise ever again to tempt Providence to the same extent. The schedule was so tight that even a puncture could have thrown it out and any breakdown of car or health would have blown it sky-high. All went without a hitch however. Between February 12th and April 18th I drove the 1951 Ford station wagon . . . 9,600 miles, not only without an accident but without seeing one. We did not have a single puncture, or even have to change a plug. I spoke an average of two nights out of three, and though we only twice spent more than two nights in one place we both kept fit . . . Providence was, of course, very kind to us. We missed all the storms (except one dust storm) though tornadoes both preceded and followed us . . . We saw what we sent to see and met those we went to meet. We enrolled a lot of new members and made a lot of new friends. We earned our expenses and above all we acquired a great deal of new information of first-class importance . . .'

The most enduring impression she had was probably of the immensity of the United States. She wrote; 'The size of the United States has to be experienced to be understood. Even though one knows that New York is nearer London than it is to Los Angeles, this really means something only when you have crossed both the Atlantic and the country at approximately the same speed (in terms of miles per day). The country contains six distinct climates. We saw the arrival of spring three times over. In 1951 the unusual experience which made the most vivid impression on my mind was my first sight of fireflies. In 1953 it was one day's driving from Atlanta, Georgia, to Jacksonville, Florida, a distance of 380 miles. It will for ever be to me a drive, not through space, but through time. in terms of the English seasons we drove from February to June in a single day. Though it had been fairly warm and spring-like in Atlanta, the trees were still bare and only the earliest flowers were out. As we proceeded, first the buds began to appear on the trees, then the tender green leaves, then they emerged more and more, until at the end of the day everything was in full leaf and full flower and it was summer. It really was an extraordinary experience, rather like living in one of those 'time lapse' films speeded up to show the growth of plants . . . Besides six climates the country has every type of scenery from tropical to arctic; but each type lasts for such a long time that you do not get the same sense of variety you do in England . . . For example we would remark to each other. 'This is rather like Cambridgeshire' or 'This is quite like the country round Tring'; but the country round Tring lasts at most for half-an-hour's driving, while its counterpart in America lasted a day . . .'

In May 1953 the memorandum on 'Ecological Research Foundation' which Eve had prepared was printed and circulated widely. The response was sufficiently encouraging at first to raise the hopes of all concerned. For the moment, however, the financial situation was far from happy. With the membership remaining apparently stuck in the region of 3,000 the Soil Association was inevitably short of funds.

One of the problems was that they attracted a broad spectrum of support, many of whom fully justified the description of crank with which the Association supporters were often branded. The big battalions of the fertiliser producers, such as ICI, were ranged against them and at this stage they could expect few, if any, companies to provide finance. They were tagged 'the muck and mystery brigade.' It was an uphill struggle to attract financial support.

In 1954 Eve managed to combine another sailing trip on her brother's yacht with Soil Association business. In the summer she successfully toured Soil Association members, lecturing, as well as filming, in Denmark, Sweden and Norway. She then met her brother's yacht by arrangement in Norway and sailed back across the North sea with him.

In February 1955 Eve had lunch with her publisher Richard de la Mare and by this time they had reached Christian name terms for she wrote subsequently on 5th March:

'Dear Dick,

'Here is a first very tentative and very summarised synopsis of how an organic farming textbook might be assembled. If you and Mr. Hills could give me your first reactions and criticisms so that I would receive them on or before 21st March I would have a very good opportunity of discussing the whole project with many Organic farming members at the forthcoming Council Conference on organic farming to be held at Cookham on 22nd and 23rd March . . . Yours very sincerely, Eve.'

Lawrence D. Hills, subsequently President of the Henry Doubleday Research Association, but then a free-lance agricultural journalist, sent in an eight-foolscap-page single-spaced report on the very skimpy synopsis with a covering letter reading in part:

'Dear de la Mare, 14th March 1955,

'Many thanks for your letter and Lady Eve's synopsis . . . Like all this type of synopsis sent by authors it tells very little . . . The question is whether she has the knowledge to write it( Yes, inserted by de la Mare) She is a great personality, but I doubt her knowledge of practical farming. She may be able to write this book but it is a very big job . . . she is taking on what looks to me like five years work . . . Lady Eve has a name, but not as an expert farmer, if it is bad the technical reviewers will jump on her with glee . . . Lady Eve as head of the Soil Association does not want to be torn apart.

'I say this because I do not know how much more she knows since she wrote 'The Living Soil, she may be able to do this book very well indeed . . .

'I hope this report will not cause trouble between yourself and an old friend, blame it on me, I do not think she likes me very much anyway. I am trying to help her and do not want her to bite off more than she can chew. I suggest six guineas for this one . . . Best wishes . . .'

It is clear there had been a misunderstanding for on the 1st of April Eve replied to de la Mare:

'Dear Dick,

'Very many thanks for sending me Mr. Hills' criticism of the synopsis. It arrived in good time and I was able to read both synopsis and criticism to some of the colleagues down at the Cookham conference.

'I think Mr Hills has one or two first class suggestions, of which, if this book does get written I shall most certainly avail myself . . . Others again I feel he would not have put like that had you briefed him properly and I really do feel that you owe him an apology for this, as he must have spent a lot of time and trouble on his criticism which, if he had realised what I was intending to do would have been saved . . . as you well know I have no intention myself of 'writing this book', even if I had the time I would not be competent to do it. If the project goes forward it will be much more in the nature of editing a book than writing one, though no doubt I will have to re-hash and put in my own language most of the material in order to retain a coherence of style . . . as I told you I couldn't begin this job before September – and I have got Mr Mayall's[1] promise that he and I will together write the chapter on Organic Ley Dairy Farming . . . If you approve of it I will then go ahead and contact the other people with whom I shall have to do likewise . . . It will take me at least a year from next September to get my material together . . . and whether I can in fact undertake it or not, will depend a little on how we get on with this first section . . . Perhaps you will pass on all this information with my thanks to Mr Hills. ever yours,

PS I dictated this just before leaving for Scotland so please excuse absence of my personal signature.'

In 1955 Eve was presented with a Bedford Dormobile by a group of Soil Association friends. In this she and KC with two companions set out for Italy, camping for the night where weather and conditions were suitable. They went down the west coast to Rome, where they met Tommasso Del Pelo Pardi[2], who with his father originated the method of contour ploughing which bears their name.

From Rome they went via Assisi and Perugio to Florence, from where they cut across to the East Coast and Venice, visiting the reclaimed area between Venice and Trieste with a local member Mr. John Walters. On the way they had noted the care with which manure and town garbage was treated and returned to the land. One thing that struck the party particularly was 'the spotless cleanliness of the cattle byres, always with fresh litter. That and the conservation of wastes and the skill with which inter-cropping was everywhere carried out . . .' Finally they made a tour through the Tyrol and Lombardy before returning home.

At the beginning of 1956 Eve made a month's tour of Kenya, where her sister Nell was one of the prominent settlers at Gilgil. Using this as a base Eve made a tour of all Soil Association members in the country and once again produced a great deal of material for lectures along with useful photographs and films to provide data for the Soil Association. On May 2nd she received a letter from de la Mare:

'Dear Eve,

'. . . First of all to ask you if you have any news at all about the proposed book on Organic Farming that we discussed over lunch at the beginning of last year . . . The second matter concerns The Living Soil . . . the book goes on selling quite well . . . and it looks as if we shall have to reprint again within twelve months . . . I so much hope we can meet again soon . . . yours ever . . .'

This received a reply on the 9th of May:

'Dear Dick,

'Thank you for yours of the 2nd of May . . .

'1. Textbook on Organic Farming . . . if you can give me until next Spring I think I shall be able during the coming Winter to arrange for help in the ferretting out process to enable me after all to produce something . . . I did just make a start a few months ago and could get down to it again next Autumn.

'2. Reprint of the Living Soil. Yes, I would like to change the chapter about the experimental work here before it is printed again . . .

'. . . finally a point of my own. There is so much of interest to report about my trip to Kenya, much of which I think has not been said before, that I am going to write it up in the form of a short book for normal publication. Do you want me to offer it to you first?

'Yours very sincerely, Eve.'

de la Mare replied on his return from the Booksellers Conference on May 23rd;

'Dear Eve.

'. . . First of all about the proposed Textbook on Organic Farming. Yes, of course we are prepared to wait and we are only too willing to give you until next Spring . . . I shall hope for the best . . .

'Next about The Living Soil, I am glad to hear that you are proposing to go through the book and to see what revision is necessary and there will be no difficulty about our carrying out any corrections . . . you may want to make . . .

'Finally about your trip to Kenya. If you 'do' write a book about it, yes of course we would like to see it . . . Yours ever . . .'

There was no reply from Eve who was extremely busy lecturing and touring for the Soil Association, instead there was a follow-up from de la Mare dated December 7th 1956:

'Dear Eve,

'There are three things I want to ask you about. First of all about The Living Soil . . . we are just giving a binding order for the last five hundred copies . . . which means I suppose that we should 'like' to have the new edition ready in a year's time. Is that going to be possible, do you suppose? 'Then, have you given any more thought to the new book on Organic Farming? I do 'hope' so for such a book is needed. But alas, I know how busy you are and I can't help fearing the worst! How nice it would be if you were to disabuse me! 'Now the third matter; I wonder if you have thought of the possibility of making a book out of what you have been writing about your tours? There is plenty of excellent material there, which I am sure many people who know it already would like to have in permanent form and if you were to make a book of it I believe it would reach a much wider public . . . and excellent propaganda for the Soil Association . . . Will you think about this.

Yours ever . . .'

Her reply to this was dated 11th December 1956

'Dear Dick, . . .

'1. Yes, I think I can undertake to have the revised edition of Living Soil ready for you probably in less than a year's time.

'2. Yes, I have given more thought to the book on organic farming We had planned during 1957 to attempt to make a survey county by county of all the organic farms in the country . . . the only limiting factor . . . is the petrol crisis (Petrol was still rationed following Eden's disastrous intervention in Suez)

'3. This is a new idea to me. I cannot see it at the moment as a book, but as something resembling a volume of essays . . . Yours ever.'

Richard de la Mare followed this up on December 14th.

'Dear Eve

'. . . I was glad that you think you can complete the revision of The Living Soil . . . in rather less than a year's time . . . I quite agree with you about the Organic farming book. Yes, by all means wait until you have completed the county by county survey . . .'I very much wish to talk with you about the suggestion I made for a book about your tours and I would be delighted if you would come and have lunch with me . . . at the Atheneum . . . Yours ever . . .'

On 18th February 1957 Eve wrote;

'Dear Dick

'. . . I will do my best to complete The Living Soil revision by the end of the year. By all means send me a reminder. Whether I can manage it or not depends very largely on how long it takes to secure the necessary finance for Haughley. At present every minute outside routine work is being devoted to that . . . Ever yours . . .'

On 23rd January 1958 de la Mare again wrote;

'Dear Eve,

'I am writing to you again about The Living Soil to ask you for news of your revision for the new edition that we have discussed more than once in the last year or two. The need for it has now become very much more urgent, because we have been asked to supply 500 copies of our own edition for America and we cannot do that without running entirely out of stock over here. I do hope we may have good news from you for we never like letting a book run out of print that is still in considerable demand . . . Yours ever . . .'

Eve's reply was not reassuring; dated 29th January 1958.

'Dear Dick, 'I have been meaning to write to you for some time because I have been suffering from a very guilty conscience in connection with my promise to revise Living Soil. I have not done it, partly because pressure of work this year has been so heavy that I genuinely have not had time . . . but also because while the future of the Haughley Experiment was so very uncertain I felt it would be quite unrealistic to attempt the revision. Now that we know Haughley is to continue for a few years at anyrate that difficulty is removed.

I have no doubt that the sudden demand from U.S.A is due to the fact that I am going there on February 18th to do a short lecture tour for the Natural Food Associates . . . I really will do my best to let you have the revision as soon as possible after my return so that you will not be out of print for long . . . I do apologise but there is a limit alas! to what one can get through. Yours sincerely'

de la Mare duly acknowledged this with an understanding letter, dated 30th January.

No doubt he knew as well as Eve the continual ups and downs of the Soil Association finances. Having been inured to recurring financial crises all her farming life, Eve was probably able to take it all with more equanimity than many others. By early January 1958 the Haughley Experiment financial situation had become so acute once more that the livestock and equipment were once again advertised for sale (in April), but after another desperate appeal the Soil Association members subscribed an amazing £10,000 per annum for a five-year period to keep it going.

The fact of the matter was, that while Eve had not expected any results in her lifetime, they were already beginning to get them after only ten years. The analysis of the fluctuations in the availability of plant nutrients showed that over ten years the field with the highest humus content and the longest history of being without chemicals had as much as ten times more available phosphate during the growing season than during the dormant period. Potash and nitrogen followed the same general pattern. It was apparent that this seasonal release of minerals could only have been brought about by biological agencies and it seems to be a natural action-pattern in a biologically active soil.

After the publication of this finding it was checked and confirmed. Previously it had always been assumed that a single soil analysis at any time of the year would show what was required.

Rumbles of discontent, however, and a lack of understanding for the need for the Experiment were still apparent. There was already a strong body of opposition within the Soil Association which made its views clear that they could not afford such expensive experiments and that a simple demonstration organic farm was all that was required. Its supporters argued that The Haughley Experiment was unique and that there were already numerous good demonstration organic farms around the country. The donation of £10,000 per annum over a five year period clearly showed that many members appreciated the value of the Experiment. This sudden reversal of fortunes was at least in part due to Eve's efforts. She had flown to the U.S.A on 17th February in a blizzard as the guest of the Natural Food Associates who sponsored her tour. During her visit the Living Soil Foundation, U.S.A, based on tax-deductible donations, was formed, with various aims, including support for the Haughley Experiment.

After an initial period in New York, Eve embarked on another very taxing tour, starting on the 11th of March and returning to London on May 3rd. In the interval she had given a total of 36 lectures and sold $600 worth of Soil Association literature. She also enrolled 25 new members. In the course of the two months she crossed and re-crossed the United States by air and train. On her return in May, before touring the agricultural shows, she set about preparing for a tour of Australia.

By 5th September de La Mare was writing again:

'Dear Eve,

'I see that I have had no news from you since I wrote to you in January about your revision . . . It is now really urgently needed . . . Dare I hope for better news than I fear you may be able to give me? . . . Yours ever . . .'

Eve wrote back promptly

'Dear Dick; On 4th November Kathleen Carnley and I start for Australia in a 12 passenger Norwegian cargo boat. I am hoping to do the revision of Living Soil during the five weeks voyage, It is then or never I am afraid . . .'

A letter on the 25th of March informed him that she had 'spent a lot of time on the voyage over, working on the revision . . . My suggestion is that I divide the book into two halves, call the first half part I

Historical (written between 1942 and 1948) and the second half Part II Development.

de la Mare acknowledged and approved this concept on May 7th

Eve and KC arrived in Freemantle in December, from there via Adelaide they went on to Melbourne and so by train to Sydney where they first saw P.A.Yeomans'[3] system of contour ploughing in operation. They also learned about Keyline cultivation and siting Keypoint dams on virgin ground, as contained in Yeomans' books: The Keyline Plan and Challenge of Landscape. They visited five Keyline properties on their way to Queensland, seeing the various results this revolutionary method of cultivating virgin land produces.

On Christmas Eve they flew from Brisbane to Woolabra the 40,000–acre sheep station of Mrs (later Dame) Alice Berry. Here there had been a drought but as they arrived a thunderstorm produced one inch of rain. Eve noted after looking at the soil 'In my ignorance I would have said it was beyond recovery, yet within 24 hours of those few points of rain the whole area had taken on a green tinge. It seemed the nearest thing to a real miracle that I have ever witnessed . . .'

After an intensive tour of numerous Queensland farms and enrolling new members as well as lecturing, Eve and KC left for Tasmania on the 16th of January. Here they spent two weeks crammed with visits and advertised lectures including a visit to Three Hummock Island farmed by Commander and Mrs Alliston, who had become the first Australian members of the Soil Association in 1946. From there a 150–mile journey took them to the width of Tasmania to the scene of their next lecture. During the next few days they were constantly travelling with a lecture almost every day until, on the 2nd of February, they caught a plane back to Melbourne.

Here in a heatwave of 105, instead of a free day on the beach as they had hoped, they were met by a full blown press reception lasting an hour in a small room. This was followed by a meeting in the evening, TV interviews, lectures and gatherings then more tours of farms in the West Gippsland area. Visits to Cheshunt and the Shepparton district followed, all interspersed with lectures. They next visited the Campaspe Valley area and saw Keyline in operation.

They went on to the Mallee Country and then made a further series of tours and lecture, including one at Geelong, where Eve gave a talk to the senior boys. This was followed by a tour of the 40–square-mile famous Werribee sewage plant, 'Melbourne's famous sewage plant.' Eve's priorities in visiting were:

'1. To meet members.

2. To see their properties if farmers

3. To learn all she could about farming conditions and problems

4. To visit research stations.

5. To see the scenery.

She noted; 'One of the oft-heard statements about Australia that turned out to be myths was that the country hotels are very bad. Perhaps they were once, but we didn't find it so anywhere . . .'

By the 6th of March they had completed a five-week tour of Victoria and flew to Sydney on the first leg of a flight to New Zealand. They arrived at Aukland and flew on to Christchurch in South Island, going on from there to Invercargil. From here they had a long drive through to Wanaka. This was followed by further meetings, lectures and farm visits before returning to Christchurch. After a month of journeying round South Island they then set out on April 9th for North Island by the 2.15 ferry.

On their arrival in Wellington there was a brief respite before the next day, April 10th, there were the inevitable press and broadcast interviews followed by a meeting in the evening. A visit to the Wallaceville Department of Agriculture's animal research station and the Soil Bureau Research at Upper Hutt they enjoyed. Then via Palmerston and New Plymouth they went to Masterton and started a very extensive tour. The rest of the month was fully occupied in visiting members, research stations, composting plants and lecturing. By May 10th they were off by air from Aukland returning to Australia.

They arrived back at Sydney on May 10th 1959, soon after which both KC and Eve went down briefly with a one day flu which was very widespread. This was barely allowed to affect their heavy schedule of visits and lectures. They were soon touring their members in the Blue Mountains, before flying on to Tamworth in New South Wales. They then went on to the New England district of New South Wales, at Bald Blair, before going on to the North coastal district. Here they had a 100–mile train journey which took all night and Eve noted; 'Some of Australia's through expresses on main lines are second to none in the world, but the average train journey in Australia has to be experienced to be believed. We arrived in the early morning with our bones well shaken up . . .'

Their next flight took them from Sydney to Canberra. On the 16th of June they visited the Snowy River catchment scheme. Here they saw the winter sports area, still in embryo. The drive itself, however, without four-wheel drive proved sufficient winter sports for them.

From there they went to members at the headwaters of the Murray River at Bringenbrong, 'one of Australia's historic houses dating from pioneer days.' They then visited a family named Ross, whose properties, named Stonehaven and Aberfeldy, betrayed their Scottish origins even if their name had not done so. From here on June 21st they moved on to the Murray Valley where they were fortunate that the Organising secretary of the Murray Valley development league was a Soil Association Member a Mr. G.V.Lawrence. Thanks to him they saw every aspect of the area before moving on to Adelaide and South Australia, where they arrived on the 10th of July.

Their headquarters for their tour of South Australia were with Professor Sir Stanton Hicks and Lady Hicks, long standing supporters of the Soil Association. From 1st July to the 10th they remained with them attending to a backlog of correspondence. From 12th July they started a busy round of visits. One particularly pleasing visit was to the Hawkers at Bungaree, one of the old original settlers homes. These Hawkers were cousins of Derry Hawker, one of the Four Bells.

They also visited the Ninety Mile desert, now largely reclaimed. Then they discovered that the ship on which they were due to return was not leaving for a further fortnight so that they had two weeks to spare. They spent these on a small safari trip from Adelaide to Alice Springs. They visited the opal miners at Coober Pedy, who live virtually underground. They then reached Alice Springs itself, where they took a mail plane tour of the various cattle stations and were fascinated to see the area from the air.

Finally on August 17th they left Adelaide for Western Australia by train on the Trans-Australian railway. This proved to be the most luxurious means of travel. They arrived at Calgoorlie, the western terminus, late in the evening and transferred to the unheated sleepers of the Western Australian Railways express. Their next stop was Perth around noon on the 21st of August.

Eve wrote; 'I expected transport to be a problem, but I reckoned without knowledge of the quite extraordinary Western Australian kindness and generosity to visitors . . . I paid a call on Mr Victor Murray of Westralian Farmers, the big stock and station agents. He at once offered me transport wherever we wanted to go. 'We have cars and drivers going everywhere all the time – nothing easier.' I did not take this quite literally, but gratefully accepted the offer of a car to drive us the 20 miles to Coorow the following Wednesday.'

They visited the Western Australian Wheat belt and a fulldays journey was arranged by the manager of the bank they visited. Throughout the month they visited many farmers in the area as well as the famous Karri Forest. Finally on the 25th of September they sailed once more for home after an amazing year's visit that had cost the Soil Association nothing, yet generated an enormous amount of good will and publicity.

As Eve explained; 'Our return fares by the Wilhelmsen Line from the European port of departure to Australia and back again amounting to a little over áá350 a head we each paid for ourselves . . . The return air fares between Australia and New Zealand and a sum of £200 to meet other inter-state transport costs and casual expenses were provided out of the Soil Association Travel Fund, a special fund donated by a generous founder-member for just such a purpose. All living expenses and nearly all transport within each State were contributed by the hospitality and private motor cars of members in Australia and New Zealand. (Without this most generous treatment the whole expedition would, of course, have been totally out of the question) . . .'

On 9th February 1960 de la Mare was forced to write again:
'Dear Eve,
'I wonder if I dare ask for news of the new edition of The Living Soil? I didn't want to bother you with a letter too soon after you got back, but . . . I feel sure there will be quite a considerable sale for the new edition when it comes . . . Yours ever.'

This brought a reply from Eve dated 12th February;
'Dear Dick,
'. . . you are very patient not to have written it earlier. My admirable intention of completing . . . the revision . . . on my voyage home proved impossible . . . I only get one or two days a week free from the pressure of current work to do any writing . . . I ought to be able to let you have something some time in April at the latest, which I hope would be soon enough for an Autumn publication . . . Ever yours.'

Meanwhile in late 1959 Ral Balfour, Eve's brother, had been cited as co-respondent in a divorce in Australia. The wife involved was a fortune-hunting Hungarian refugee, who had reached Melbourne via a divorce in New York, and thought she now saw the opportunity of a title as well. To his surprise, he suddenly found himself an object of interest to every scandal sheet in the business. He sought sympathy from his sisters and received a mixed reception. From Nell, always strong on religion, he predictably received a rebuff. Eve wrote firmly:

'Sep.1960.

'Darling Ral,

'. . . You really are not in a position to complain about anything others may do, as though you were the innocent injured party.

'One can't have anything in life without paying the price for it in one form or another.

'The price of privilege is responsibility and duties. You were born to the privileges of . . . position, name and the possession of a landed estate and the ability to influence others. The responsibilities and duties that go with that include acceptance of certain recognised standards of behaviour . . .

'You are certainly not the first person who has decided to kick over the traces and throw them to the wind, but nobody can do this and retain the privileges!

'You have decided that everything you had is well lost for E. All right then, but in that case what, as Beb would say, are you belly-aching about?

'All of us have to learn the lesson and most of us do so while quite young, that you cannot have your cake and eat it. I am most terribly sorry for both you and E that you are apparently having to learn this lesson for the first time so late in life, but you have got to face it now . . . there is still time to think again . . . darling Ral . . . love . . . Eve'

Her approach was straightforward enough.[4] She refused to take sides and remained friendly with both Ral and Jean, who refused to divorce him, without favour to either. It is plain from the file of correspondence on the matter, however, that it was difficult at times. Unlike her other sisters, she was, however, very fully involved with the Soil Association, which continued its roller-coaster economic performance.

On the 7th of July 1961 there was a familiar plea from Richard de la Mare:

'Dear Eve,

'I expect you will guess what I am writing to ask! The perennial question whether there is any chance . . . of our getting your revised copy for the new edition of The Living Soil? We keep being asked for the book and it does seem a great pity that it is no longer available. But I know how busy you must have been and that is why I haven't pestered you more often. Do forgive me, but I would love to see the book in print again. . . .'

Eve replied on the 15th of July:

'Dear Dick,

'You have been very patient. I have one more Australian article to do . . . but I am badly in arrears with correspondence. Since last November I have been and still am, locum farm manager here. This, added to the tremendous amount of work involved in the Haughley Appeal, made it quite impossible hitherto to attempt to get back to The Living Soil. I am in sight of being able to, but the job itself still puzzles me . . . We are planning to bring out next spring a comprehensive booklet . . .'The First 15 Years at Haughley' . . . this would seem to be the logical data to include in a revised version of Living Soil. If I could get everything done except that, that could almost be added ready made at the last minute direct from the booklet.

'As I am writing, have you thought any more about publishing my Australian and New Zealand letters as a travel book? In a week or two's time I could send you the whole series to have a look at . . . Ever yours . . .'

Ten years earlier Eve would have taken on the challenge of finishing a new version of The Living Soil by simply burning the candle at both ends. Now, however, she had begun to consider the matter of her retirement. After the pace she had set herself in the two decades since the war even she must have been beginning to feel the effects. In 1961 she saw a cottage at Theberton, near Leiston, in Suffolk, which attracted her. It was close to old friends and she liked the area. Priced at £350, it was at the end of a row of old cottages, possibly once occupied by a verger at the nearby church. Although very dilapidated she saw its possibilities and bought it at once.

During the next three years she and KC spent much of their spare time renovating, decorating and painting the house, (4 Rattla Corner) both internally and externally. The work included such basic features as laying concrete driveways and major interior structural renovations, quite apart from getting the garden of over an acre into order. This was a fairly major feat for someone in their mid-sixties let alone for KC who was now well over seventy. However they not only managed to make steady progress, eventually transforming it into a very comfortable home, but also continued their usual hectic round of Soil Association activities.

Although continuing as Field Director from 1964 onwards Eve was now over 65 years and well past the normal female retirement age. A nominal pension was provided by the Soil Association, but with her characteristic disregard for money she used most of it in the service of the Association. There were, however, changes taking place in the Soil Association, although the membership still remained static at around 3,500.

To start with, the editor of the magazine Mother Earth Jorian Jenks[5], a practical farmer and foundation member of the Soil Association, who had turned successfully to journalism, died in late 1963 and a new editor was brought in. Changes in the Council were also starting to be felt. It was argued once again that the title of the quarterly journal Mother Earth was a handicap, labelling the readership cranks. The perennial argument was also being raised yet again that The Haughley Experiment, which to Eve and those who understood its purpose still remained vitally important, was a financial millstone and that it should become simply an organic experimental farm.

At this stage Eve was glad to welcome an old ally to Haughley. Professor Lindsay Robb,[6] now 78 and supposedly retired, arrived to live at Haughley, taking on the post of Consultant to the Soil Association. His daughter Mrs Margaret Smith, better known to all as 'Maggie' became secretary to the Association working at Haughley. In many ways it was natural for Eve to regard the group who lived and worked at Haughley as her friends and something akin to family. To a large extent the feeling was reciprocated, although she could appear a formidable figure at first to those who did not know her well. A letter from Richard de la Mare on 25th November 1965 indicated clearly that there had been no progress in the interval. Even he had begun to give up hope as is apparent:

'My dear Eve,

'Many thanks for your letter of the 22nd of November which I was delighted to get. It is certainly good news that you hope to be able to do the revision of Common Sense Compost Making (which had been written by her friend and colleague May Bruce and which required up-dating) quite soon and that you may be able to let us have it by the end of January . . .

'Alas! we discussed the Australian book again at our meeting' yesterday . . . and we do feel now that it is far too late in the day for us to consider publishing it with any hope of making a success of it . . . I'm afraid it really is too late now.

'But of course the book that we are really hoping to get from you is a new edition of The Living Soil. However I assume that by this time it wouldn't be so much a matter of revising the old book as writing quite a new one? I wonder if there is any prospect of you doing that? . . . I am sure it would be widely welcomed . . .

'I am very pleased to know that you expect things to ease up for you somewhat and I certainly hope this will be so. Yours ever'

On 26th November Eve replied . . .'The Living Soil is a problem. I am not prepared to commit myself on anything yet, but I have it mind.' To this de la Mare replied; ''I note what you say about the Living Soil and I am glad to know that even though you cannot commit yourself to anything just now, you do have it in mind.' The fact was that internecine politics in the Soil Association were once again taking up a lot of Eve's time. The 'young Turks' were intent on unseating the 'old guard, as they saw it, and as ever Eve was cast in the uncomfortable role of peacemaker.

By 1966 Eve had been given the somewhat anomalous post of Consultant along with Professor Lindsay Robb. The Resident Research director at Haughley was a newcomer, Douglas Campbell, who had been an agricultural field director in Basuto land. Inevitably he developed his own ideas as he was given a freer and freer hand by the Council and was probably encouraged to do so by some of the members.

After the Council Meeting in 1966 one of the members wrote:

'Dear Eve, 3rd March 1966

'What fun it was to see you again and your quite delightful little place . . . I feel sure that a fundamental change in approach is necessary not only to meet the financial crisis but to make the Soil Association a body that can be understood and accepted by ordinary practical people.

'It is very hard I know for anyone who has been in it from the beginning like you . . . to bear the sight of young 'upstarts' like Douglas Campbell and me (!) apparently determined to change everything even if it seems disloyal to you founder members. But we have got the principles firmly implanted in us . . . So many people I have met feel as I do, but are loathe to speak out for fear of hurting you. I believe you would prefer complete frankness, hence this letter. I do hope you will be able to put your complete trust in Douglas and those who are helping him form a fresh policy for the S.A and Haughley . . . Otherwise we shall . . . fail to attract a practical membership . . . Yrs ever . . .'

Eve replied on March 14th

'Dear . . .

'How good of you to take the time out of your busy life to write to me at such length . . . the only thing that disturbed me slightly in your letter was the information that my other friends have such a poor opinion of me that they could think I would be hurt by frankness or opinions that I don't happen to share.

'I have never had any 'personal' ambitions about Haughley or the Soil Association and if I had they would be totally unimportant. I don't know if you will understand this but I have never felt that any of my work for either has been 'chosen' by me of my own volition. I hold a teleological view of the Universe (if that's how you spell it) and what I have tried to do just seems to have been my 'job'. What I incarnated for perhaps – as such I have most of the time felt 'directed'. This means looking at any 'check' with an attitude of mind open to receive directions for a 'new' direction if this should be intended, while retaining complete faith that if this 'not' intended the ways and means to surmount the check will be forthcoming. The materialist would probably regard this as a mechanism of the subconscious to achieve peace of mind – well that is a good end in itself too!

'In so far as I have any ambitions 'for' the Association and Haughley, holding the philosophy I do, it is obvious that I want them to fulfil their allotted task – whatever that may be – in the plans being worked out by the 'Higher Powers' for the ultimate redemption of the planet. If there are 'Lower powers' too they may want to prevent this, but they could only succeed if the majority of the Soil Association members turned materialist, which is a contradiction in terms. Glad we are to see you in May. Yrs Eve.'

By 1967 Eve had been appointed an Honorary Vice President and was more or less fully retired, although taking a great deal of interest in proceedings from the sidelines. At the annual meetings she remained a formidable presence listened to with considerable trepidation by those members of whose actions she disapproved. She was still a forthright and trenchant speaker able to make her presence felt with considerable power. Her comments were hard to answer unless people had an equally scientific background, which increasingly less and less of the Council members could boast.

Under the new director, however, the Haughley Research farms were producing strange results. In 1966–7 it appeared, for instance, that the organic section was losing fertility, although the results were open to varied conclusions. This was seized on by those who anyway were against the Experiment as a reason for discontinuing it, although Eve was naturally against any such suggestion.

The financial outlook, however, was once again uncertain as the Farms were now controlled by a Trust set up by a supporter of the Association, Lady Elizabeth Byng, who had waived the rent. However, the Trustees now felt that in the interest of the beneficiaries of the Trust they should consider selling. Then a millionaire business man, a Mr. Jack Pye, stepped in and bought the farms for £60,000, leasing them back to the Soil Association and donating the sum received back to them. Controversy over the Experiment, however, still continued.

In late April and early May of 1968 Eve was invited to visit Israel for a fortnight as an honoured guest of the Israeli Ministry of Agriculture. Her itinerary was, as usual, fairly intensive, including visits to organic centres, kibbutz, the Balfour Forest, a tour of Jerusalem, Co-operative farms and even a bird sanctuary. As niece of A.J.Balfour, of the Balfour Declaration, and as an Organic expert closely associated with the Haughley Experiment, she was doubly welcomed. It proved an exhausting but rewarding fortnight.

By this time she had reached the age when many of her older friends were dying and some of her contemporaries. In late 1968 while in hospital for a small operation, her brother Ral had a pulmonary embolism and died. It says much for Eve's even-handedness that she continued to correspond with his mistress providing her and his widow with equal comfort. The former, however, had ensured that she was well provided for and within six months secured the second of her ambitions by marrying a retired general with a knighthood. That proved rather more than Eve was prepared to accept.

In 1969 Lady Howard, Eve's fellow Vice-President of the Soil Association died. In the same year Eve visited the Alentejo with KC, to stay with Huldine Beamish, author of The Hills of Alentajo, whose farms were run on largely organic lines. There she enjoyed a pleasant protracted holiday, although, of course, unable to miss the opportunity of visits to organic farms.

Meanwhile at Haughley a majority of Council members were urging that the Organic Section should be a convincing demonstration of productive Organic farming. Mr Pye, the new owner, who appears to have been more at ease discussing management matters with men than with women, seems to have taken this view and at this point the Director of Research took a group of Council members round the

Research Farms. Only two of them were qualified to evaluate what they were seeing. Neither Professor Lindsay Robb, nor Eve, were present to give them a clear picture of the Experiment, indeed both were apparently deliberately excluded. In the circumstances it was perhaps scarcely surprising that at the subsequent Council Meeting it was decided by a majority vote to change matters. The decision was finally taken to end the Experiment.

NOTES ON CHAPTER ELEVEN

1. Sam Mayall: Studied at Wye, Agricultural College. Started farming in 1923 at age of 22 at Lea Hall near Shrewsbury, farming 600 acres of light to medium land. Turned organic in 1947. Highly successful farmer and keen Soil Association supporter. His farm was regarded as a key example of successful organic farming.
2. Tommaso del Pelo Pardi: Born in 1901 and studied as an engineer. With his father developed the system of contour ploughing which bears their name and is found to counter erosion effectively. It is described in his book 'La Systema de Terreno' translated into English by the University of Wales.
3. P.A.Yeomans. Born in New South Wales in 1908 and trained in banking and mining. Took up farming on the unexpected death of a brother in the 1940's. With his engineering experience developed the revolutionary method of contour land-use, which was named after him. Member of the Soil Association and contributed greatly to the success of Eve's Australian Tour. Author of Keyline Plan and The Challenge of Landscape. Eve was later to say:' I think he contributed as much to organic agriculture as anyone this century.'
4. straightforward enough. Eve conducted her own affairs with a great deal more discretion. During the latter years of the war she was closely involved with a married man who was killed shortly before hostilities ceased. Although her sisters were aware of the affair they never knew the name of the man involved.
5. Jorian Jenks: Born in 1899 and educated at Haileybury and Harper Adams Agricultural College, obtaining diploma of Agriculture in 1920 after service in 1914–18 War. Served in department of Agriculture in New Zealand, returned to U.K. in 1928 and did post-graduate work at Balliol College, Oxford, lecturing for a year before farming in Sussex. Ill-health forced him to retire in 1939 and take up journalism. Successfully edited 'Mother Earth' from 1945 to his death in 1963.
6. Lindsay Robb. Born on the Ayrshire farm of a well known-cattle breeder in 1885 he served in the 914–18 war before qualifying at Glasgow University Agricultural College. He went on to become head of the Agricultural dept. at London University. (Wye) He then joined – before in the mid-thirties becoming Professor of Agriculture at Pretoria University S.A. During the 1939–45 war he was Director of Agriculture for Tripolitania as a Lt. Col. After the war he was appointed to F.A.O.,(United Nations Food & Agriculture Organisation) as chief of mission to Costa Rica from which he retired aged 75. He then joined the Soil Association as Consultant, lecturing around the world, until his death in 1972.

23. Rattla Corner in the late 1960s with KC at work in front.

24. Eve at an Israeli reception in 1968.

25. Eve & KC on tour in the late 1960s.

26. Eve in the late 1970s.

27. In the mid-1980s looking piratical but characteristically
with a cat instead of a parrot.

28. In 1989 still sampling the soil.

# CHAPTER TWELVE

# The 'Retirement' Years

## 1970–1990

*'When I started . . . I didn't expect to see any results in my lifetime . . . but we did see some results and I think it has played a part . . .'*

Eve in a speech on her 90th birthday at a party given by the Soil Association.

IN MAY 1970, Mrs Helen Zipperlen, of Camp Hill Village, Copake, New York, who before her marriage had served on the Council of the Soil Association as Helen Murray, wrote to the Secretary enquiring what had happened about the Haughley Experiment. After her initial letter a joint statement by Eve and Douglas Campbell, the Director of Research, appeared in the Soil Association News Letter, Span. This merely prompted Helen Zipperlen to send a further series of penetrating questions, including the direct query as to whether the Experiment had been discontinued. Asked to contribute answers, along with Dr.R.F.Milton, and Douglas Campbell, Eve's answers to what may well have been inspired questions were revealing, as follows:

'1. Was the original purpose of the Haughley Experiment to compare three farming systems? Yes.

a. If so, is it true to say that from the outset none of the systems at Haughley were representative of typical farming systems because the matters to be investigated concerned the consequences of the various treatments which might be masked in farming practice? Yes

b. Is it true to say that from the outset all the systems were closed so far as possible? Yes.

c. Arising from this is it true to say that the most Interesting comparisons are to be made between the 'organic' and the 'mixed' sections? Yes.

2. Is it possible for the 'organic' section to maintain or increase its fertility without imports and with the continual export of surpluses in the form of milk, eggs and some animals, etc? This is one of the things we hoped to find out. No answer to it had emerged when the Experiment was stopped . . .

5. Is the 'organic' section losing fertility? Opinions vary over this – the evidence, in any case, was very inconclusive

a. If so by what signs and from what experimental results is this deduced? Soil analysis indicated a reduction in humus and in the total nitrogen bank. It was also argued by some that the crop yields were falling, but this is not borne out by the printed reports and records.

b, When did these signs first appear? About 1966/7?

c. Where are the published data referring to them? There is none; only opinions.

6. Is it not logical to suppose that a decline in the fertility of the 'organic' section should have begun many year sago? Yes.

a. If so is it true to say that the delay in the onset of this decline is itself one of the most interesting challenges the Experiment has produced? Yes.

b. Is it not important to observe and document the downward trend, in order to determine why it has occurred and why it occurred at a particular point? Undoubtedly.

7. Is it true that a number of monthly analyses of soil and plant and animal materials have been discontinued? Yes

a. If so, what were dropped and for what reasons? Practically all – no money was allocated to cover them.

b. What tests replaced them and what is the justification for breaking the continuity of techniques, apparently just as a new trend was appearing in the comparison of the 'organic' and the 'mixed' sections? Nothing replaced them. The 'justification' was twofold;

i. The majority of the Council deciding that demonstration and applied research had become more important than fundamental research and

ii. Withdrawal of adequate financial support to continue fundamental research.

c, How is it proposed to follow this trend during the next rotation period or two? The Experiment being now terminated this question is no longer relevant . . .

8. Is it true that no more money is available and that the whole Experiment must be discontinued? Yes.

a. Is it true that it has served its purpose anyway and its resources should be diverted to other purposes? Many members think so, probably a majority . . .

10. Is it true that the Experiment is to continue as before, but that it is to be modified by permitting imports of organic matter to the 'organic section? The three sections are to be retained, but a larger number of modifications are being made.

a. If so does this not in fact mean that the Experiment is being terminated, since no further useful data will be available ertaining to the original Experiment? Yes. THE Experiment has been terminated.

b. If the original Experiment is to be terminated is a new Experiment to begin? Yes.

c. If a new Experiment is to begin by whom has it been set up, what questions does it ask, by what section of the membership has it been approved? The Pye Charitable Trust and the Directors of Haughley Research Farms Ltd.,

Its purpose is less to ask questions than

i. to provide and make available research material for others to study the effect of the three systems of farming on a number of current problems such as soil structure, eutrophication, animal nutrition, etc. and

ii to contribute to the establishment of a practical advisory service in organic husbandry.

b. The majority of the Council, and as only a small minority of members have objected, presumably by the majority of members too,

11. Is it true that after 20 years the 'organic' section began to lose fertility and at the mere undocumented suggestion of this the Association has altered the terms of the Experiment? Yes, but I think the 'suggestion' was seized upon as a welcome excuse by those who wanted to change it anyway.

a. If this is so, does it not suggest a bias tending toward the production of experimental data to support an opinion already held? Yes, but I expect this was an element in the situation . . .

13. Arising from the joint statement by Lady Eve and Douglas Campbell Do the changes proposed amount to a termination of the Experiment? Yes Signed. E.B.B 14/4/71

Footnote.

I have tried to give these answers as truthfully as I know how. I think we have a better chance of finding an agreed form of words for publication if, at this confidential discussion stage, we are absolutely honest.

It was a subject on which emotions ran high and even in 1990 Helen Zipperlen could still write with deep feeling:' The muddle-headedness and total lack of understanding by the members of the Council of what was involved in the Haughley Experiment is hard to understand. This simple yet highly rigorous experiment was beginning to show that health can be cultivated and fostered, that a healthy agriculture naturally produces surpluses without depleting itself and that chemical additives, rather than enhancing the process, may actually inhibit it. Thus the Mixed Section, farmed well and carrying the same amount of animals as the Organic Section, should have been improved by its chemical supplements. Over the long term, however, this was not the case as Dr. Milton's analyses proved.

It is only possible to conclude that the fact that the Organic section appeared to show signs of decline alarmed them. Theoretically, since it ran on its own strength entirely, importing nothing beyond a few bags of seaweed and exporting milk, meat, eggs and some crops, it should have deteriorated fairly steadily, but for at least 21 years it had not done so. This was remarkable to say the least.

To close the original Experiment, analyse and publish Dr. Milton's findings, and write up the results would have been an acceptable, if short-sighted, solution. To 'change it a little' simply destroyed the integrity and continuity of the whole 21 years and was worse than useless. It was a mindless betrayal.'

Eve, however, appears to have taken the final ending of the Experiment with that amazing resilience she possessed. She had carried through 21 years of specific research, where she had hoped for only ten, and she was determined to publish the results in due course.[1] Recrimination, as she saw it, was pointless. By this time, having travelled widely around the world, while still firmly holding to her own views, Eve was able to see the larger picture.

As she indicated to an interviewer some years later the enormous improvements in crop production over the post-war decades were largely attributable to the remarkable feats of the seed geneticists. The results of their research had increased average yields to an almost unbelievable extent. This, of course, had absolutely nothing to do with the work that had been done at Haughley and did not in any way invalidate it.

In 1970 there was danger of yet another schism in the Soil Association when the Earl of Bradford, who had proved an able President for many years was forced to resign because of increasing deafness. Eve was asked by an old supporter to allow her name to go forward for nomination as his successor, but wrote back conclusively:

'I have given much thought to your suggestion . . . The more I think about it the fewer good reasons, and the more objections I see . . . I will try to enumerate the latter, not necessarily in the order of priority, but as they present themselves:

'Objections on principle.

1. It would be putting the clock back – like a retired actress trying to make a come-back in her original parts; it would be a flop and an anti-climax.

2. My influence would be negligible, for the simple reason that the majority of the Council no longer hold my views.

3. It is in the Articles of Association that the President is Chairman of the Council and I am A VERY BAD CHAIRMAN – ask anyone who has suffered under my chairmanship and they will confirm this. I can't keep order and I can't refrain from talking too much.

4. If the Articles were changed so that the President need not be Chairman, the President would, to all intents and purposes become a figure-head. In what manner could such a one guide?

5. A new leader must be sought for a new decade and generation. A leader if possible on the right side of middle age and in full vigour. Not an old and tired one, and one, moreover, belonging to a previous era.

6. The myth in the name would probably (though not certainly) get me elected, but over half the Council would resent the appointment bitterly. so that there would be a split team and disruption; too high a price to pay for the negative reason of keeping some other people out of office.

7. The right way for us of the old gang to influence the future direction is as back-room boys behind the scenes, not by seeking to get back into office again.

Practical Objections

1. You pointed out that I have my health. This is true, but I am very conscious of being fully stretched, so that I could not possibly add anything to my existing activities. So if I took on more work or responsibility for the Soil Association than I have had I would have to give up some other activities. How to achieve this, even if I wished to, which I definitely don't, would in itself present a whole host of other difficulties.

2. Financially I am, at present, completely dependent on my Soil Association pension. You brushed this aside as unimportant, but it

isn't. As a member of the Council (which the President has to be) I am not allowed to receive any financial benefits. To wangle or fiddle to get round this would be highly undesirable and the Council would not and indeed could not possibly approve. Nor indeed would I be a party to it. (She received £2,500 per annum)

3. As indicated in 1. above I have since my retirement taken on many commitments and responsibilities which take all my time and energy.

4. And perhaps most important, I have had a taste of comparative freedom following 20 years hard slogging for the Association – I have no heart for going back into that kind of harness at my age. I would have no confidence that I could make a success of it, in fact a strong conviction that I couldn't.

5. I still have enough enthusiasm to be very willing to back up and help the new President and General Secretary as consultant (if they wish it) but not to shoulder the responsibility of office again.

General Conclusion.

We must get the right candidate – and I will do all I can to help over this.'

In the end Dr Ernest F. Schumacher, whose book, Small is Beautiful, was to make as much impact as Eve's The Living Soil, when it was published in 1972, was elected as President of the Soil Association. At last the Soil Association had a first-class organiser and business mind at the helm. From then onwards its progress forwards was inexorable. From the moment they met both he and Eve found an enormous amount in common and their liking and admiration was mutual.

As the detailed rebuttal of her would-be supporter quoted above demonstrates, Eve had little time for false posturing. She was well aware that in some circles she amounted to a cult figure and she discouraged this whenever possible. When any of her over-earnest admirers appeared scandalised that she would occasionally drink alcohol or smoke a cigarette, she would reply with her disarming smile.

'I feel that if you stick to whole food and a sensible diet 95% of the time you are entitled to backslide for the odd 5%, if that gives you any pleasure.'

Even so, Carol Twinch, who worked in a junior capacity in the Soil Association office at Haughley in the early seventies, still recalls how whenever Eve was due to put in an appearance there was a palpable feeling of of excitement and ezpectancy in the air. Since launching the

Soil Association she had lived through the grey days of the fifties, when rationing was only slowly being eased, and the liberated flower-power days of the 'pill,' drugs and sex of the sixties, almost without noticing them. She had been too busy acting as 'a clearing house for information' around the world to pay much attention to ephemeral changes. The same applied to the strike-bound seventies in Britain, when the dead weight of the Unions seemed to be suffocating the country. Through it all she had been steering the Soil Association past one financial crisis after another, continuing to spread the organic message and slowly increasing the membership. In the process it was scarcely surprising that she had achieved an almost legendary status amongst those who only knew her by reputation.

Although well past retiring age, she continued to be involved in her work, touring and lecturing frequently both at home and abroad. In 1970 The Living Soil was put forward belatedly by the Soil Association for a Nobel prize, but scarcely surprisingly at this late stage the recommendation came to nothing. However in 1972 Richard de la Mare received a letter out of the blue from a Hugh de las Casas, a reprint publisher which read in part;

'12th April 1972;

'Dear Mr. de la Mare,

'I was talking recently to Lady Eve Balfour about the possibilities of making a reprint edition of her book 'The Living Soil' . . . she tells me that you still hold the rights.

I have suggested to Lady Eve that we would like to reprint the book with a new introduction and some amendments. I understand that you were once interested in producing another edition but that the project has since faded. Would you be prepared to negotiate the rights . . . ?

Scarcely surprisingly de la Mare wrote on 20th April politely informing de las Casas: 'if . . . (Lady Eve) is now ready to do some work on the book, then we would certainly want to re-issue the book ourselves.' The following day in a very restrained letter de la Mare wrote to Eve:

'Dear Eve The Living Soil

'I am sending you a copy of a letter I have just received from Mr. Hugh de las Casas . . . and I couldn't help wondering if he has reported you accurately. Of course I very much hope that what he says is true and that you now think you can spare the time to revise the book for a new edition, the possibility of which I have asked you about many times over the years. But, needless to say, if you do revise the book as seems to you necessary for a new edition, we would want to publish it ourselves, for that is something that we have always hoped to be able to do eventually . . . Yours ever.

In an internal office memo dated 9th of May 1972 Eileen Brooksbank, Richard de la Mare's personal assistant, noted; 'Lady Eve telephoned last week to discuss this . . . Lady Eve has always felt that it would be extremely difficult to bring the book right up-to-date . . . and felt that the part dealing with the Haughley Experiment was still fluid and changing. However, the latter situation no longer remains and she is in fact now writing an account of the Haughley Experiment for the Soil Association . . . She wonders if that could then make the second part of The Living Soil . . . I . . . simply said that I knew you'd be interested . . . but that you'd want to discuss this very thoroughly before coming to any decision . . .'

In 1973 Douglas Campbell left as Director of Research at the Haughley farms and Eve was again asked to take on the post of Consultant. Despite the fact that the original Haughley Experiment had now been terminated, Eve agreed to take on the extra work involved and initiate Campbell's successor, Dick Widdowson, when he had been selected, into the job of running the new Experimental farms. During the same period there were several new appointments including a new editorial team for the journal.

It was in September 1973 when Eve was on a visit to Canada for a brief lecture tour that there was further correspondence on the subject on The Living Soil. Then de la Mare and she had a meeting in London when she gave him a copy of her account of the Haughley Experiment to read. He wrote to her on 8th November:

'Dear Eve,

'I have now read your account of the Haughley Experiment and I have much enjoyed doing so. I didn't find it difficult to read or hard going and it seems to me you have succeeded very well in making it suitable for the general reader . . . So I do think it would be a good plan to publish this together with your shortened and revised version of The Living Soil in one volume and that is something that we would like to do. But I am a little worried about the cost of setting the tables in the appendices, so before we make a final decision I think we ought to prepare a preliminary estimate of the cost of production . . . Yours ever . . .'

On 16th of January 1974 another internal memo from Eileen Brooksbank summed up developments;

'I spoke to Lady Eve on the telephone yesterday and explained that to publish the book without illustrations but with a 10% royalty we would need a subsidy of £1,000 and explained that in the circumstances we thought it best to pay a royalty, especially if the Soil Association were going to help and that in any case it wouldn't make all that much difference to the price if there were no royalty. She seemed to think this very reasonable and said that even if the cash came from private contributors they'd probably be encouraged to know that the royalties would eventually be going to the Soil Association. She seems to think it very likely that she'll be able to raise the money and on that basis is perfectly happy to go ahead with the work she has to done revising The Living Soil and she'll get down to this when she's in Kenya and will get in touch with us as soon as she can after her return . . . on February 24th . . .'

On 25th January de la Mare wrote;

'Dear Eve,

'. . . I am very happy to confirm that we would like to publish The Living Soil and The Story of the Haughley Experiment on the following terms: we would pay you a royalty of ten per cent of the published price, which we expect to be in the region of £13.50 . . . To do this we shall require a subsidy of one thousand pounds . . . a quarter of it on signature of the agreement and the balance at a later date . . . When we have confirmation of these agreements we will draw up a contract . . . I can't tell you how greatly I look forward to its publication . . . I can only say I hope . . . you will have . . . a really successful and enjoyable visit to Kenya . . . yours ever . . .'

On February 12th Eve wrote from Kenya:

'Dear Miss Brooksbank,

'Triumph, I have finished the revision of The Living Soil! . . . As soon as I get home (Feb 28th) I will get the new paras into type and then (transport permitting) (there was a national rail strike) will come up to London, I hope first week in March . . . I and my friend (she was with KC) are having a wonderful holiday . . . we are of course loving the sun, but everywhere is fearfully dry and longing for rain . . . We have been to both Treetops and Samboru game reserves where we were very lucky in the amount and variety of birds and animals we saw . . .' On 19th April Eve dictated a letter from the Soil Association office now at Walnut Tree Manor:

'Dear Eileen,

'Many thanks for your letter. I am replying to it from Haughley so as to leave a copy of my letter with yours for Brigadier Vickers (The S.A.Secretary) to see since he is not here today and I could not discuss it with him.

'I am very anxious if possible not to involve the Soil Association officially via its Council in the subsidy. I am practically certain I can get the necessary money from Soil Association groups and individuals and I shall make a contribution myself in so far as I am able. So what I would like you to ask Dick is that in the wording of any contract would he accept my undertaking to see that the subsidy is forthcoming? If the Brigadier is not in agreement with this letter he will write to you direct . . . Yours sincerely,'

This was duly acknowledged and the usual flurry of pre-publication correspondence followed. Eve's cheque for £250 and the signed contract was sent on 15th May. By September 9th a 'Subsidy Fund' which had been started to finance the publication had reached £527 with small voluntary contributions. By 15th January 1975 negotiations with Devin Garrity of Devin Adair, the U.S.publishers who had published the original, resulted in them asking for a quotation for up to 2,500 copies.

On 6th October Eileen Brooksbank wrote from Faber:

'Dear Eve,

'I hope you don't think we have all gone to sleep here! . . . life has been full of the usual complications . . . now about publication plans for The Living Soil, which we are, barring any unprecedented accidents, going to bring out on November 24th . . . the delay is entirely due to our having had to wait for the American order to be confirmed, so that we could print their edition with ours . . . Author's copies usually go out about 4–5 weeks ahead of publication so you won't have to wait much longer . . . the text looks very well set out and clear to read . . . Yours ever . . .' Eve replied on 17th October:

'Dear Eileen,

'. . . tho' when I first heard of the further delay in publishing date I was dissapointed, I think it may result in capturing more Christmas sales . . .

'Second, the Soil Association as holders of my subsidy fund await your request for payment of the £750 balance whenever you want it.

'Third – don't forget to prepare something for me to sign to the effect that until such time as you may receive other instructions all royalties are to be paid to the Soil Association to whom I donate them . . . It will be interesting to see if it sells. I feel at £5.25 it is a gamble . . . ever yours . . .'

A post card dated October 20th arrived noting: 'The book arrived this morning. I like its looks very much. Please congratulate all concerned.'

On 30th of January 1976 the only distinctly critical review of the new version of The Living Soil was written by Margaret Duggan in The Church Times. This made some valid points forcefully enough, even if it was naive to expect personal revelations in a book of this nature.

'If only Lady Balfour could construct a book, or if only her publishers had been tougher as editors, what a much more readable, informative and evangelistic book this new edition of The Living Soil would be . . . it consists of the first seven chapters of the original The Living Soil which was published in 1943 and which says the blurb ' the author has specially edited for this 1975 edition.' As far as one can see the 'special editing' consists of a short paragraph at the beginning of each chapter . . . But The Living Soil is dated by more than its data. A lot of the highly selective and often anecdotal evidence for the benefits of organically-grown food looks very unscientifically presented to a generation for whom research project reports and elaborately set up sociological surveys with proper controls and balanced arguments are part of the daily diet of information.

'What was acceptable in 1943 . . . does not sound so impressive now, which is a pity, for The Living Soil was a very important book in its day . . . anticipating the whole ecological movement of the last decade.

'The second part of the book is given to The Haughley Experiment 'a dramatic and very human story of struggle, frustration, sacrifice and achievement' (again according to the blurb). One only wishes it was.

'The setting up of a Farm under the aegis of the Soil Association to do basic research into the different results in quality to be obtained from organic methods and proper composting as opposed to artificial fertilisers could have been a fascinating personal story set about – as it obviously was by controversy even amongst its backers. But Lady Balfour eschews the personal narrative that could so hold the lay reader who loves to know about farming without getting mud on his boots . . . Instead we get what reads like a pile of notes from which a fascinating book might one day be written . . . We do not get the human story of Lady Balfour's part in all this, who worked with her and the personal frustrations, sacrifices and achievements. We get the very barest outline of the dissension that blew up in the Soil Association Council that brought the Experiment to an end.[2]

'The Council did not understand the full importance of what was being done at Haughley. Perhaps it was that Lady Balfour and her associates were not very good at telling their story.'

In the event this sole dissenting voice, described by Eileen Brooksbank as 'distinctly hackle-raising', proved only too accurate, or perhaps it was a little over-priced as Eve had suggested. Anyway the book only just sold out its U.K edition with the aid of a fire at the printers which destroyed over 1,500 sheet copies unbound. The U.S edition of only 1,500 taken eventually by Universe Books was almost entirely unsold and the bulk was bought back to sell through the Soil Association.

In 1976, while visiting friends in Yorkshire, Eve's old friend KC died. Almost ten years older than Eve, she had been growing deaf and noticeably frailer for some time, but retained her indomitable sense of humour to the very end. It was, however, a great personal blow to Eve. They had been together more or less continuously for almost fifty years barring a few months. As fellow workers in the farm and subsequently working together for the Soil Association they had shared similar hopes and aspirations over the years. Eve was admittedly always the stronger partner physically although KC was strong for her size and mentally quite capable of holding her own. However KC, despite her Yorkshire forthrightness, possessed a tact and unobtrusive but sensitive judgement of people which undoubtedly aided Eve greatly on many occasions. Eve herself was not always a good judge of people as events often proved, As her companion on many of the tours and as one who fulfilled all the functions on which Eve was weak, such as housekeeping and domesticity, she also was invaluable, allowing Eve much more time for her work than would otherwise have been the case.

It says much for Eve's remarkable resilience that even at this stage, approaching eighty, she took over her own domestic problems. For the first time in her life she began to cook. With that remarkable ability of her's to laugh at herself and at the same time to interest herself in any subject, she read cookery books and within a year or so was cooking very successfully. It was again characteristic of her that it was straightforward cooking such as oxtail stews with potatoes in their jackets which attracted her most. Her interest in food, nutrition, diet and the soil continued unabated with yet another dimension being added to it in the stockpot. The addition of several glasses of good red wine to such dishes was not something she overlooked.

In 1977 it came as a considerable shock when Ernest Schumacher died suddenly on a train in Switzerland. He had already revitalised the Soil Association in the four years of his Presidency. Eve especially felt it greatly. She read a passage from Corinthians at his Memorial Service with a depth of feeling which impressed all who heard it. His death, so unexpectedly while still in his late sixties, was a loss not only to Eve but to the Soil Association too.

He had been travelling to a Conference of the International Federation of Organic Agricultural Movements (IFOAM) held at Sissach where Eve read a paper entitled 'Towards a Sustainable Agriculture.' Now without the support of her old companion KC, Eve herself had travelled through France by road on this occasion accompanied by Mary Langman, who had been involved in the Peckham Experiment and among the founder members of the Soil Association. Typically she had used the journey as an opportunity to visit a number of French organic farms on the way. Despite the severe shock of Schumacher's premature death she addressed the Conference with her customary vigour. Her speech on that occasion was a powerful presentation of her beliefs and it was clear that her intellect had not weakened with advancing years for she gave a penetrating and succinct address presenting up-to-the-minute views and a sound analysis of the case for organic farming in a global framework.[3]

Having lived for nearly four score years, however, it was scarcely surprising that her old friends were dying. Her other even older friend Beb Hearnden, who had formed one of the original Four Bells, was now bedridden and Eve had been given power of attorney for her, installing her in a hospital in Ipswich. Here she could visit her every week and see that she was well cared for. It is, however, as anyone knows who has experienced such matters, no pleasure to see an old friend or relative visibly dying before one's eyes and when she too finally died in 1978 it was almost something of a relief.

All this had drawn her closer to her sister Mary again, who was now living with her younger sister Kathleen close to their old home of Whittingehame in East Lothian. Here Eve, still driving her own car, would come up to visit two or three times a year. Her eyesight by this time was troubling her and one eye in particular, her left, was proving troublesome, so that occasionally she was forced to wear a patch over the glasses she wore. While this had a slightly piratical look at times the effect for the most part was more of an aged kindly bloodhound, with red-rimmed eyes. Painful and tiresome though this handicap must have been she did not complain and continued to run her garden of an acre and a half with great enjoyment, looking after herself.

In August 1980 Eve learned via an enquirer that the new edition of The Living Soil was out of print and wrote a letter to Eileen Brooksbank enquiring if the rights had now reverted to her. She received back an apologetic letter dated 29th August;

'Dear Eve,

'Thank you for your letter . . . I feel guilty that you should learn from anyone but me that The Living Soil . . . is out of print What actually happened was that Burns, one of the binders we use most, had a major fire . . . and a considerable number of unbound sheets were destroyed, including The Living Soil, of which there just over 1,000 sets. By that time we had sold around 3,500 copies (including the 1,500 American copies and we have since sold the rest . . . making 3,678 in all . . . a pretty respectable total for a pretty specialist book . . . So the upshot . . . is that the rights now revert to you . . . Yours . . .'

Eileen Brooksbank followed up this letter by checking with Universe Books in the U,.S.A and on 7th October wrote again:

'Dear Eve

'Universe Books tell us they have about 1,200 copies left and suggest that the Soil Association might be willing to buy back 'a fair number' of them at about $1,50 a copy, plus the shipping cost . . . at around $,40 or $.50 a copy.'

'This sounds to me quite a good deal especially now that the pound is getting stronger and especially if the book were sold here at £5.95 its price at the time it went out of print . . . the best plan would be for you or the Soil Association to communicate direct with Universe Books . . . do please let me know if there is any further help or advice I can give you . . . Best wishes. Yours ever . . .'

In 1980, while Eve was visiting East Lothian yet again, her sister Mary died peacefully. Arrangements were made to bury her at the family graveyard in Whittingehame, beside her brother Ral. Meanwhile Eve continued visits north to her youngest sister Kathleen and also to visit her sister-in-law Jean who was now in hospital in East Lothian after a stroke. In 1981 not unexpectedly Jean also died. Once again Eve found herself visiting the family graveyard at Whittinge-hame where Jean was finally re-united with her husband.

In 1982 Eve, who had been acting as Hon. General Secretary of the Soil Association Council announced at the meeting that year in Edinburgh that she wished to resign on the grounds of age. She was after all by this time 84. It was also obvious to her that yet again a new generation of young members were eager to take over in ways which did not entirely match with hers.

She was, however, still full of life as her account of a journey back from Portugal in 1982 demonstrates very clearly. She had visited the Alentejo via Lisbon once again and on her return was held up by a national rail strike. This resulted in a lengthy saga. Her subsequent account of the journey undertaken and written at the age of 84 superbly illustrates her sense of humour and attitude to life and events. She wrote; 'The railway authorities undertook to transport any passengers who had reserved seats on the international 'Sud' Express by coach to the Spanish frontier to connect with the train there. On 7th of March . . . my train for Paris should have left Lisbon at 2.30 p.m. – instead two motor coaches were provided, one for 1st class passengers and one for 2nd – I was on the latter.

It left Lisbon station at 2 p.m. and . . . started off on a motorway. It was not very comfortable for me because the distance between the rows of seats was insufficient for my long thighs, I had to sit either with knees far apart, or sideways, thereby encroaching on my neigh-bour's space (he was a little man, whose legs gave him a clear 2'). I am glad that I didn't know at that stage that the drive would take seven hours.

It was not long before we left the dual carriageway . . . The route took us through very well cared for agricultural country and there was much of interest to look at . . . It was a gorgeous, clear, sunny day.

As time went on the route we took became ever narrower, more twisty and more rural . . . when we suddenly pulled into a gateway and stopped – luckily under the shade of some trees, as it was very hot by then.

The driver got out and went round the bus looking at all four wheels – 'Oh dear!' I thought. 'We've got a puncture' but I hadn't felt a tyre go down. However, after having also inspected something under the bonnet, the driver disappeared behind the bus re-appearing with a bucket. By this time about half the passsengers had also descended and stood around, quite relaxed and smiling . . . There was no grumbling and no shouting . . . which I am sure there would have been with an English or French group in similar circumstances.

Obviously water was required, so my next idea was radiator . . . one of the passengers went off with the bucket, the way we had come, presumably to houses we had recently passed. In the meantime the driver got himself into a pair of mechanics overalls. The whole procedure was immensely leisurely. On the arrival of the water . . . water was transferred to something under the bonnet and at the same time the driver disappeared under the bus by the right rear wheel with a screw driver. Then at last I tumbled to the trouble, there must have been a leak in the hydraulic braking system of that wheel . . . I suppose the whole episode must have taken about three quarters of an hour.

The next rather startling thing to happen was that we turned off onto a brand new and as yet unsurfaced road. it struck straight across uninhabited open country . . . and it reduced our speed to between 10 and 15 miles per hour . . . We came off it eventually onto a tarred road running beside one of Portugal's many new man- created lakes . . . This part of the journey lasted a long time . . . but eventually we pulled up into the one big open space of a scattered village opposite a scruffy looking cafe.

My neighbour and I had become quite pally by now. He was a Portuguese business man of sorts, on his way to Luxembourg – we communicated in French.

Most of the passengers got out at this stop and he told me they were going to the cafe for a drink. Taking my courage in both hands (because some people had been addressing me as 'Senor') I asked him if he happened to know if the place possessed a 'toilette des dames' . . . He said 'yes' and he would conduct me there, which he did with the utmost courtesy – for this I was very grateful for it turned out to be off an unlit, very dark passage and I would never have found it on my own.

Not long after this we took another 'short cut' on an unmade road . . . The sun was setting by now . . . We went through . . . soon after dusk . . . a very large village, which also obviously had some very fine old buildings- these included a typical Portuguese church right in the 'fairway', the road dividing to pass it on each side. We took the left, but it was too narrow . . . and we stuck!! At this precise moment the double doors of the church opened and the congregation from the Sunday evening mass poured out. We provided a wonderful entertainment for them. Once again all stood round in calm content (apparently) no one shouting or giving advice. It was quite dark by this time, but . . . an inch at a time the driver managed to get out without causing any damage and just . . . succeeded in circumnavigating the church on the right hand side . . . we arrived at 9.30 p.m at our destination . . . a tiny rural station . . . in the depths of the country with one building . . . Opposite the one building was a single rail track. On this to the left were two unlit rail coaches and to the right two more lit, which turned out to be for the 1st class passengers, the unlit ones for the 2nd class.

With the help of a torch and two fellow passengers I succeeded in locating my reserved seat. The coaches were not very full and when the lights did come on it appeared that I was only to have one other passenger in my compartment – a large, burly, friendly Portuguese man who mercifully spoke French . . . owing to the strike . . . everything was noticeably less clean than on the outward journey.

No attendant appeared and my fellow passenger and I erected our couchettes and hauled our pillows and blankets down from the top shelf. It was some time before we were hitched up to an engine and where we eventually joined the rest of the 'Sud' Express I have no idea.

As soon as we had fixed our bunks my companion announced his intention to go to bed and I went along the corridor for a rather inadequate wash (no hot water). When I came back my companion demonstrated that the catch on the compartment door did not work so that the door kept sliding backwards and forwards with each lurch of the train. There was an inside lock that he asked me to fasten, which I did. Afterwards, lying in my bunk in the dark, I had a quiet internal chuckle to myself, reflecting what the reaction of some females might have been at being asked to lock themselves into a carriage for a night journey alone with a strange male foreigner!! Daylight revealed the most spectacular scenery I have ever seen, towering crags of fantastic shape and awe-áinspiring grandeur – so stark and dry it looked as if no rain had fallen for years. Within an hour or two . . . still high mountainous country, but so water-logged it looked as if it hadn't stopped raining for years . . . Waterfalls were torrents and much land under water, An incredible weather contrast so close together.

The train did provide a breakfast car which was very welcome, but this was removed at the French frontier and not replaced . . . miraculously we arrived on time at Paris. I took a taxi across Paris and managed to get some food at Gard du Nord with difficulty . . . I didn't book a couchette on the boat train because it . . . got to Dunkerque at

3 a.m . . . I got home eventually at 4 p.m. on Tuesday the 9th having been continually travelling since 8.30 a.m. on Sunday the 7th – three days and two nights without taking my clothes off. It was an interesting journey to have done, but I wouldn't do it again voluntarily . . . When I was asked why I was going by train I said partly because it was cheaper and partly because I think it will be an interesting new experience. I think my guardian angel (who throughout the holiday worked overtime . . .) thought if I wanted experince it would be a good joke to see I got it! I liked him all the better for this . . .' All this taken in her stride at the age of 84 sums her up in her own words far better than any biographer can hope to do.

In 1983 Council members of the Soil Association had another fundamental disagreement when yet again a younger faction felt that the 'old guard' were losing their way. Certain older members accused them of materialism. This led to a major split in views. Jack Pye, who had taken over financial control, at Haughley, perhaps understandably became disillusioned. He decided to turn Haughley into an organic farm and discontinue it as an experimental farm, even under the very changed form it had taken since 1971. Yet again the Soil Association seemed to be in crisis.

Eve had already announced her wish to retire on the grounds of age after one further year in 1982. She was after all by then approaching 85. She could have had nothing to do with the controversy that arose, but unwisely she allowed herself to be drawn into it. For once her even-handedness failed her. Had certain of her old friends, such as KC or Beb Hearnden, still been alive it is possible that she might not have acted as she did. As it was the old lioness gave a final roar. The real reason behind her participation was that, rightly or wrongly, she was persuaded that the staff at Haughley, whom she still regarded in a sense as 'her' family, or her responsibility, had been badly treated by the Council.

Summoning her resources and still considerable backing she called an extraordinary general meeting. Despite strong support she failed to secure her object. Her resolution, though lucidly and powerfully presented, was outvoted. Although accustomed to dealing with committees, none better, politics and behind-the-scenes political manipulations were never her scene. She was too straightforward to be at home in the twisting corridors of power.[3]

It says much for her that she continued thereafter on good terms with many of those who had voted against her resolution. She was doubtless glad to leave the hurly burly at last. She had after all wished to retire for some time. Even so she remained in touch and applauded the fact that the Soil Association went on to flourish successfully, growing steaedily in numbers, power and influence. Her role, as 'a clearing house for information,' had been amply fulfilled. Her information had been disseminated round the world and her ideas had taken root and were growing well.

By this time, although still active, she was at last becoming visibly less strong than of old. She was by now an almost legendary figure regarded as an awesome personage by those who did not know her. She still, however, continued gardening every day and even took over the care of an elderly neighbour who was in her late nineties. Her younger neighbours and local friends, who were numerous, were now unobtrusively keeping an eye on her too, but she was remarkably fit for her age as well as lucid and able to follow world events with keen interest. Her chief problem was a slowly deteriorating eyesight. At the age of 86 she still managed to drive unaided and alone up to Scotland, with an overnight stop at friends on the way. After that her eyesight deteriorated too much for such lengthy journeys, although she continued to visit Whittingehame by train. Her garden at Rattla Corner continued to provide her with fresh vegetables and fruit throughout much of the year and she continued to work in it whenever possible despite difficulties with her eyesight and increasing frailty.

In 1989 as her ninetieth birthday approached she became the focus of considerable media coverage. She was the subject of a number press and magazine articles from around the world and interviews on radio and T.V. On these also she showed that she had not lost her old skill in dealing with interviewers and in presenting a lucid and balanced case spiced with humour.

In an interview with Derek Cooper on the B.B.C Food Programme, during which she had given a very succinct account of the formation of the Haughley Experiment and the Soil Association she was then asked: 'Nowadays your views, of course, are highly acceptable, but in the early days did people regard you as something of a crank?'

Eve was too old a hand at interviews to rise to such an obvious bait.

'Oh yes,' she replied, with that wonderfully rich chuckle of hers. 'Crank! Muck and mystery! Mind you, I never minded muck and mystery, because life still is a mystery I believe. As for a crank I agree entirely with what Dr. Schumacher said. He said, 'What's wrong with a crank? It's a small instrument. It's comparatively inexpensive. It's comparatively non-violent and it causes revolutions.'

Towards the end of the interview it was put to her that nobody who started a crusade in the way she had done could travel through life without hope and she was asked:

'Hope is still there is it?'

'Oh yes,' she replied. 'Fundamentally I am an optimist. I don't think we have passed the point of no return.'

In Organic Growing, the magazine published by the Organic Gardening and Farming Society of Tasmania recalling the Haughley Experiment she was well quoted as follows: •

'Another significant result was the analysis of the fluctuations in the availability of plant nutrients which showed, over a period of ten years, that in the field with the highest humus content and the longest history of no chemicals as much as 10 times more available Phosphate was recorded in the growing season than in the dormant period.

'Potash and Nitrogen followed the same general pattern. It was clear from the fact of the closed cycle, that this seasonal release of minerals could only have been brought about by biological agencies, abd it appears to be a natural action-pattern of a biologically actrive soil. When this finding was first published it was taken up by a Scottish University, repeated, confirmed, and is now generally accepted. Previously it had been assumed that a single spot analysis at any time of the year would show what the soil required.'

An interviewer for the magazine Country Living also discussing the Haughley Experiment with her wrote:

'Lady Eve discovered that soil can be as dependent on chemicals as any drug addict; 'Everybody who has done this sort of research agrees that organic farming yields 15 per cent more product per food unit, whether it's beef. milk, wool or whatever.' After the third generation she was convinced that the organic section's stock was more contented: 'Not the sort of thing you can put into figures. They were healthier, we had the vet less often.'

In the BBC's Radio 4's programme 'Prophets Returned' she remarked revealingly: 'I am just surprised to see that what I stood for all my life is no longer derided, but more or less accepted.'

On the 11th of August the Soil Association gave a special celebratory lunch party in honour of her ninetieth birthday at the home near Ipswich of her old friends the Marland family. John Marland, J.P., and his son Angus, the former an early pupil and both past Council members, were present as well as many other old friends. Eve was in great form and in reply to a speech by George McRobie, President of the Soil Association, she said:

'. . . Anybody that had what the world would call common sense at all, would never have started the Haughley Experiments . . . because we started it without any money. It was founded on faith, and the fact that we were able to keep it going, and basic research is terribly expensive, for 25 years, and produce some results which are significant, was remarkable. When I started on that, which is of course what started the Soil Association . . . I didn't expect to see any results in my lifetime . . . but we did see results and I think it has played a part . . .'

Later in the year a family party was arranged for her at Whittingehame attended by numerous relatives, including her nephew, the 4th Earl of Balfour and various other nephews and nieces, as well as grand-nephews and nieces. Some of the latter she was meeting for the first time and it was noticeable that she at once established a rapport with them uncommon between generations so far apart. Her sister Kathleen, of course, was also present, the only surviving relative of her own generation. Still a keen photographer, Eve herself took most of the photographs on this occasion.

This was to be her last visit to her old home at Whittingehame. She had a stroke at her house in Theberton in the late Autumn of 1989 on the same day, ironically, that an invitation arrived from No. 10 Downing Street to attend a gathering of eminent ecologists there. She was moved to the local cottage hospital, but after it became apparent that she would not recover she was flown back to Scotland. There, at a cottage hospital near Dunbar in East Lothian, close to Whittingehame, she saw one final New year in, her ninety second, in the company of her sister Kathleen and with many relations within visiting range.

In the New Year's Honours List of 1990 she was awarded an O.B.E, a belated and it might be thought rather inadequate public acknowledgement of her services over the years to issues at last recognised as of the first importance. She had never sought recognition for herself and at this stage it really meant very little. That she had lived to see so much of what she had campaigned for recognised as of vital importance was probably reward enough. However it was at least a public acknowledgement of her work and she no doubt saw it as such.

One welcome and unexpected visitor to her at this time was Helen Zipperlen from New York, as Helen Murray one of her early pupils and a very old friend, now a director of the internationally-known Camp Hill Village Trust. Another visitor was Angus Marland co-founder of the newly created Organic Farming Centre, a joint project between the Edinburgh School of Agriculture and the University of Edinburgh's Centre for Human Ecology. He was able to tell her about this recently created centre, which has substantial backing from the European Commission, from the Scottish Development Agency and from Safeway plc. Eve greeted the news with all her old eagerness, for this was in effect a further evolution of the Haughley Experiment. Even at this stage her enthusiasm for fresh developments bridged the gap of time and generations.

On the 14th of January 1990 she finally died peacefully. Such a free spirit would not have wished to continue a half existence away from her own garden and dependent on others. To the end, however, her resonant voice and powerful personality were apparent and her spirit remained undiminished. A memorial service[3] was held subsequently but, according to her wish, she was cremated and her ashes buried in her sister Mary's grave at a private service in the family cemetery at Whittingehame. Thus the two sisters were united once more in the Whittingehame where they had been brought up together, where they had dreamed of farming and where they formed their childhood resolution to do so. Their dreams had been more than fulfilled and the reality was a remarkable life.

After years of tireless campaigning at home and abroad she had seen the gist of her message generally accepted, that Man and his Environment are one and indivisible and that if we poison our planet we poison ourselves. Far ahead of her contemporaries in thought and vision, indefatigable in spreading her message that every part of the food chain – the soil, plants, animals and man – were interconnected and interdependent, she refused to give up in the face of powerful opposition at the highest levels. The Organic Movement is now spreading globally. In a manner which neither she nor anyone else could have envisaged when she first planned the Haughley Experiment and went on to found the Soil Association. Her message resonates around the world and her work goes on internationally with a now unstoppable momentum. It is only right to close this final chapter with these two words:

'The Beginning'[5]

## NOTES ON CHAPTER TWELVE

1. due course: They were, of course, published in her enlarged edition of The Living Soil, but a Summary presented prior to her Paper to the International Federation of Organic Agriculture Movements in 1985 read:

The Haughley Experiment implemented in 1939 by Lady Eve Balfour and continued by the Soil Association from 1945 onwards may be regarded as the first agricultural research project that was consciously founded on ecological principles. It was planned to fill a gap in the evidence for organic husbandry.

In this project three agricultural systems were compared with each other.

1. Biological System: Farming with stock, with exclusive use of farm-yard manure. Total renunciation of use of readily-soluble mineral salts and pesticides.

2. Mixed System:

Farming with stock, recycling farm-yard manure and additional use of readily-soluble mineral fertiliser and pesticides as required.

3. Stockless System:

Exclusive use of mineral fertilisers and pesticides.

The analytical investigations in connection with the Haughley Experiment have shown how wastefully modern commercial agriculture uses the natural reserves and resources and how with the cyclical cultivation technique in the closed cycle the nutrients are not only returned to the biological system, but are more readily available, given that methods are used that suit the ecological factors.

Functional differences between the three systems became particularly clear through the investigation, as illustrated by the following three examples.

1. In the biological cultivation system apparently significant growth inhibition during the early growing periods was regularly observed. Nevertheless, closer investigations showed that the plants developed an intensive root-system during this period, so that by the end of the growing period the above-ground growth had overtaken both other systems.

2. Although both systems 'biological' and 'mixed' received equal quantities of organic manure it was possible to prove unequivocably that the fields in the mixed system had become dependent on the additional mineral fertiliser.

3. In the dairy herds and with hens a similar production level (milk, meat, eggs) was achieved, although 12 to 15% less feed was required for the biological system.

2. to an end: It is quite conceivable that at the time Eve, in common with many others, may have been completely unaware of one of the possible causes. It is probably true to say that Jack Pye, the property developer, who had come in as a white knight to rescue the Soil Association, was never as interested in its' aims as his wife and clearly became increasingly disenchanted over the years.. He was also described as never totally at ease with women, nor, as a businessman, was he likely ever to be very happy with committee decisions. Helen Zipperlen was probably right to smell a rat when the Experiment ended. She blamed collective stupidity and may have been at least partly right but failed, however, to ask the classic detective's question, cui bono, who benefits, also who was in a position to influence the Committee? As a business man he would have seen the Experiment as the financial millstone it undoubtedly was and may well have regarded its' supporters as unbusiness-like idealists as some undoubtedly were. Who was in a

better position to influence employees and for that matter steer the Committees than their financial benefactor and guide? Once freed of the financial burden of the Experiment and without anything really any longer to tie them to Haughley it was not long before the Soil Association decided, or was persuaded, to move its' offices to a more central position in Bristol. New Bells, which had been bought for around £70,000, as a Charitable Trust with the on-going encumbrance of the Experiment and the presence of the Soil Association, was then freed of both and had increased in value ten or even twenty fold over the years - a very satisfactory investment indeed even allowing for the inevitable expenditure over the years.

3. global framework Having outlined the basis of the Haughley Experiment she continued: 'In addition to carefully recorded field observation, an extensive range of sample analyses (soil and products) was carried out by the consultant bio-chemist Dr R.F.Milton. These included analyses for available plant nutrients in every field every month for a period of over ten years, The outcome of this huge number of individual analyses, running into thousands, was a new discovery. It was one of the most important single findings to come out of the experiment, because it was so conclusive and, surprisingly, hitherto unsuspected by orthodox agricultural chemists – namely that the levels of available minerals in the soil fluctuate according to the season, maximum levels co-inciding with the time of maximum plant demand. These fluctuations were far more marked on the Organic Section than on the other two, where, moreover, they could be partly related to fertiliser application. On the Organic Section, which received no fertilisers, the fluctuation was so marked that, for example, in the field with the highest humus content and the longest history of no chemicals, as much as ten times more available phosphate has been recorded in the growing period of the year than in the dormant period. Potash and nitrogen followed the same general pattern. It was clear from the closed cycle, that this seasonal release of minerals could only have been brought about by biological agencies, and it appears to be a natural biological pattern of a biologically active soil. When this finding was first published it was taken up by a Scottish University, repeated, confirmed and is now generally accepted. Previously it has been assumed that a single spot analysis at any time of the year could show what the soil required.

4. memorial service: This was held on May 8th at Marylebone Parish Church and attended by numerous friends, supporters and representatives from the Soil Association, also the bodies closely associated with it, the British Organic Farmers, the Organic Growers Association, the Elm Farm Research Centre, and many others from every branch of the Organic Movement. Her local MP and, co-incidentally, Minister for Agriculture, John Gummer, gave an address. This was followed by a moving tribute from Lawrence Woodward, OBE, director of the Elm Farm Research Centre

5. The Beginning. When Eve finally retired as Honorary General Secretary of the Soil Association Council in 1983 the membership had risen to over 4,000. Today it is around 20,000 and still rising steadily with MPs and men and women of influence among its members as well as many working farmers. The Prince of Wales is Patron. Green issues were regarded as easily ignored in the 1980s. Today governments around the world ignore them at their peril and awareness of her message that mankind, animals, crops and the soil are one and indivisible and that

if we poison the soil we poison ourselves is now at the forcefront of many minds in government and in the conference rooms of global conglomerates. Green party candidates are now to be found in many governments around the world and their power is growing. As Founder of the Soil Association and a constant campaigner for the Organic Movement around the world, when no-one appeared to be listening, she was truly the Voice of the Organic Movement.

# *Index*